Jeffrey Lyons'
101 GREAT MOVIES
for

Kids

Jeffrey Lyons

A Fireside Book

Published by Simon & Schuster

New York   London   Toronto   Sydney   Tokyo   Singapore

FIRESIDE
Rockefeller Center
1230 Avenue of the Americas
New York, NY 10020

Copyright © 1996 by Jeffrey Lyons
All rights reserved, including the right of reproduction
in whole or in part in any form.

FIRESIDE and colophon are registered trademarks
of Simon & Schuster Inc.

Designed by Jeanette Olender
Manufactured in the United States of America

10   9   8   7   6   5   4   3   2   1

Library of Congress Cataloging-in-Publication Data
Lyons, Jeffrey.
Jeffrey Lyons' 101 great movies for kids / Jeffrey Lyons.
p. cm.
"A Fireside book."
1. Motion pictures for children—Catalogs. I. Title.
PN1998.L97 1996
016.79143'75—dc20   95-49088   CIP
ISBN 0-684-80339-9

For my children,

Benjamin Leonard Lyons and Hannah Madge Lyons,

and my wife, Judy,

the most understanding, patient, supportive,
and fascinating woman in the world.

Contents

Contents

10

Introduction

The night before I became a film critic, in 1970, I had dinner with Ruth Gordon, the great Oscar-winning actress/screenwriter, who advised me to remember at all times "Think twice before knocking somebody else's work." I've never forgotten that advice, which I've adopted as the basic tenet of my career on TV, radio, and in print.

People constantly ask me which films to see, which films are worth their time and money. There is never an easy answer. Tastes vary, comedy is subjective, and everyone has individual perspectives. But one thing is certain: great films are always the exception, never the rule. Great films make sitting through all the mediocre movies worthwhile.

When I became a parent fourteen years ago, my entire perspective on movies changed. I became more cautious, more aware of the effect a movie can have on a young viewer. With the introduction of video to the masses in the late 1970s, nearly every movie ever made is now available for home viewing. For parents, the task of diligent selection can be daunting. Video stores have vast collections of films, but many are unknown to the latest generation of parents. Wonderful titles gather dust on video store shelves as frustrated parents reach for more familiar but inferior titles.

While one child may love gentle animation, another may prefer live action. What interests a child one month may seem boring the next. Over the years, I've accumulated a collection of videos which is now as large as that of some stores. As far as I can guess, I've seen about twelve thousand movies, averaging five a week, plus countless old or little-seen movies on television. From those, I've selected one hundred of my favorites for young viewers.

You won't see *E.T.*, *Bambi*, or *Pocahontas* in this guide. You don't need me to tell you those are brilliant works. My favorite Disney movie of them all, for instance, is *Lady and the Tramp*. But I'd be merely a keen observer of the obvious if I included a film like

12

that here. How many ways can one dissect such a classic?

The purpose of this book is to provide alternative choices. When parents search frantically for that one video to please their children, they can now turn to this guide to find forgotten, overlooked, or unknown movies for wholesome, challenging, and sometimes thrilling entertainment.

Along with the hidden gems, I have also included some popular titles, such as *The King and I* and *My Fair Lady.* The movies are divided into general categories of comedy, adventure, drama, and musical. When they overlap, or when the actors listed have appeared in other films in the book, it will be so indicated.

Too often great movies from earlier generations are forgotten. Ask a hundred adults to identify Spencer Tracy, Clark Gable, or Deborah Kerr, and chances are you'll get a few blank stares. This book will help change that, so that when a parent comes across Danny Kaye in *The Secret Life of Walter Mitty,* for instance, or Gary Cooper in *Friendly Persuasion,* they'll stop and consider those wonderful alternatives to today's commercial blockbusters.

Since the intended age group for these selections ranges from about five to thirteen years old, the entries will obviously vary. Older children will enjoy the action and adventure movies, some of which occasionally contain some violence. But most of those films I've chosen were made when directors didn't feel the need to depict explicit gore. What was implied was sufficient.

Lavish musicals are a thing of Hollywood's past. But there are some musicals every young person should see and enjoy. Each of these, and many of the other movies I've included, have interesting histories, especially concerning the lives of the stars themselves. Every performance is part of a body of work, and I've put that film in the general context of the artists' careers.

I've tried to raise my children so that they know some of the great stars and films of the past; at the same time, I can appreciate how far movies have come, and what great contributions those filmmakers whose works are included here have made.

Jeffrey Lyons
New York

The Adventures of Milo and Otis

Category: Drama. Featuring the voice of Dudley Moore. Screenplay by Masanori Hata. 76 minutes. 1989. Rated G. Columbia Home Video.
Director: Masanori Hata.
Suggested Age Group: 5 and older.

The Story This story is about the adventures of a kitten named Milo and a pug puppy named Otis who live on a farm. One day, Milo is accidentally swept away down a small stream. His friend Otis follows, trying to rescue him, and soon encounters a bear cub who is threatening Milo. Otis fights the cub off and leads him into the woods, away from Milo. Still, Otis is unable to rescue Milo and must continue chasing his friend down the river.

Thus begins an amazing movie about a most unusual friendship. At one point, Otis is stranded on a rock off a nearby shore, and in an astonishing sequence, Otis makes it safely back to dry land on the back of a friendly sea turtle! All this in a live action movie, with two of the best-trained animals in recent movie history.

There are no human players in this film, which was originally released in Japan. It was brought here and given witty narration by Dudley Moore. Along the way, we meet a fox, a snake, baby chicks, and other delightful creatures.

The film has a happy ending, with Milo and Otis reunited, and Milo even finds love with a beautiful white cat named Joyce. For his part, Otis strikes out for home on his own, and, in a snowstorm, encounters Sandra, a female pug. Shortly thereafter, Milo and Otis become fathers in adjoining parts of the same cave, safely out of the wrath of the raging winter. In the spring, all the animals come out to frolic with their new families. Finally, Milo and Otis lead their families back home to the farm.

Background: The secret of the success of *Milo and Otis* is that it never talks down to children nor perpetuates stereotypes. The fox that Otis encounters, for instance, is never depicted as "sly."

The turtle never speaks slowly, and the bear never talks with a Goofy-like voice, as in so many other movies of this type.

This is the sort of movie which will mesmerize children and adults alike. One sequence, in which Milo the kitten and a jittery fawn nuzzle one another and eventually curl up to sleep together, just might bring a tear or two to young and older eyes alike.

The Adventures of Milo and Otis was a sleeper hit in 1989, one of those unheralded little children's movies which soon found its audience by word of mouth and did well at the box office. It loses none of its charm on video, and in fact the intimacy of home viewing only adds to the experience. Parents should be warned, however, that they won't be allowed to look away from the screen for a moment, as each new scene introduces an adorable new member of the cast.

The Adventures of Robin Hood

Category: Adventure. Starring Errol Flynn, Olivia de Havilland, Claude Rains, Basil Rathbone, Alan Hale, Eugene Pallette. Screenplay by Norman Reilly Raine and Seton I. Miller, based on the novel *Ivanhoe* by Sir Walter Scott and the opera *Robin Hood* by De Koven–Smith. 102 minutes. 1938. Warner Bros. Home Video.
Directors: Michael Curtiz and William Keighley.
Suggested Age Group: 8 and above.

> **The Story**

In 1191, King Richard the Lionhearted, returning home from the Crusades, has been taken hostage by King Leopold of Austria and held for ransom. Back home, his evil brother, Prince John, has removed Richard's appointed regent and put himself in the position of king, levying heavy taxes on the people of England, especially the Saxons. Ostensibly John's intention was to free Richard, but the real consequence of his actions is that he has installed himself on the throne permanently.

But deep inside Sherwood Forest, Sir Robin of Locksley (Robin Hood), a dashing, fearless Saxon, leads his newly formed band of Merry Men in a campaign to fight the forces of Prince John and John's aide, Sir Guy of Gisbourne.

"You speak treason!" charges Sir Guy to Robin Hood, early in the story in a confrontation at the court in Nottingham Castle. "I speak it fluently!" replies Robin Hood defiantly, before taking on the prince's entire force single-handedly, then making his escape. This remarkable scene is played out to the wonderment of Lady Marian, the royal ward who witnesses his escape.

Thus begins the most swashbuckling of all swashbucklers ever filmed, culminating in the most exciting sword fight of them all! This masterpiece has lost none of its appeal over five decades. To view it again today is akin to opening a treasured old book that has remained on the shelf for years but offers as much luster and as many thrills as the first day it was opened.

Background: In 1938, the movie was filmed for a budget of $1 million, only enough money to feed a crew for a few days on one of today's blockbusters, but back then, an enormous sum. It was the first widely successful live-action Technicolor movie, released the year before *The Wizard of Oz.*

Only one actor of that era could portray Sir Robin of Locksley. Just as Douglas Fairbanks, Sr., owned the genre in the first generation of movies, so Errol Flynn, the Tasmanian-born star, was born to play the role in his age. By 1938, the onetime newspaper columnist had already starred in *Captain Blood, The Charge of the Light Brigade,* and *The Prince and the Pauper.*

When he made *The Adventures of Robin Hood,* Flynn had just completed *The Perfect Specimen* and would follow this movie with *Four's a Crowd,* reteaming him with director Michael Curtiz and costar Olivia de Havilland.

Flynn spent much of his free time on his yacht, an income-producing luxury. He rented it out to anyone willing to pay his price, including Orson Welles, who chartered the yacht for his honeymoon with Rita Hayworth. On board, the newlyweds discovered a monkey which they fed and tended.

When he received the bill from Flynn, Welles discovered an extra charge of $75 a week for the monkey, listed as "Entertainment."

Parents of young viewers should be cautioned that there is reference in the film to various forms of torture, and lots of men, usually the evil Norman soldiers, meet their ends with arrows in the back. And one scene, in which a daughter pleads for her father to be spared, might disturb younger siblings. Nevertheless, *The Adventures of Robin Hood* is a marvelous tale come to life, with incandescent color, one of the most charismatic stars in movie history, and an action-packed story children will love.

Angels in the Outfield

Category: Comedy. Starring Paul Douglas, Janet Leigh, Donna Corcoran, Keenan Wynn, Spring Byington, Ellen Corby, Lewis Stone, the voice of James Whitmore. 102 minutes. 1951. Black and white. MGM/UA Home Video.
Director: Clarence Brown.
Suggested Age Group: 7 and over.

The Story A gruff, foul-mouthed manager of the Pittsburgh Pirates named Guffy McGovern can't get his team out of last place. One night, after another loss, he's visited by an unseen angel. They strike a bargain: Guffy is to stop baiting and arguing with umpires, clean up his language, and be nice to his fellow human beings. In return, the angel just might help him win a few games. Maybe even the pennant.

A newspaper reporter named Jennifer Paige befriends the manager while on assignment to do a story about him, and after some predictable romantic sparring between the two opposites, they begin to forge a friendship.

When a little girl named Bridget White, who lives at a nearby Catholic orphanage, attends a game, she claims she can see angels standing behind every Pirate player. Since no one else can see the angels, the little girl is ignored. But soon she gets to meet the manager, who wants to know what his unseen angelic friend looks like.

The Pirates keep winning, but just before the pennant game, there is a dramatic twist in the story that puts the team's efforts in jeopardy. This twist lends the film a wonderful irony and a human touch.

Since both Guffy and Jennifer are unmarried and Bridget is an orphan, you can pretty much guess the rest. Add a nasty radio announcer named Fred Bayles who has it in for Guffy and brings the "angel issue" before the baseball commissioner, and you have a thoroughly delightful fable. It also offers some genuinely touching moments, and the transformation of Guffy from tough-as-nails manager into a lovable father-to-be is totally believable.

Angels in the Outfield will leave you laughing and shedding a tear, and it might even convert you to a Pittsburgh Pirates fan!

Background: This is a vintage fifties comedy, with familiar supporting players in minor roles. Some of the baseball shots look authentic, since the real Pittsburgh Pirates were used as extras, including the Pirates' greatest all-time home run hitter, future Hall of Famer and long-time Mets announcer Ralph Kiner. Even in scenes where the skyline of Pittsburgh is superimposed over the stands, it looks pretty real.

Watch for cameo appearances by a slightly nervous Joe DiMaggio, then in his last year with the Yankees, and even Ty Cobb, displaying uncharacteristic good humor. One wonders how many takes were required to get the thoroughly nasty Cobb to smile and appear pleasant for a few seconds. In another scene, Bing Crosby, then a part owner of the real Pirates, attempts a long putt on a golf course and prays for angelic intervention.

In 1994, a color remake of this film was released, in which the angels were made through state-of-the-art special effects that Hollywood could conjure. In contrast, the original left the angels invisible, requiring viewers' imagination.

Angels in the Outfield isn't really a movie about baseball. It's about faith, the virtues of living a clean life, of believing in something beyond what we can see, and winning life's battles through kindness and cooperation. Could there be a better message for children?

Around the World in 80 Days

Category: Comedy/drama/adventure. Starring David Niven, Can-
tinflas, Shirley MacLaine, Robert Newton; with cameo appearances
by Trevor Howard, Ronald Colman, Charles Boyer, Joe E. Brown,
John Carradine, Charles Coburn, Hermione Gingold, Sir Cedric
Hardwicke, Luis Miguel Dominguin, Buster Keaton, Frank Sinatra,
Peter Lorre, Victor McLaglen, Colonel Tim McCoy, Sir John Mills,
Alan Mowbray, Edward R. Murrow, Beatrice Lillie, Jack Oakie,
George Raft, Marlene Dietrich, Gilbert Roland, Cesar Romero, Red
Skelton. Screenplay by S. J. Perelman, based on the novel by Jules
Verne. 167 minutes. 1956. Warner Bros. Home Video.
Director: Michael Anderson.
Suggested Age Group: 6 and older.

The Story Phileas Fogg, an upper-crust gentleman in London
in 1872, enters into a wager with his friends at a
posh men's club. He's certain he can go around the
world in eighty days, or as he puts it: "One thousand, nine hundred twenty hours, or 115,200 minutes." Fogg is a notorious stick-
ler for details. He is the sort of man who every morning insists,
for example, that his toast be a specific temperature. Fogg brings
his valet Passepartout along with him, as he purchases a hot-air
balloon to get to Paris. Thus begins an extraordinary adventure,
as they land not in France as planned but in Spain at a bullfight,
in a makeshift arena in the main square of a village.

By ship, railroad, elephant, and wind-driven boxcar, Fogg and
Passepartout continue on their sometimes perilous journey. All
the while, a detective is trailing Fogg, convinced he's just robbed
the Bank of England. The detective, Inspector Fix, is determined
to thwart Fogg and arrest him the next time they reach British
territory.

Through it all, Fogg maintains his stiff upper lip, encountering
adventures and dangerous situations en route to London in time to
collect on his bet. They rescue an Indian princess from a funeral
pyre, witness a buffalo stampede, survive an attack by hostile In-
dians, and race back to England just as their time runs out.

The long movie ends when the princess sets foot in Fogg's club, the first woman to do so. "This could spell the end of the British Empire," says Fogg. "This *is* the end," proclaims fellow club member Robert Morley, before the wonderful closing credits begin.

Background: *Around the World in 80 Days* was the first movie to make extensive use of cameos—brief appearances by stars—whose presence kept the audience involved and eager to inspect every frame. The cameos were the brain child of producer Mike Todd, the most flamboyant showman of his era.

Todd made a fortune from *Around the World in 80 Days,* but he wasn't always right. When, for instance, he'd seen *Oklahoma!* in its out-of-town tryout before its Broadway opening, he'd said: "No girls. No gags. No chance." The Theatre Guild, which produced the show, gloated about that remark when the show became a sellout, tacking the phrase ". . . and no tickets" on to the end of his comment for their advertising.

When his wife, Elizabeth Taylor, gave birth to their child, Todd had all the hospital furniture moved from her room and substituted Louis XIV pieces. Working for him in *Around the World in 80 Days,* David Niven said: "It was like riding a runaway amphibious tank."

Bad Day at Black Rock

Category: Drama. Starring Spencer Tracy, Robert Ryan, Lee Marvin, Ernest Borgnine, Walter Brennan, Dean Jagger, Anne Francis, John Ericson. Screenplay by Millard Kaufman from the story "Bad Time at Hondo" by Howard Breslin. 81 minutes. 1955. MGM/UA Home Video.
Director: John Sturges.
Suggested Age Group: 13 and older.

The Story Shortly after the end of World War II, a mysterious one-armed man in a dark business suit gets off a Santa Fe train in a tiny, dusty California town; the conductor tells him it's the first time the Streamliner has stopped there in four years. It isn't a town, really, just a collection of a few rickety old buildings, a grimy café, a seedy hotel, and one dusty street.

The stranger in town, a Mr. John J. MacReedy, encounters two drifters who are curious about his presence there, and soon they learn that he's arrived to present a medal to a Mr. Komoko, whose son, a Japanese-American, had been killed in action in the war after saving MacReedy's life.

Soon he meets Reno Smith, the unofficial head of the shabby town, who puts on a friendly but cautious face for the nosy stranger. MacReedy becomes suspicious at the unfriendly attitudes of the drifters hanging around the café, notably Hector David and Coley Trimble, who soon make it clear that he is not welcome in town and that questions might lead to trouble.

Doc Velie, the local physician, and Tim Horn, the boozy figurehead sheriff, are the only people who seem remotely friendly, but at first they too are unwilling to talk or tell the stranger where he can find Komoko.

After making inquiries and finally facing down his enemies in some shocking confrontations, MacReedy learns that the day after Pearl Harbor, Smith and the others had tried to enlist in the army in a nearby town, but they were turned down. They returned, drunk, and took out their anger by killing Komoko. The shabby town's deep, dark secret had remained hidden until uncovered by MacReedy's unexpected visit.

The next day, his enemies vanquished, MacReedy agrees to Doc's request to give him Komoko's son's medal, to provide for the town "something to build on." Then MacReedy hails the train headed in the other direction, and when the conductor remarks that it was the first time the train had stopped in the town in years, MacReedy says simply: "Second time."

Background: This is a tough, gritty little movie most people don't seem to remember or even know about. Perhaps its short length or the fact that the same year had better-known movies like *Marty* and *Mister Roberts* contributed to its obscurity. Nevertheless, this story of an underdog with a righteous cause, an ordinary man moved to extraordinary courage, is thrilling in a quiet sort of way and will win the hearts of young adults. One of the first films made in the new process called CinemaScope, *Bad Day at Black Rock* has a parched look to it. You can almost taste the dust and sweltering heat of Death Valley, where it was filmed, and sense the despair of wasted lives and people desperate to cover up the truth.

Spencer Tracy, whose career is reviewed under the chapters on *Captains Courageous* and *Inherit the Wind,* made *Bad Day at Black Rock* in between *Broken Lance* and *The Mountain,* two of his less important movies. Except for narrating *How the West Was Won* in 1963, this was his last film at MGM, where he'd been one of the studio's biggest stars.

Tracy won his fifth Oscar nomination for his performance; Ernest Borgnine, his principal tormentor in the movie, would become a star after winning the Oscar for Best Actor for *Marty* that year. Lee Marvin, who played Hector, another of the town thugs, would also win an Oscar in later years as the drunken gunfighter in the comedy Western, *Cat Ballou.*

The Bear

Category: Adventure. Starring Bart the Bear, Douce the Bear, Jack Wallace, Tcheky Karyo, Andre Lacombe. Screenplay by Gerard Brach, based on the 1917 novel *The Grizzly King* by James Oliver Curwood. 93 minutes. 1989. Rated PG. Columbia Home Video.
Director: Jean-Jacques Annaud.
Suggested Age Group: 8 and older.

The Story This remarkable movie, set in British Columbia in 1885, centers around two Kodiak bears: one is an orphaned cub, played by a young bear named Douce, whose mother is killed early in the movie in a rock slide. The cub soon learns to adapt to the wild and comes upon a full-grown male, played by the movies' only trained grizzly, Bart the Bear. The furry giant had been wounded in the shoulder by a hunter.

At first the adult bear will have little to do with the cub, but the cuddly critter tags along nonetheless, trying to forge a relationship. With the indefatigable energy of youth, he is confident that he will ultimately succeed.

Meanwhile, the hunters pursue the big bear, eager to finish him off. One hunter returns to civilization to summon a third hunter and a pack of tracking dogs, while the other stays behind to track the wounded giant.

The cub is eventually captured by the hunters, who treat him well and hope to lure the big bear using the cub as bait. In a climactic scene on an isolated mountain ledge, the adult bear corners the hunter who shot him, growling at him, about to strike. The hunter, played by Tcheky Karyo, is paralyzed with fear and unable to reach for his rifle. He begs for his life, and somehow, through an almost mystical communication, the bear seems to understand his plea and finally, a few terrifying moments later, lumbers off.

Understandably, the hunter races for his rifle and lines up the bear in his sight, but now that the bear has spared his life, he is unable to pull the trigger. Going one step further, he yells: "Hide!

Hide!" at the big bear, fearful that the other returning hunters will kill him. When another hunter does in fact arrive and raises his rifle, Karyo pushes it away, having made peace with the huge animal. Then they free the cub and leave the mountains.

Background: Though set in the Canadian wilderness, this fascinating movie was actually filmed in the Italian Alps, which required the transporting of two bears to the remote shooting location. Bart the Bear did not have to be captured in a national park somewhere, of course. He works often, as Hollywood's one trained Kodiak bear, and anytime you see such a magnificent creature in a movie, it's old Bart, the one bear filmmakers can trust with stuntmen.

This mesmerizing movie has very little dialogue, which contributes to its documentary-like style. Younger viewers may be put off a bit by scenes of the bleeding bear or a hunting dog which has to be destroyed. But by the time these scenes appear, their effect is minimal.

Director Jean-Jacques Annaud, a veteran of hundreds of TV commercials, made his debut behind the lens with *Black and White in Color,* which won the Oscar for Best Foreign Language Film of 1977. His 1982 movie *Quest for Fire* is in some ways a precursor to *The Bear,* as that film was the most realistic caveman movie ever made. Like *The Bear,* it too has sparse dialogue, makes excellent use of animals, and conveys a brilliant sense of reality.

The Bear is at once an adorable movie and a brutal look at hunting. But it is never preachy or heavy-handed. Just fascinating.

The Big Country

Category: Drama. Starring Gregory Peck, Jean Simmons, Carroll Baker, Burl Ives, Charlton Heston, Chuck Connors, Charles Bickford. Screenplay by James R. Webb, Sy Bartlett, and Robert Wilder, based on a book by Donald Hamilton. Music by Jerome Moross. 166 minutes. 1958. MGM/UA Home Video.
Director: William Wyler.
Suggested Age Group: 10 and older.

The Story

Sometime in the 1880s, a handsome sea captain named James McKay arrives in Texas, where he is to marry Patricia Terrill, the rich daughter of landowner Major Henry Terrill. As soon as McKay arrives, however, he and his fiancée are subjected to hazing from a group of cowboys on the way to the huge Terrill ranch. Surprisingly, McKay refuses to fight back, and Patricia is enraged.

Soon McKay learns that the Terrills are involved in a range war over water rights with a neighboring family, the Hennesseys, some of whom had harassed him. Living in shacks on their adjoining property, and ruled by the blunt leader of the family, Rufus, the rough-hewn Hennesseys apparently will stop at nothing to get their rights to the river which separates their lands.

Slowly McKay begins to realize that Major Terrill relishes the clash with the Hennesseys, and it becomes clear that Patricia wants McKay to stand up to Rufus and his loutish son, Buck. But McKay is a gentleman, and prefers to seek peaceful alternatives. He starts to see that Patricia may not be the ideal choice for a wife after all.

In town McKay meets a schoolteacher, Julie Maragon, whose late father Clem owned the land which divides the Terrills from the Hennesseys and who in fact controls the Big Muddy, the dividing river. McKay, still intending to marry Patricia, is nevertheless attracted to Julie, and offers to buy her ranch as a wedding gift. He would thus become a neutral party in the dispute, offering free access to water for all. Despite McKay's attempt at arbitration, however, Major Terrill longs for a showdown. When

Julie is kidnapped by Buck Hennessey and held at the Hennesseys' ranch, McKay sets out to rescue her. The final, stirring confrontation comes after Terrill's men, led by foreman Steve Leech, ride up Blanco Canyon to force a showdown with the Hennesseys.

Background: *The Big Country* is one of the most sprawling, thrilling Westerns ever made, featuring huge vistas of endless acres, confrontations between men and women of opposing characters, and a brave protagonist who doesn't feel the need to demonstrate his courage just to satisfy himself.

The highlight of this rousing Western adventure comes in the showdown between Gregory Peck and Chuck Connors, who plays the hot-tempered Buck Hennessey. What makes this movie appropriate for older children, despite this brief and stunning violent confrontation, is the fact that the hero is a man who wants to resolve the conflict peacefully. The bloodshed is minimal.

Peck and William Wyler, who coproduced this movie, had worked together on the engaging *Roman Holiday* three years before. That film won an Oscar for newcomer Audrey Hepburn and made her a star. But they quarreled on the set of *The Big Country* over the size of the herd of cattle they needed to hire.

"As a producer," said Peck, "I saw things in a completely different light. When I was just an actor, I worried about today's work. But a producer has to worry about tomorrow, too." He and Wyler, incidentally, made up at the Academy Awards ceremonies, where the movie was nominated for Best Original Score, and Burl Ives won Best Supporting Actor. Peck's career is reviewed in the chapter on *The Yearling*.

The Big Country is enhanced by arguably the most beautiful score ever written. Curiously, though he wrote the music for *The Adventures of Huckleberry Finn; The Cardinal; Rachel, Rachel;* and *The Proud Rebel,* Jerome Moross achieved the most recognition for the score to this movie, as it conveys the endless prairies and growing tensions of a range war.

The Big Country is one of the most stirring, exciting Westerns ever filmed, offering larger-than-life characters in a tableau as big as has ever come across a screen. It is a classic Western saga.

The Bishop's Wife

Category: Comedy. Starring Cary Grant, Loretta Young, David
Niven, Monty Woolley, Elsa Lanchester. Screenplay by Robert E.
Sherwood and Leonardo Bercovici, from the novel by Robert
Nathan. 108 minutes. 1947. Black and white. HBO Home Video.
Director: Henry Koster.
Suggested Age Group: 8 and older.

The Story   An angel comes to earth to help a bishop who has
lost some of his humanity; his marriage is strained
and he is having trouble raising money for his
church in New York. It's Christmas time, naturally, and soon the
angel begins to impact the lives of everyone he meets, especially
the bishop's wife.

This is an endearing tale, full of wonderful observations and
meaningful gestures that reaffirm the positive values of life. There
is a moment, for example, when director Henry Koster uses ex-
treme close-ups to emphasize the increasing closeness between
the angel and the bishop's wife. The angel tells her that the only
things in life that don't change are youth and beauty, and that
"the only people who grow old were born old." He rekindles her
love of life and eventually her love for her husband, who had
grown distant due to the stress of his calling.

The Bishop's Wife is like a mysterious present sitting in a far
corner under the Christmas tree, waiting to be opened and to
show its magical glow. While not a film that is generally known,
families will surely adore it.

Background: While occasionally shown on TV around Christmas, *The Bishop's Wife* seems to have been lost in the horde of
better-known holiday classics like *It's a Wonderful Life* or *Miracle on 34th Street* and *A Christmas Carol*. But this film has a
warmth all its own, without ever getting sappy or overly sentimental.

Cary Grant, who plays the angel, had made fifty-three films
prior to this. In this movie, he is seen, as usual, in a well-tailored

suit. Off the set, he had his own clothes made to order in Hong Kong, where his tailor displayed a sign on the street: a life-sized cutout of Grant, wearing a suit, pointing to the entrance.

Loretta Young, the film's title player, won the Oscar for her other movie that year, *The Farmer's Daughter,* and would win a nomination two years later for *Come to the Stable.* She retired from films and became a TV star on her own show in 1953, but in films like *The Doctor Takes a Wife* and *The Stranger,* among many others, she remains one of the most beautiful women ever to grace the screen.

The Bishop's Wife is an understated but gentle story that will warm every heart and delight young viewers. Its use of special effects, such as when the angel trims the tree or fills a drink with a flick of his finger, is appropriately judicious. Offering the charm of Cary Grant, the incandescent beauty of Loretta Young, and the message that the world is good, that people are luckier than they know, and that things seem to work out for the best, this film is a classic in family entertainment.

Black Beauty

Category: Drama. Starring Sean Bean, David Thewlis, Jim Carter, Peter Davidson, John McEnery, Peter Cook, Eleanor Bron. Screenplay by Caroline Thompson, based on the novel by Anna Sewell. 102 minutes. 1994. Rated G. Warner Bros. Home Video.
Director: Caroline Thompson.
Suggested Age Group: 6 and older.

The Story Narrated by Beauty himself (the voice of Alan Cummings), this is the heartwarming tale of a horse who goes from owner to owner in late Victorian England. "I remember everything," he tells us, as he recounts his life.

We begin, appropriately, with Beauty's birth and early life spent with other horses and a pony on a large estate in the English countryside. Merrylegs is a mischief-causing pony, Ginger is the mare Beauty eventually falls in love with, and Joe is the head groom at the idyllic estate.

But of course Beauty's life isn't all contentment. The wife of the landowner falls ill, and Beauty is soon sold to another, wealthier landowner whose foolish, demanding wife treats him and Ginger as mere beasts of burden.

Beauty suffers pain and sadness for the first time, as his odyssey through life begins. Later on, he is bought by a poor carriage driver and must learn to navigate the crowded cobblestone streets of Edwardian London. Luckily, this driver is kindly, but Beauty's journey doesn't end there. He changes owners again, and he's put to work pulling heavy loads. In the movie's tenderest moment, Beauty has a poignant reunion with Joe, his groom and friend from the estate, who goes on to rescue him from his unhappy plight.

Background: *Black Beauty* didn't find a theatrical audience for long and was soon gone from theaters. But it paints a beautiful, poignant picture at the life of a working animal a hundred years ago. The lush, sweeping estates of the English countryside are depicted in stark contrast to the grimy streets of the London slums, and *Black Beauty* calls both of these locales home throughout the film.

The cast is made up largely of unknowns, but Eleanor Bron, who was in *Two for the Road, Alfie, Bedazzled,* and *Help!,* appears in a small role as the silly, somewhat cruel Countess of Wexmire, oblivious to the pain she causes the horses pulling her carriage. The late Peter Cook, also of *Bedazzled* and *The Wrong Box,* and cofounder of the famous "Beyond the Fringe" group at Cambridge with Dudley Moore, appears briefly as the Count of Wexmire in his last screen role.

Produced by the same team that brought us *The Fugitive, Under Siege,* and *Cliffhanger, Black Beauty* has a look that is as much a character as the horses and humans themselves. Production designer John Box, who made *Lawrence of Arabia* and *Doctor Zhivago,* is no stranger to first-class work, and his experience in creating the look of old London for *Oliver!* is evident here.

Black Beauty does have some scary moments, such as when a barn catches fire, threatening the horses, and some sad sequences, when Beauty's future looks bleak with his owner. "We don't get to choose the people in our lives," Beauty tells us. "For us, it's all chance."

This is a touching, beautifully filmed remake of the familiar old story.

The Black Stallion

Category: Drama. Starring Kelly Reno, Mickey Rooney, Teri Garr, Hoyt Axton. Screenplay by William D. Wittliff, Melissa Mathison, Jeanne Rosenberg, based on the novel by Walter Farley. 118 minutes. 1979. Rated PG. Warner Bros. Home Video.
Director: Carroll Ballard.
Suggested Age Group: 5 and above.

The Story   An eleven-year-old boy and his father are traveling on a ship when the boy comes upon a beautiful black Arabian stallion, who is tied up and frightened. The horse has been mistreated by his owners and is confined to a stall.

The boy's father wins a trinket in the shape of a horse in a poker game, and he explains to his son that it represents Bucephalus, the horse that only young Alexander the Great could tame and ride. He presents it to his son, just as a violent storm hits the ship. A fire quickly breaks out, sinking the ship and everyone aboard. Everyone, that is, except the boy, who washes up on a deserted Greek island.

Soon after he regains consciousness, the lucky youth realizes that he's not alone. The other survivor of the ship is the stallion, who cautiously approaches the boy upon his awakening. Gradually they form a bond that is strengthened after the horse saves the boy from a deadly king cobra snake.

After the two unusual friends begin to adapt to life on the island, the boy is rescued by some Greek fishermen who drag him away, leaving the horse behind. Ultimately, though, the horse is also recovered, and he and the boy wind up back in America in the boy's hometown.

The boy keeps his new friend in the backyard, but one day, the horse is spooked and runs away, followed closely by the boy. He finally finds the horse on the property of a onetime horse trainer who explains that the mysterious horse is endowed with tremendous speed. Soon the boy and the trainer prepare the stallion for a big race against the two rival thoroughbred champions. Before you know it, a track announcer at Belmont spies the horse in a late-night training session, and soon the boy is weighing in with the professional jockeys before the big race.

Since "the Black," as the horse is known, has never raced before, he shies away from the starting gate, then rears and hesitates once the race has begun. Nonetheless, as expected, he wins the race. The racing sequence, intercut with flashbacks of the boy and horse racing on a sandy beach, makes for a stirring, exciting, and unforgettable scene.

Background: The early part of this Francis Ford Coppola production was filmed on the beaches of Sardinia, which doubled for the Greek island where the boy and his horse are marooned. Nearly twenty minutes go by with no dialogue whatsoever. Nevertheless, the boy and the horse speak volumes as their close relationship begins to take shape.

This is a movie which demands just a bit of a suspension of disbelief. For example, it's never explained, when the boy returns home, how he's allowed to keep his horse. And there are some needless ethnic stereotypes, such as the depiction of an Arab man stealing the boy's life jacket. These minor flaws, however, do not diminish the magical beauty of this special film.

Kelly Reno, who plays the lead, has yet to enjoy a major screen career, though he did star in the sequel to this film, *The Black Stallion Returns,* and the now-forgotten *Brady's Escape.*

In contrast, Mickey Rooney, who plays Henry Dailey, the old horse trainer, has enjoyed one of the longest, most distinguished careers in the history of the movies. Born Joe Yule, Jr., in 1920 in Brooklyn, he made his debut in show business not by performing with his vaudevillian parents but by wandering onstage and standing on his head during the performance of another trouper named Sid Gold.

Rooney, no stranger to movies about horses, also costarred in *National Velvet* in 1944. In one of his early movies, he played a midget and even lost a baby tooth while puffing on a cigar. He also played a midget in his movie debut, *Not to Be Trusted.*

Eight wives (including actresses Ava Gardner and Martha Vickers) and a trip to bankruptcy court did not derail his career. *The Black Stallion,* which won him a Best Supporting Actor nomination, helped to revive his career. He won an Emmy for his sensitive title portrayal of a learning-disabled man named *Bill* in 1983, and today remains one of the true giants in Hollywood history.

The Black Stallion is a movie about a remarkable friendship and dream that comes true. The screenplay, cowritten by Melissa Mathison, who would write *E.T.* and *The Indian in the Cupboard,* never goes over the top emotionally. The bond between boy and horse is always plausible, never sappy or sentimental. *The Black Stallion* remains one of the best family movies of recent years.

The Boy Who Could Fly

Category: Drama. Starring Bonnie Bedelia, Lucy Deakins, Jay Underwood, Colleen Dewhurst, Fred Savage, Fred Gwynne, Louise Fletcher. Screenplay by Nick Castle. 114 minutes. 1986. Rated PG. Warner Bros. Home Video.
Director: Nick Castle.
Suggested Age Group: 7 and older.

 The Story Charlene, a widowed mother with her children, Milly and Louis, move into a new home where their next-door neighbors are Eric, an autistic teenager, and his alcoholic uncle Hugo. Since his parents were killed in a plane crash when he was five, Eric often sits on his roof outside his bedroom window, slowly flapping his arms, pretending to be an airplane.

Charlene and her children soon begin to adjust to their new home and school, though Louis has trouble paying attention and does poorly in class. Furthermore, he's bullied by some tough neighborhood kids and constantly flees to his backyard.

The strange, lonely boy next door intrigues Milly. At school, Milly's teacher, Mrs. Sherman, asks her to look after Eric and try to form a friendship with him. As she spends time with him, Milly searches in vain for some response, some smile or outward communication from Eric, but to no avail. Finally one day Milly coaxes a smile out of him and, encouraged, she intensifies her contact with him, trying to get him to respond further. One day, as they are watching a baseball game in the park, a fly ball threatens to hit Milly on the head, but Eric reaches out and catches it, much to her astonishment and delight.

Despite such small triumphs, though, Milly has persistent suspicions about Eric. He leaves a flower in her room, but she can't explain how he could've crossed over to her house without . . . flying!

When Milly suffers a slight concussion in a fall, she dreams she is flying with Eric, and when she awakens, she can't believe it was only a dream. Eric's uncle's drinking increases to the point where Eric must be taken to an institution to be cared for. When

Charlene and her children attempt to visit him, he tries to fly out a window.

Soon after this frightening incident, Milly finds Eric back in his home, having escaped from the institution. When the authorities return to take him back, he and Milly flee, first to the school, then to a nearby roof. With two security men closing in, Eric and Milly jump off the roof. Just when it appears they'll fall to their deaths, with Charlene watching in terror, they fly! A huge crowd gathers, and finally Eric returns Milly to her room and flies away.

Several weeks later, Eric still hasn't returned but his uncle has stopped drinking and gotten a job. Louis, with the help of his dog Max, finally takes on the neighborhood bullies. And the film ends with Milly looking skyward, thinking of her unusual friend.

Background: If ever there was a movie which deserved the warning "Don't try this at home, kids," it's this one. The notion, furthermore, that an untrained classmate can somehow break through to a severely autistic friend is a bit of a stretch. But with a tender and sensitive portrayal, lead actress Lucy Deakins convinces the viewer that she cares deeply for the boy.

Jay Underwood is believable as Eric. Always stoic, he nevertheless conveys the sense of someone trapped inside himself.

Fred Savage, who plays Louis, made his screen debut in this movie, and soon followed afterward with *The Princess Bride, Vice Versa, Little Monsters,* and *The Wizard.* He also starred in the delightful TV series *The Wonder Years.*

Bonnie Bedelia is the quintessential screen mother here. The real-life aunt of child star Macaulay Culkin, she was trained in ballet and first appeared in *The Gypsy Moths; They Shoot Horses, Don't They?;* and *Lovers and Other Strangers* before making her starring debut in *Heart Like a Wheel,* in which she played race driver Shirley Muldowney. She is perhaps best known as Bruce Willis's oft-endangered wife in the first two *Die Hard* movies, and more recently costarred in *Speechless.*

It is typical of the professionalism of the late Colleen Dewhurst that she took a small role as Mrs. Sherman, the teacher, in *The Boy Who Could Fly.* She was one of the great stars of the theater, and received several Tony Awards. A onetime president of Actors Equity, Ms. Dewhurst led the fight to save several theaters on Broadway from the wrecker's ball.

Fred Gwynne appears here in a small but memorable role as

Eric's alcoholic Uncle Hugo. Best known for two TV series, *Car 54, Where Are You?,* which ran from 1961 to 1963, and *The Munsters,* from 1964–66, he was also terrific as the Yale-educated southern judge bewildered by the sleazy demeanor of neophyte New York attorney Joe Pesci, the defense attorney, in the hilarious 1992 comedy *My Cousin Vinnie,* his final film before his death in 1993.

The Boy Who Could Fly is a sweet, endearing movie in which children and parents are honest with one another and learn to deal with unusual problems sensibly. Although its ultimate message that dreams sometimes really can come true may be a bit trite, it's a film families won't soon forget.

Breaking Away

Category: Drama. Starring Dennis Christopher, Dennis Quaid, Daniel Stern, Paul Dooley, Barbara Barrie, Robyn Douglass, Hart Bochner, John Ashton. Screenplay by Steve Tesich. 100 minutes. 1979. Rated PG. Fox Home Video.
Director: Peter Yates.
Suggested Age Group: 12 and older.

 Filmed in Bloomington, Indiana, near the campus of the University of Indiana, *Breaking Away* centers around Dave Stohler, a local boy who spends his days swimming in a nearby rock quarry with his friends, sunning himself, and wondering about the direction his life will take. What distinguishes him from his three friends, Mike, Cyril, and Moocher, is that he has begun to act as if he's Italian.

Dave speaks with an Italian accent, covers the walls of his room with posters of Italy, and rides a bicycle fully attired in the outfit of an Italian racer. When he learns that the real Italian bicycle team will be coming to Bloomington to compete in a race, he's beside himself with joy. His unconventional behavior does not sit well with his used-car dealer father, but his mother thinks he's just going through a phase.

The action picks up when Dave meets Katherine, a beautiful college student. Still pretending to be Italian, he serenades her outside her sorority house one night. Again this behavior causes a conflict, but this time it's Katherine's boyfriend, Rod, who is upset. As tensions between the college students and the locals (called "cutters," short for stone cutters) begin to boil over, it's all the local policemen can do to keep them apart.

When the inevitable fight breaks out, the students and the cutters are hauled into court, where the judge suggests a solution. To settle the dispute between the temporary residents of Bloomington and the locals, the judge proposes a bicycle race between the two groups.

When the long-awaited Italian team comes to town for an exhibition race, David rides alongside them. But his illusions are suddenly brought crashing to reality when one of the riders causes the awestruck David to fall off his bicycle. So he shucks his Italian persona, comes clean to Katherine about his true identity, and pulls down all the posters of Italy from his walls, making the ultimate break.

Finally, in the big race held between the college boys and the cutters, Dave finds vindication at last.

Background: Curiously, though *Breaking Away* was favorably received and did well at the box office, its star, Dennis Christopher, never went on to anything quite so successful again. Even with a bit role, ironically, in *Fellini's Roma,* a part in Robert Altman's *A Wedding,* and an appearance in *Chariots of Fire,* the Philadelphia-born actor hasn't had much luck since.

The same cannot be said, however, of Christopher's costars Dennis Quaid and Daniel Stern. Quaid, who plays Mike, the leader of the cutters, had just begun in films back in 1979, with three forgettable pictures to his credit. But ahead for the rising star lay *The Big Easy, The Right Stuff, Everybody's All-American,* and *Postcards from the Edge.* He is one of those actors who has not quite achieved enormous stardom, but he's certainly well-known enough to be more than just a working actor. He met his wife, Meg Ryan, when they costarred in *Innerspace.*

Daniel Stern, who plays Cyril, one of Dave's cutter buddies, made his screen debut in *Breaking Away.* Soon his career began to take on some interesting credits, such as *I'm Dancing as Fast as I Can, Diner,* which really propelled him to widespread recognition, and *Hannah and Her Sisters.* He then found real stardom as one of the two bumbling thieves in *Home Alone,* the most successful comedy in movie history. He returned in the sequel, and more recently appeared in *Rookie of the Year* and *Bushwacked.*

Breaking Away is, to date, the highlight in the varied career of Paul Dooley, who plays the hard-working if somewhat narrow-minded Mr. Stohler, David's bewildered father. He also played Dennis Christopher's father in *A Wedding* the year before, one of several movies he's made with director Robert Altman. Dooley, who cowrote the film *Health* with Altman, has appeared in dozens of commercials, and in fact heads his own company to produce them. His other films of note include *Death Wish, Endangered Species,* and Altman's highly touted *The Player.*

Barbara Barrie, who won an Oscar nomination for her small

but memorable role as David's mother, is best known for her work on TV shows like *Barney Miller, The Mary Tyler Moore Show,* and in films such as *Private Benjamin.*

Director Peter Yates is perhaps most remembered for *Bullitt,* one of the best crime thrillers of the sixties, which features a car chase against which all others (save *The French Connection*) will forever be measured. *Breaking Away* is a quintessential American movie, though its screenwriter and director came from Europe. Yates, born in Surrey, England, also directed *John and Mary, The Hot Rock, The Deep, Eyewitness,* and *An Innocent Man.* His 1992 movie *Year of the Comet* was an intriguing film with great potential, but unfortunately few saw it.

More recently, Yates directed the touching *Roommates* and the compelling *The Run of the Country,* both released in 1995. For *Breaking Away,* Yates was nominated for Best Director. The film was also nominated for Best Picture, but it ultimately lost out to *Kramer vs. Kramer.*

Breaking Away is a study in class distinctions, and it offers a slice-of-life portrait of a small college town. It shows a subtle quality of wistfulness and a sense of longing for a better life.

Some of the film's language is harsh, so parents of younger viewers should wait a few years before sharing it with them. But older siblings will love *Breaking Away* and may pedal their bicycles with just a bit more determination after seeing it.

Brian's Song

Category: Drama. Starring James Caan, Billy Dee Williams, Jack Warden, Bernie Casey. Screenplay by William Blinn, based on the book by Gale Sayers, *I Am Third*. Music by Michel Legrand. 74 minutes. 1970. Rated G. Columbia Home Video.
Director: Buzz Kulik.
Suggested Age Group: 10 and older.

 This is the true story of the brief but intense friendship between two pro football players, Chicago Bears rookies Brian Piccolo and Gale Sayers. The former was an unheralded backup running back from Wake Forest, the latter the number-one draft choice from the University of Kansas who, despite an injury-shortened career, would nevertheless be remembered as one of the greatest running backs who ever lived.

Piccolo and Sayers were roommates in the Bears' preseason training camp and on road trips during the regular season, the first interracial roommates among pro athletes of any sport.

Sayers was an immediate sensation, returning kickoffs and scoring touchdowns almost at will. When a severe knee injury (which would eventually end his career prematurely a few seasons later) cut short his rookie season, Piccolo filled in for him. He performed adequately, but it took several seasons for him to make his own mark on the field. Finally, he was moved to the starting lineup, but as a fullback.

Soon after being added to the starting lineup, however, Piccolo's performance begins to slack off. And he can't keep his weight up. No matter what he eats or what exercise regimen he tries, he keeps losing weight, until head coach George "Papa Bear" Halas takes Piccolo out of the lineup and orders tests. Cancer is detected and surgery performed. Piccolo seems on the road to recovery. But more tumors are detected, and soon it becomes evident that the young athlete is terminal. Through it all, until the end, he and Sayers maintain their special bond of friendship.

Background: This is one of the most acclaimed sports movies ever made. It had a huge audience when it was aired on TV, but now that two decades have passed, younger audiences might easily overlook it in the video store.

James Caan's portrayal of the doomed football player is one of the highlights of his sometimes turbulent career. Caan's background as an amateur athlete is obvious, for he is quite convincing as he goes through the film's vigorous football drills alongside real players. Caan worked frequently after this picture, and his other films of note are *El Dorado* with John Wayne, *T. R. Baskin* opposite rising actress Candice Bergen, *The Godfather, The Gambler, Cinderella Liberty, Funny Lady, Rollerball, Thief, Gardens of Stone,* and a funny role as a sleazy Las Vegas gambler in *Honeymoon in Vegas.*

Billy Dee Williams captures the essence of the shy superstar Gale Sayers. He'd made a strong impression opposite Diana Ross in *Lady Sings the Blues* and later costarred in *The Bingo Long Traveling All-Stars & Motor Kings,* an excellent comedy about baseball's Negro Leagues. His film career has not lived up to its early promise, however, though he made his mark in two parts of the *Star Wars* trilogy, *The Empire Strikes Back* and *Return of the Jedi.*

Michel Legrand's music adds a poignant dimension to *Brian's Song.* Although never overwhelming, its recurring theme will certainly tug at your heart. His many memorable credits include the scores for *Summer of '42* and *The Thomas Crown Affair.*

Brian's Song is a beautiful story of friendship and courage in the face of tragedy. The football sequences look authentic, including judicious use of file footage of the real Sayers, cutting his way across opposing backfields on his way to the Pro Football Hall of Fame, and footage of the real Brian Piccolo. For one scene, Caan and Williams were captured sitting on the Chicago Bears bench during a real game. In it, the actors radiate that special glow that is all too rare; they knew what they were doing was heartfelt. None of this is maudlin. *Brian's Song* is continually inspiring and uplifting.

The Bridge on the River Kwai

Category: Action adventure. Starring William Holden, Sir Alec
Guinness, Sessue Hayakawa, Jack Hawkins, Geoffrey Horne, James
Donald. Screenplay by Pierre Boulle, based on his novel; screenplay
cowritten by Michael Wilson and Carl Foreman, uncredited. Music
by Malcolm Arnold. 161 minutes. 1957. Columbia Tristar Home
Video.
Director: Sir David Lean.
Suggested Age Group: 11 and above.

> **The
> Story**

During World War II, in a remote Japanese prison
camp in the dense jungles of Burma, a tyrannical
camp commander named Colonel Saito keeps his
prisoners in check with heavy labor and harsh discipline. "Be
happy in your work," he commands with irony.

A new contingent of British POWs enters the camp in crisp
formation. Despite being prisoners, however, they obey only the
command of their own leader, Colonel Nicholson, not their
Japanese captors.

This recalcitrance becomes a sticking point in the relationship
between Saito and Nicholson, especially when Saito insists that
British officers work alongside enlisted men constructing a bridge
across the river Kwai, a clear violation of the Geneva Convention. Eventually, Saito tosses Nicholson into a steamy box-shaped
hut called "the oven" to try to break his spirit.

These power struggles are witnessed from a nearby infirmary
by wounded and bedridden prisoners, including an American
officer named Shears, whose cynicism is his principal weapon.
He knows the ropes of the camp, and recognizes that the idealistic, by-the-book English officer will soon succumb to the Japanese commander's fury.

Shears soon manages to escape the camp and make his way
through the jungle back to British lines. While relaxing on the
beach with a new female friend, he is summoned to a commando
headquarters and confronted with the accusation that he'd faked
his officer's rank to get better treatment from the Japanese.

As punishment, Shears is forced to "volunteer" to join a three-man commando team sent into the jungle to return to the camp, find the strategically important bridge, and blow it up.

Meanwhile, back at the camp, Saito has come to the realization that the only way he can get the vital bridge built on time is to let the POWs work under the direct command of their own officers. This is a critical but vital loss of face for the proud, traditional Japanese officer.

Work on the bridge is moved down river and begun again, and everything goes smoothly. When the bridge is finally completed, both Nicholson and Saito proclaim it a splendid structure. Nicholson sees it as a permanent monument to the ingenuity and engineering skill of British soldiers, who are superior even to their captors. Saito sees it as an example of Japanese-led labor. But in reality, he is shamed at his loss of face.

After a perilous trek through the dense jungle, the commandos and their porters arrive at the campsite and set up their mortars for a diversionary attack. During the night they wire the bridge with explosives while, down below, the POWs stage a musical revue for their last night in the camp.

The next morning a completion ceremony is held on the bridge, and the prisoners have nailed a plaque to the side of the sturdy wooden structure saying it was built by British POWs. But for the commandos, the dawn brings a crisis. The river has receded overnight, exposing the telltale detonating wires. When Colonel Nicholson, by now full of pride in completing the bridge, spots the wires he exclaims in utter horror: "Someone is trying to blow up the bridge!" Accompanied by Colonel Saito, he uncovers the hidden position of one of the commandos down river on a sandbar. Refusing to let his proud achievement be destroyed, Nicholson tries to stop the commando, who manages to knife Saito but is then killed by Japanese snipers.

Seeing this, Shears swims frantically across the river and tries to kill Nicholson and push the detonator himself. But a sniper wounds him in the leg, then shoots him in the back. He falls just a few feet short of his goal, when Nicholson recognizes him and begins to realize at last what's going on. Diversionary mortar fire from the commandos finds its mark and hits Nicholson. Realizing the folly of his deeds, the mortally wounded officer asks: "What have I done?" Rolling his eyes heavenward, Nicholson staggers, collapses, and dies, falling on the mortar detonator, which blows up the bridge just as a flag-draped train load of

Japanese soldiers and officials passes over the bridge and plummets into the river Kwai below.

The last words heard in the movie are uttered by a British medical officer named Clipton, a POW who'd witnessed the disaster from an overlooking ridge. Surveying the devastation, he says simply: "Madness. Madness," addressing the folly and waste of war.

Background: *The Bridge on the River Kwai* was based on true events. There were in real life two bridges: a wooden structure that was later demolished and a steel bridge with a concrete base. However, the movie wasn't filmed where the events actually took place, as locations in Thailand and Burma were deemed inappropriate. Instead, producer Sam Spiegel shot the film in the dense jungles of what is today Sri Lanka, along the Kelani River.

Naturally, other changes were made to the story as well. In Pierre Boulle's novel, Colonel Nicholson actually thwarts the destruction of the bridge, which was closer to the real events. But director Sir David Lean and producer Spiegel prevailed upon Boulle and credited screenwriters Carl Foreman and Michael Wilson to write in a final, huge explosion of the bridge.

Why, you might ask, would I recommend *The Bridge on the River Kwai* in a book for young viewers, given its subject matter and several scenes of violence? Simply because it is one of the greatest adventure films ever made. Its appeal is universal; when it was shown for the first time on network TV in September 1966, an estimated national audience of 60 million viewers tuned in. It went on to win seven Academy Awards, including Best Picture, Best Actor for Alec Guinness, and Best Screenplay.

The Bridge on the River Kwai was Sir Alec Guinness's sixteenth film to be released in this country, coming just after *The Swan* and before *All at Sea,* two modest performances compared to this masterpiece.

"The first time I was sent the script," Guinness once said to me, "I didn't want to do it. It just looked like something out of a jungle movie, with women wearing fruit on their head, elephants, things like that." Revisions on the script soon changed his mind.

Guinness became a star with this movie. His other notable films include *Kind Hearts and Coronets, Tunes of Glory, Lawrence of Arabia, The Man in the White Suit,* and *The Lady Killers.* He is probably the greatest "inside-out" actor of his generation, changing his entire appearance and carriage to fit the role.

In addition to making Guinness a star, this movie revived the career of Sessue Hayakawa, who was brilliant as Colonel Saito. He'd enjoyed success in silent films and made many more movies here, in Europe, and Japan, but *Bridge on the River Kwai* is the movie that made him famous. The success couldn't have come at a better moment, for he'd fallen on difficult times. Hayakawa went on to receive an Oscar nomination for his role as Saito, but he lost to Red Buttons for *Sayonara*.

William Holden, who played Shears, was born William Franklin Beedle, Jr., in tiny O'Fallon, Illinois. He was already a star going into *Bridge on the River Kwai*. He'd become an overnight star as the lead in *Golden Boy*, was perfectly cast as the writer-gigolo to Gloria Swanson in *Sunset Boulevard*, tutored Judy Holliday in the hilarious *Born Yesterday*, won an Oscar for *Stalag 17*, and starred in *Sabrina* and *Picnic*.

Holden did a smart thing when he made *The Bridge on the River Kwai*. Rather than work for a straight salary, he worked for a small stipend, plus a percentage of the movie's gross, which earned him $2 million.

The Bridge on the River Kwai remains one of the greatest adventures ever filmed, offering vivid characters and exploring the tensions and sublimated emotions of war. It is a plea for sanity in a world gone mad, taking what is in reality a minor incident and making it a monumental and heroic struggle. It is a film every young adult is sure to enjoy.

Brigadoon

Category: Musical. Starring Gene Kelly, Van Johnson, Cyd Charisse, Elaine Stewart, Barry Jones, Hugh Laing. Screenplay by Alan Jay Lerner, based on the play by Lerner and Frederick Loewe. Songs by Lerner and Loewe. 108 minutes. 1954. MGM Home Video.
Director: Vincente Minnelli.
Suggested Age Group: 8 and older.

The Story — Two American hunters on holiday stumble upon an uncharted village in the Scottish Highlands. A wedding is scheduled to take place there and the whole town is abuzz. It doesn't take long, however, before the Americans discover that this is no ordinary hamlet. It is, in fact, a village from 1754 whose inhabitants awaken only one day every one hundred years. The hunters just happened to have come upon the village on that century's one special day.

One of the Americans, Tommy Albright, is engaged to marry a woman he doesn't really love back in New York. But in Brigadoon, he's quickly attracted to Fiona Campbell, the bride-to-be's older sister. They dance together romantically in the heather, but soon Tommy's cynical friend, Jeff Douglas, convinces him to return to New York and leave Brigadoon behind.

After a month back home in New York, listening to dull conversation from his fiancée, Tommy and his friend Jeff return to the outskirts of Brigadoon. To Tommy's chagrin, though, Brigadoon has now disappeared, but as Tommy's been told, if you love someone, anything is possible. Before his wondering eyes, Brigadoon suddenly reappears through the mist, and Tommy rejoins Fiona for eternity.

Background: This is the movie version of the Broadway musical which opened on March 13, 1947, and had a respectable run of 581 performances. Made during the waning years of MGM's golden age of musicals, it was shot on the back lot at MGM instead of on location in Scotland.

The result is the film's stagy, artificial look, which attracts attention to the obvious sets and contributes a sometimes claustrophobic interior sensation to the outside shots. Nevertheless, the intimacies among the characters are not lost in the transition to the large screen. *Brigadoon* has several standard songs, most notably "Almost Like Being in Love," one of those songs you've always known but really never associated with this or any other show.

But what makes *Brigadoon* spectacular is the choreography by Gene Kelly himself, no doubt inspired by Agnes de Mille's choreography for the Broadway version. Kelly and Cyd Charisse are perfect dancing partners and enchanting together.

By the time he made *Brigadoon,* Kelly had already established himself as the heir to Fred Astaire. The onetime apprentice bricklayer, soda jerk, and dance teacher was spotted by Richard Rodgers in *One for the Money.* He made his mark in the title role in *Pal Joey,* signed a movie contract with David O. Selznick, was loaned to MGM in *For Me and My Gal,* and soon became an MGM contract player. Films such as *Du Barry Was a Lady, Thousands Cheer, Anchors Aweigh,* and *An American in Paris* followed, after which he made the movie for which he is best known, *Singin' in the Rain,* which also featured Cyd Charisse, though not in a leading role.

After a capable dramatic stint as a cynical reporter in the riveting *Inherit the Wind* in 1960, Kelly turned to directing, and though *The Tunnel of Love, Gigot,* and *A Guide for the Married Man* were flops, he did direct Barbra Streisand in *Hello, Dolly!* and has since enjoyed his status as one of Hollywood's greatest song-and-dance men. His performance in *Brigadoon* is a bit forced, especially when he's called upon to sing, but put him in the arms of Cyd Charisse and it's pure magic.

Cyd Charisse might have been an unlikely choice to play the Scottish Fiona Campbell, since she was born Tula Ellice Finklea in Amarillo, Texas. But she handles the obligatory Scottish accent capably. Given her livelihood, she was probably born too late, because by the late 1950s, the lavish Hollywood musical had begun to lose favor; subsequently, she found work in dramatic roles.

By the time she made *Brigadoon,* Charisse's movie résumé included *The Harvey Girls, Fiesta, Singin' in the Rain,* and *The Band Wagon,* and she would go on to make *It's Always Fair Weather* and *Silk Stockings.*

Director Vincente Minnelli was one of the giants of his craft and one of MGM's greatest filmmakers. He began as a director and designer on Broadway and was brought to Hollywood by Arthur Freed, who produced twelve of Minnelli's sixteen movies. This was one of four movies he made with Gene Kelly, along with *The Pirate, Ziegfeld Follies,* and *An American in Paris.* He also directed *Meet Me in St. Louis, The Band Wagon,* and *Gigi.* But he didn't restrict himself to musicals. He also directed *Lust for Life,* the mesmerizing biography of Van Gogh with Kirk Douglas, *Bells Are Ringing,* the comedy with Judy Holliday, as well as other dramas. The onetime husband of Judy Garland and the father of Liza Minnelli, he died in 1986.

Van Johnson, who plays Kelly's cynical best friend, Jeff Douglas, was one of Hollywood's great "other men" as well as a distinguished leading man. This was especially true during World War II, when most of the other stars were in uniform. The Newport, R.I. native was one of Broadway's *New Faces of 1936* and ironically, later understudied none other than Gene Kelly on Broadway in *Pal Joey.*

A leading lady at MGM was once asked if she wanted a chance to act in *A Streetcar Named Desire.* "Sure," she replied, "but if I don't land that role, I'll settle for a Van named 'Johnson.'"

In 1943 he nearly lost his life in an auto accident; a huge gash across his forehead nearly decapitated him. But Johnson made an astonishingly-quick recovery. At first, his doctors couldn't understand this, but then Johnson explained he'd made 12 donations to the Red Cross Blood Bank program, thus making his body accustomed to the rapid creation of new blood, saving him from bleeding to death.

The actor, whose trademarks are red socks, still performs in dinner theaters, and starred in more than 100 movies, most notably *A Guy Named Joe, Thirty Seconds Over Tokyo, In the Good Old Summertime* (in which he and Judy Garland escort the then-three-year-old Liza Minnelli in the finale), *The Caine Mutiny,* and *Miracle in the Rain.*

To this day he insists he has no regrets for turning down the leading part in a TV pilot, portraying Eliot Ness in *The Untouchables.*

Brigadoon is an underappreciated musical, rich in style and a throwback to the grand days of MGM. Its mood is enchanting, and Kelly and Charisse show us why they were one of Hollywood's greatest dance teams. It is a film to enthrall every member of your family.

Captain Blood

Category: Adventure. Starring Errol Flynn, Olivia de Havilland, Basil Rathbone, J. Carrol Naish, Guy Kibbee, Lionel Atwill. Screenplay by Casey Robinson, based on the novel by Rafael Sabatini. 119 minutes. 1935. Black and white. Warner Bros. Home Video.
Director: Michael Curtiz.
Suggested Age Group: 11 and older.

 Dr. Peter Blood is an Irish physician living under the iron-handed rule of King James II in 1685, when anyone questioning the authority of the Crown was deemed a traitor. After he is summoned to treat a wounded man who'd opposed the king, Blood is arrested. Sentenced to die, he is saved when it is decided that all traitors should be sent to Jamaica to be slaves.

Soon after he arrives, Blood spies Arabella Bishop, the beautiful daughter of a plantation owner. Enduring the brutality of his captors, Dr. Blood is soon summoned to treat the colonial governor, who suffers from gout. From this point forward, he becomes a frequent visitor to the governor's bedside.

Later on, when the Spanish fleet arrives and conquers the island, Blood and some other slaves escape, becoming pirates sailing the Caribbean. Blood forms an alliance with a French pirate named Levasseur, and he establishes a code of conduct for the team. Their alliance is short-lived, however, as Levasseur captures Arabella. Blood, determined to free her, defeats his sometime partner in a duel. After the evil King James is dethroned by William of Orange, Blood wins a naval commission. As Captain Blood, he defeats two French galleys, after which he replaces the corrupt governor of Jamaica and chooses Arabella as his bride.

Background: This was the movie which made Errol Flynn a star. But as is so often the case, he wasn't the first choice for this swashbuckling adventure. Robert Donat, a much more established name in 1935, was originally to star with Jean Muir. But

Donat was reportedly ill, so studio head Jack L. Warner took a chance on the little-known, twenty-three-year-old Flynn and paid him a whopping $300 a week, hardly enough compensation for Flynn's suffering through a case of malaria during the shooting. Warner also cast nineteen-year-old Olivia de Havilland, who would go on to be Flynn's greatest costar. "I was in love with him the moment I laid eyes on him," she said years later. Her passion shows through every one of her scenes with the Tasmanian-born star.

Parents should be aware that several scenes in *Captain Blood* might cause some fearful reactions in younger viewers. Although not shown on camera, one slave is branded on the cheek, and there are some fierce battles between pirates and French soldiers. But they are filmed in that old-fashioned thirties style that will probably leave even young viewers wide-eyed rather than cringing.

Captain Blood takes its time in finding its pace. Flynn looks uncomfortable in the early part of the film, before he becomes the free-spirited pirate roaming the Caribbean with his men. Once he assumes that role, however, it's easy to see that he was born to play such parts the way no other actor before or since ever could.

Captain Blood is a rousing adventure made in a style Hollywood stopped using decades ago. Although over half a century old, it remains undiminished by the passing years.

Captains Courageous

Category: Drama. Starring Spencer Tracy, Freddie Bartholomew, Lionel Barrymore, Mickey Rooney, John Carradine. Screenplay by John Lee Mahin, Marc Connelly, and Dale Van Every, based on the novel by Rudyard Kipling. 116 minutes. 1937. Black and white. MGM/UA Home Video.
Director: Victor Fleming.
Suggested Age Group: 10 and older.

The Story   Harvey, a rich, spoiled little boy, is so unbearable that he is expelled from his school and taken on an ocean voyage by his father, in an attempt to get closer to his troubled son. But the boy is swept overboard and saved by a Portuguese fisherman named Manuel Fidello.

The fishing vessel is out of Gloucester, Massachusetts, and not about to head back to port before filling its nets. So Harvey is stuck on the ship until the fishing trip is over. Of course among the ship's crew, only Manuel can stand the boy, and gradually their friendship deepens. Over the course of the voyage, the boy is transformed into a sensitive, caring young man with a heart.

Parents should know that Manuel dies in an accident during a storm, but his death scene is incredibly poignant and depicted in a very gentle way.

Background: Even though his version of a Portuguese accent might be laughed off the screen today, Spencer Tracy won his first Academy Award for this, his thirty-second film. He would make forty-two more movies, but this is one of his finest. It was his first of two consecutive Best Actor awards (the second was for *Boys Town*), a feat matched only one other time in history, by Tom Hanks in 1993 and 1994.

Spencer Tracy was one of the giants of Hollywood's golden age, from the middle of the 1930s through the postwar period. His film legacy would include, besides *Boys Town, Bad Day at Black Rock* (an underappreciated little thriller), his movies with Katharine Hepburn (such as *Keeper of the Flame, Woman of the*

Year, Pat and Mike, and *Desk Set*), and *Dr. Jekyll and Mr. Hyde.* Other Tracy films worth renting include *Father of the Bride, The Old Man and the Sea,* the great political saga *The Last Hurrah,* and *Inherit the Wind..*

"I'm no Method actor," Tracy once proclaimed, referring to the intense approach to the craft espoused by Brando, Newman, and other famous New York–based actors. "I'm no good at playing a teapot."

Freddie Bartholomew, who plays Harvey, was the leading young actor of his generation. Born Frederick Llewellyn in London in 1924, he was perfectly cast as the upper-crust, spoiled young man who makes a gradual but dramatic transformation of character. Bartholomew, who died in 1992, was unsuccessful at landing many roles after adolescence; his work here and in the title role of *David Copperfield* two years earlier represent the high points of his career.

Director Victor Fleming will forever be known for having taken over directing *Gone With the Wind* from George Cukor, as well as helming *The Wizard of Oz. Captains Courageous* is part of his film legacy that includes *Treasure Island, Tortilla Flat,* and *A Guy Named Joe.*

Captains Courageous takes a bit of time to get going, but once Harvey is in the care of the fishermen, his transformation is beautiful to behold.

Carousel

Category: Musical. Starring Gordon MacRae, Shirley Jones, Cameron Mitchell, Richard Deacon, Gene Lockhart. Screenplay by Henry and Phoebe Ephron, from the Broadway musical by Rodgers & Hammerstein, based on Benjamin F. Glazier's version of Ferenc Molnar's play *Liliom*. Music by Richard Rodgers, lyrics by Oscar Hammerstein II. 128 minutes. 1956. Fox Home Video.
Director: Henry King.
Suggested Age Group: 8 and older.

The Story Billy Bigelow, a swaggering New England carnival barker, is attracted to a simple farm girl, Julie Jordan. She confides her concerns about him to her friend Carrie Pipperidge, but eventually they meet and profess their love in a sweeping ballad. Marriage soon follows. But Billy and his sinister pal Jigger pull a holdup to get money for Billy and Julie's expected child. In the attempt, Billy falls on his knife and dies. Fifteen years later, he returns to earth to instill confidence in his daughter, Louise, and helps her in a way to avoid the mistakes he made in his life.

Background: Following the success of *Oklahoma!,* another musical remake of an old play, the Theatre Guild decided to try to repeat the process. Whereas *Oklahoma!* sprang from the play *Green Grow the Lilacs, Carousel* was based on a successful 1921 play called *Liliom,* written by the Hungarian Ferenc Molnar. But Rodgers and Hammerstein realized that they would have to Americanize the musical for wider audience appeal, so the character of Liliom became Billy Bigelow. The musical was a big hit on Broadway when it opened in April 1945. John Raitt (known today as the father of singer Bonnie Raitt) starred with Jan Clayton. The show enjoyed a successful run of 899 performances and has been revived over the years, most notably with a well-received production in 1993 at New York's Lincoln Center.

As with *Oklahoma!,* many of the songs in *Carousel* have taken on lives of their own. Best known among them is "You'll Never

Walk Alone," perhaps the songwriting team's most inspiring song ever; "If I Loved You," one of their most beautiful romantic ballads; and "June Is Bustin' Out All Over," which is as rousing a number today as when it was written half a century ago.

The history of the movie version of *Carousel* is almost as intriguing as the film itself. As with *Oklahoma!,* it took ten years to begin filming *Carousel,* under the aegis of 20th Century–Fox mogul Darryl F. Zanuck. The first choice for the character of Billy Bigelow was to be Frank Sinatra! However, "Old Blue Eyes" abruptly quit just after filming began. The movie was to be shot in CinemaScope using a 55mm process, which would require each scene to be done twice, and Sinatra didn't fancy doing double the work for the same salary. Gene Kelly was reportedly considered for Billy, too, but he balked at having his misty singing voice dubbed by someone else. John Raitt, who originated the role on the stage, and Howard Keel were also considered, but Gordon MacRae, fresh from *Oklahoma!,* finally landed the part.

Unlike the stage version, the movie begins after Billy Bigelow has died, playing as one long flashback. While flashbacks are often risky in movies, it hasn't seemed to hurt the structure of *Carousel.* Nevertheless, director Henry King never gets too cinematic, employing straightforward camera angles and shots. The songs and the book are too good to risk ruining the feel of the film with excessive stylization.

Because of its themes, *Carousel* is a sometimes sobering experience rather than your typical sweeping Rodgers and Hammerstein musical. Indeed, it was given short shrift for Oscar promotion that year, in favor of another Rodgers and Hammerstein masterpiece, *The King and I.* Still, it is often enchanting, and the chemistry between Shirley Jones and Gordon MacRae is magical.

A Christmas Story

Category: Comedy. Starring Peter Billingsley, Darren McGavin, Melinda Dillon. Screenplay by Jean Shepherd and Bob Clark, based on a book by Jean Shepherd. 98 minutes. 1983. Rated PG. MGM/UA Home Video.
Director: Bob Clark.
Suggested Age Group: 7 and older.

 This autobiographical story is set in a small city in Indiana in the 1940s, when families gathered around the radio to listen to serials, when children would bring apples to school for their teachers, and when Christmas was the biggest event of the year.

A nine-year-old boy named Ralphie lives with his parents and younger brother. As Christmas approaches, he dreams of only one gift under the tree: a Red Ryder Daisy BB Air rifle. But Ralphie knows his mother thinks "it'll put your eye out," so he holds little hope for getting his wish.

Ralphie and his little brother must walk past a bully on their way home from school every day. One fateful day, after receiving a C+ on a paper about what he wants for Christmas, on which his teacher had written that a BB gun would "put your eye out," he turns on the bully and beats him up, much to his brother's astonishment.

The action of the film then takes on a bemused if somewhat bizarre perspective of childhood events. Ralphie's schoolmate gets his tongue caught on a frozen pipe, and Ralphie receives a long-awaited Little Orphan Annie decoder ring in the mail; such scenes conjure the memories of an innocent childhood. But Ralphie learns a lesson about life when he decodes the secret message broadcast on that night's radio show, for it turns out to be nothing more than a commercial for Ovaltine. He feels betrayed.

In a last-ditch effort to make his Christmas morning dream come true, Ralphie goes to a department store where he meets a child-hating Santa Claus, who tells him that a BB gun "will put your eye out" and kicks him down a slide.

On Christmas morning, Ralphie opens his big gift: a hideous pair of pink bunny pajamas made by his aunt. His mother forces him to try them on, but it ends up being worth it, because he finally does get his Daisy Air rifle! Of course, all is not well that ends well. The family's Christmas turkey is accidentally ruined, and they wind up eating duck in a deserted Chinese restaurant.

Background: *A Christmas Story* is a heartwarming, nostalgic look back at the tender years in the life of radio raconteur Jean Shepherd, who narrated the film and makes a quick cameo as an impatient parent in line with his child at the department store to meet Santa. Shepherd has an absorbing style and a wry sense of humor, and he obviously loves waxing nostalgic about that time of his life.

To date, *A Christmas Story* is the only notable film in the career of young Peter Billingsley; his other credits include *Death Valley, Beverly Hills Brats, Russkies,* and *The Dirt Bike Kid*—none of which were exactly blockbusters.

Darren McGavin, who plays Ralphie's bombastic father, is a veteran of New York's Actors Studio and the Neighborhood Playhouse. He was first noticed in 1955 as the young painter in the movie *Summertime* with Katharine Hepburn. Other movies of note on his résumé include *The Court-Martial of Billy Mitchell, The Man with the Golden Arm,* and later *The Natural* in a memorable but unbilled appearance. But he is best known as TV's original Mike Hammer in the popular fifties series; he returned to TV in the seventies in the popular series *The Night Stalker.*

It's difficult to believe that this warm, gentle, nostalgic comedy was directed by the same man who made the sleazy comedy *Porky's,* but it's true. Canadian filmmaker Bob Clark, who cowrote the screenplay with Jean Shepherd, has made other must-miss films, like the *Porky's* sequel, *Rhinestone* (a Sylvester Stallone musical, for goodness sake!), and *Turk 182!. A Christmas Story* seems to be an aberration for a routine director. But what a delightful, funny aberration it is!

A Connecticut Yankee in King Arthur's Court

Category: Musical comedy. Starring Bing Crosby, Rhonda Fleming, William Bendix, Sir Cedric Hardwicke, Henry Wilcoxon. Screenplay by Edmund Beloin, based on the novel by Mark Twain. Includes songs by Johnny Burke and Jimmy Van Heusen. 107 minutes. 1949. MCA Home Video.
Director: Tay Garnett.
Suggested Age Group: 8 and older.

The Story Hank Martin, a mild-mannered inventor and mechanic from Hartford, Connecticut, played by Bing Crosby, is touring an old English castle. Somehow, it all seems vaguely familiar to him and after continually interrupting the guide, he's summoned to see the lord of the manor, portrayed by that wonderful character actor, Sir Cedric Hardwicke. Hank then explains to the old man how he seems to know the castle so well. After being rendered unconscious from a fall, he'd awakened with a lance at his chest, the prisoner of Sir Sagramore, a Knight of the Round Table in the Court of King Arthur in sixth-century England.

Still unable to understand how he'd traveled back in time, Hank comes to Court, uses some of his twentieth-century knowledge of science, and convinces the king and his scheming advisor, Merlin, that he has supernatural powers.

Hank quickly zeros in on the beautiful Alisande la Carteloise (played by Rhonda Fleming), whom he quickly names, in the modern vernacular, "Sandy." This does not sit well with the scheming Morgan le Fay, who is suspicious of Hank and fears he will get on the good side of the king. Meanwhile, Sir Lancelot, played by veteran actor Henry Wilcoxon, challenges Hank, by now known to one and all as "Sir Boss," to a joust.

The late forties special effects, employing speeded-up action, look momentarily clumsy. But young viewers will quickly find it an amusing touch. As Crosby croons love songs to Fleming, the main action begins. At Hank's suggestion, the benign old king dons a disguise and goes among the peasants to see what life away from the splendor of Court is really like. Merlin the Magician, his duplicitous advisor, seizes this opportunity to wrest power away from him.

The story is a gentle fable, and although there is one reference to "Aunt Jemima" which may be offensive, it will surely go over the heads of young viewers. In another scene several people face the executioner's ax; however, it's done off-camera, so its potential for upsetting a child is minimized.

The film is a continual delight, milking its time-travel premise to the hilt. Throughout Hank uses knowledge from the early part of the twentieth century to astound the superstitious people of the Court. He manages, for instance, to extricate himself and the king from certain death by accurately predicting an imminent solar eclipse. He also uses some funny magic words to cast a "spell," fooling his captors, and he even refers to Shakespeare as a "new boy coming up."

Background: There was a 1921 silent version of this Mark Twain tale and a sound version a decade later with Will Rogers, Maureen O'Sullivan, and Myrna Loy. But this version, starring the crooner Bing Crosby, is the best known.

By the time Paramount released *A Connecticut Yankee in King Arthur's Court* in 1949, Crosby had already made three "Road" pictures with his good friend Bob Hope, and had copped the Best Actor Oscar for 1944's *Going My Way*. He received additional nominations for *The Bells of St. Mary's* in 1945 and *The Country Girl* in 1954. Parents may enjoy seeing another side of the Crosby screen persona in the latter, a riveting Clifford Odets drama.

The Court Jester

Category: Comedy. Starring Danny Kaye, Glynis Johns, Basil Rathbone, Cecil Parker, John Carradine, Mildred Natwick, Robert Middleton, Michael Pate. Screenplay by Norman Panama and Melvin Frank. 101 minutes. 1956. Paramount Home Video.
Directors: Norman Panama, Melvin Frank.
Suggested Age Group: 6 and older.

The Story Uneasy lies the crown on the head of King Roderick I, who sits unlawfully on the throne of England after usurping the crown from the rightful king. But a member of the royal family survives; an infant bearing the regal birthmark (a purple pimpernel) on his backside. He is protected by a loyal subject, the "Black Fox," an adventurer not unlike Robin Hood. He heads a band of rebels living in the forest, striving to restore the rightful king to the throne.

The Court Jester has a vast array of characters, including an ersatz king, his two scheming ministers plotting his murder, a court jester who is really a hired assassin, a beautiful maid, and a carnival performer named Hubert Hawkins. Helped by Maid Jean, Hawkins overpowers the jester and assumes his identity; he gets inside the castle to spy and to open its gates for the rebels. The king's fair-haired daughter, her lady-in-waiting, and a knight betrothed to the princess round out the principal characters.

Hawkins, disguised as the jester, is hypnotized by the princess's lady-in-waiting who, at the snap of a finger, changes him into a daring swashbuckler. He then sweeps Princess Gwendolyn off her feet, smothering her with kisses. Still under the spell, he makes a spectacular exit out the window, swinging down the side of the castle on a vine. The zany comedy and fast-paced dialogue, laced with tongue-twisters and other verbal tricks, move the intentionally silly story along.

Especially funny is the scene in which Princess Gwendolyn proclaims her love for the jester. Not realizing she's referring to him, he sings: "Light up the oil, this man must boil." Hawkins is then exposed as an impostor, and is even suspected of being the "Black Fox," leader of the rebels.

Hawkins, now under arrest, is then knighted so he can presumably be killed in a contest with a rival suitor for the hand of Princess Gwendolyn. His "test" of bow and arrow, and combat against a "wild boar" (really a piglet) is hilarious. So is his being caught in the formation of a precision drill team before being engaged in mortal combat.

This prolonged sequence of delightful silliness leads to a climactic sword fight with Ravenhurst, the scheming minister to the king, who is tossed off the ramparts into the sea. The rightful king of England (the baby with the purple pimpernel on his left buttock) is then restored to the throne, and Hawkins wins the hand of the beautiful Maid Jean, who'd helped him all along during his masquerade as the court jester.

Background: "Those who try to tangle with my derring-do, wind up at the angle that herring do," sings Danny Kaye as Hawkins, the carnival-performer-turned-jester in the witty opening number.

Danny Kaye, who was the Robin Williams of the late forties and fifties, was never better than in *The Court Jester*. For Kaye, this role was ideal, affording him the chance to sing, dance, do accents, play a Lothario, and be the hero all at once. And he was more than up to the challenge, adding an air of unpredictability that makes it hilarious and a bit daring, too.

The spoofing of the Robin Hood–type movies, added to a script in which characters had names beginning with G (Gwendolyn, Griselda, Griswold, and Giacomo) was another effective comedy tool, which Kaye and the others in the cast exploit skillfully.

But of course the most famous highlight in the movie is the classic "Pellet with the poison's in the flagon with the dragon" routine, which continues about "the vessel with the pestle has the brew that is true." It's doubtful any other actor could've pulled off such dialogue so skillfully. Later, Robert Middleton as Sir Griswold, Kaye's adversary in the joust, tries to say the tongue twister, but you'll quickly notice his labored effort in comparison to Kaye's smooth delivery.

Kaye's climactic sword fight against Basil Rathbone is equal in intensity to that in *The Adventures of Robin Hood,* and not coincidentally against the same opponent, Basil Rathbone. The spoof of the classic swashbuckler is obvious but effective.

Danny Kaye was one of the most colorful performers ever to grace the screen. You never knew what to expect from him, on screen or off. He once bought an airplane, determined to fly it himself. But in order to get his pilot's license, he had to demonstrate a proficiency in mathematics. So Kaye, who'd left school at a young age, sought out his daughter Dina and had her teach him long division. On another occasion, on a trip to Berlin, Kaye scooped up all the local newspapers and began scanning them. "I didn't know you read German," said a friend. "I don't," he replied, "but I can spot 'Danny Kaye' in any language."

Director Norman Panama specializes in light comedy fare, although he did codirect and write *Above and Beyond,* about the dropping of the first atomic bomb on Hiroshima.

The Court Jester is a witty sendup, with devastating spoofs of familiar movie swashbuckler types, and with running gags throughout. Characters say, for example, "Get it. Got it? Good!" or "What did the Doge do? When the Doge did his duty and the Duke didn't . . ."

Don't be surprised if children start reciting the "vessel with the pestle" speech verbatim!

Damn Yankees

Category: Musical. Starring Tab Hunter, Ray Walston, Gwen Verdon, Robert Shafer, Shannon Bolin. Screenplay by George Abbott, based on the play by George Abbott and Douglass Wallop from Wallop's novel, *The Year the Yankees Lost the Pennant*. Music and lyrics by Richard Adler and Jerry Ross. Choreography by Bob Fosse. 110 minutes. 1958. Warner Bros. Home Video.
Directors: George Abbott, Stanley Donen.
Suggested Age Group: 8 and older.

The Story Joe Boyd is a realtor in his late fifties, living in Washington, D.C. Year after year, he suffers the indignities of his beloved baseball team, the Senators, the perennial doormat in the American League. Every year, the New York Yankees beat them, and the climb to pennant contention looks hopeless. Then one day, while watching another Senators loss on TV, Boyd is visited by a mysterious man who calls himself "Mr. Applegate." He offers Boyd a chance to become a twenty-two-year-old slugger who will save the Senators and lead them to the pennant, in exchange for his soul at the end of the season.

But the realtor wisely inserts an escape clause, in case he wants to call the deal off at the last minute. Thus begins a rousing musical, certainly the best ever written about baseball and one of the best musicals of the fifties. Joe Boyd is transformed into young Joe Hardy, a rookie who can hit the ball out of sight. He's signed by the Senators and begins to lead them out of the basement and toward the pennant.

Applegate, fearing that Boyd misses his wife and his old identity, sends Lola, a beautiful 172-year-old witch to woo him and make him forget about his bargain. It all comes down to the pennant game, Boyd's second thoughts, and that lucky escape clause.

Background: *Damn Yankees* opened on Broadway on May 5, 1955, at the 46th Street Theater, won the Tony Award for Best Musical, and went on to play 1,019 performances. The premise is, of course, a clever updated version of the Faust legend. Stylistically, the show was a sequel to *The Pajama Game,* employing the same songwriters and directors to create a fast-paced romp.

Although Stephen Douglass played Joe Hardy on Broadway, Tab Hunter got the screen role opposite Ray Walston and Gwen Verdon, who re-created their Broadway roles as Applegate and Lola, respectively. The songs include "Heart," one of the best songs about sports ever written, "Shoeless Joe from Hannibal, Mo.," "Whatever Lola Wants," and the song every spouse of a baseball nut should memorize, "Six Months Out of Every Year." Bob Fosse choreographed both the stage and screen versions.

Marilyn Monroe was considered for the part of Lola, but she wasn't the dancer that Gwen Verdon was. Others who made the leap from Broadway were Robert Shafer as the world-weary Boyd, Shannon Bolin as Mrs. Boyd, and Jean Stapleton as Sister, twelve years before she would join the cast of the watershed TV comedy *All in the Family.*

When Yogi Berra went to see *Damn Yankees,* he sat through the number in which the Yankees sing in the shower. Berra, then the Bronx Bombers' star catcher, turned to a friend and said: "They gotta change that scene. We never do that."

Some people had reservations about the casting of Tab Hunter in the movie version of *Damn Yankees,* because despite his athletic, all-American look, he had a weak singing voice. Nevertheless, they muddled through the production, disdaining any notion of dubbing in another voice. Hunter hasn't made many other movies of note, but in 1982, he coproduced and appeared in *Lust in the Dust,* a cult favorite from director-writer John Waters.

Gwen Verdon, who plays the alluring witch, Lola, is primarily a Broadway star, winning the Tony for *Can-Can, Damn Yankees, New Girl in Town,* and *Redhead.* She is the former wife of Bob Fosse, who choreographed the Broadway and movie versions of *Damn Yankees.* Her other screen appearances include *The Cotton Club* and *Cocoon.*

Although he never became a big star, Ray Walston owned the role of Mr. Applegate, for which he won the Tony Award on Broadway, and was brilliant in the film. Born in New Orleans, he is best known to younger audiences as the title player in *My Favorite Martian,* the sixties TV situation comedy, and as Judge Henry Bone on the drama *Picket Fences.* The staccato-speaking actor's films of note include the classic *The Apartment,* in which he played a philandering executive, and *The Sting,* in which he played a con man who helped Paul Newman and Robert Redford pull the scam on Robert Shaw.

George Abbott, the greatest, most prolific producer in Broadway history, handled the staging of *Damn Yankees,* while Stanley Donen, who had more experience in film techniques, handled the camera angles. Abbott, who died at the age of 107 in 1995, was a tall, elegant man, a Harvard graduate who directed, wrote, and produced scores of shows, including *Pal Joey, On the Town, Where's Charley?, A Tree Grows in Brooklyn, Wonderful Town,* and *The Pajama Game.* Abbott and Donen teamed up for *The Pajama Game* before *Damn Yankees,* a work Abbott lived to see revived again on Broadway in a hit 1993 production.

Damn Yankees is a bit stagy, but it's to be expected, considering its Broadway origins. Nevertheless, it effectively conveys the look and feel of fifties baseball, the gut-wrenching emotions evoked by a losing team, the promise of a mythical hero, and the expectations of a devil seeking his due.

The Devil's Disciple

Category: Drama. Starring Burt Lancaster, Kirk Douglas, Laurence Olivier, Harry Andrews, Eva Le Gallienne, Janette Scott. Screenplay by John Dighton and Roland Kibbee, based on the play by George Bernard Shaw. 82 minutes. 1959. Black and white. MGM/UA Home Video.
Director: Guy Hamilton.
Suggested Age Group: 10 and older.

The Story Set during the American Revolution, *The Devil's Disciple* opens with the imminent execution of an American patriot named Dick Dudgeon. British General John Burgoyne, who is in the process of moving his forces from Boston to Springtown, speaks tersely to his stiff, by-the-book aide, Major Swindon. It is soon obvious that the general is a perceptive, perhaps even fair-minded man, who claims that "martyrdom is what these people like. It is the one way to achieve fame without ability."

A few miles away at his pulpit in the small town of Webster-bridge, Anthony Anderson, a small-town minister, is quickly summoned to Springtown to rescue Dick Dudgeon from his impending demise. Meanwhile, General Burgoyne faces the challenges presented by the British War Office, which has supplied him with twice the number of cavalry officers as horses, and cannons so large that half the roads are unable to support them. But pig-headed Swindon is confident that the British forces will prevail.

"Be a little less generous with the blood of your men," Burgoyne admonishes. The general knows he's outnumbered by six to one, and that his forces are made up of Hessians, German dragoons, and Indian scouts with knives. "Suppose the colonists find a leader. What shall we do, Swindon? What shall we do?"

Thus begins a delightful look at an incident of the American Revolution that focuses on a general whose cause has been lost due to bureaucratic bumbling, and a minister and a rogue who temporarily switch identities to fool the British and wind up exchanging their stations in life.

This is a wry, offbeat little film that provides young audiences with an opportunity to get a taste of history and be entertained at the same time. The action comes in quick bursts, and the interplay between characters is marvelous.

Background: *The Devil's Disciple* was made as a coproduction between Kirk Douglas's Bryna Productions and Burt Lancaster's own company. It was the combined power of these stars, who had worked together a handful of times, that enticed Laurence Olivier to do the part of General Burgoyne.

Despite the superb interplay between Douglas and Lancaster, in many respects it is Olivier who walks away with *The Devil's Disciple.* His portrayal of "Gentlemanly Johnny" Burgoyne is riveting, capturing perfectly the general's subtle disdain for his hopeless assignment.

Director Guy Hamilton took over the reins of *The Devil's Disciple* at the last minute, replacing Alexander Mackendrick. Born in Paris, he is an unspectacular director, but his major credits include five of the best James Bond movies: *Goldfinger, Diamonds Are Forever, Live and Let Die, The Man With the Golden Gun,* and *Funeral in Berlin.*

In retrospect, it is possible that since *The Devil's Disciple* was released in the same year as *Ben-Hur, Anatomy of a Murder,* and *North by Northwest,* three heavily hyped and more successful films, it hasn't been given its proper place in movie history. Oddly, considering its all-star cast, it received little publicity and turns up in few film anthologies. However, the sharp-witted dialogue, the narration, the stop-action shots of toy soldiers, and the interplay among the three major stars moves the story along swiftly, making it soft-sell education while providing first-rate entertainment for young viewers.

The Ernest Green Story

Category: Drama. Starring Morris Chestnut, Ossie Davis, Ruby Dee. Narrated by Ernest Green. Written by Lawrence Roman. 101 minutes. 1993. Walt Disney Home Video.
Director: Eric Laneuville.
Suggested Age Group: 11 and older.

> ### The Story

This is the inspiring, true story of a Little Rock, Arkansas, high school junior named Ernest Green. After segregation was ruled illegal in 1957 by the U.S. Supreme Court, he decided to join eight underclassmen and spend his final year at all-white Central High. This groundbreaking first step toward integration touched off a controversy and a series of confrontations that brought reactions from all over the world.

Initially, Governor Orval Faubus tried to block the students' entry by positioning Arkansas National Guardsmen and police outside the school. But when Washington ordered the students admitted, they sent in federal troops to ensure their safety.

Soon the troops were removed from inside the school, however, and Ernest and his fellow black students were on their own. They faced degradation and abuse from their white classmates. The school administration itself was not eager to have them and prohibited their membership in the glee club, in the orchestra, on athletic teams, or in any other extracurricular activities.

Still, the students persevered. All but one remained, all the while determined to endure any abuse in school by practicing nonviolence. When Ernest's physics notes were destroyed by white students, he enlisted a tutor to help him study for an important exam administered by a teacher who especially disliked him.

The end of the school year saw Ernest passing his courses and ensuring his admission to Michigan State University. In a touching scene, he bicycles past his elated grandfather while humming a college fight song. "Hey, that's the University of Michigan song, not Michigan State's," corrects his grandfather. "I know," replies young Ernest. "I haven't learned Michigan State's yet."

The movie ends with the school's graduation ceremony that Ernest attends, despite a last-minute request from the principal that he skip it and receive his diploma in the mail. But Ernest Green, who later had a position in the Carter administration and was an NAACP executive, said he couldn't let down his grandfather, who'd waited years to witness this occasion. Dr. Martin Luther King, Jr., also attended the historic event, but it is Ernest's joyous grandfather who is seen leading the applause for his courageous grandson.

Background: Morris Chestnut, who is just a bit too old for the part of Ernest Green, isn't yet a household name. His résumé includes an appearance in *Boyz N the Hood,* director/writer John Singleton's riveting 1991 film about life in the inner city of Los Angeles. He turns in an inspiring performance as a principled young man bucking the odds.

However, it is Ossie Davis, the veteran actor, who is the real joy here as Ernest's grandfather, the only father figure in his life. Davis, the civil rights activist, renowned stage actor, and director, has appeared in *No Way Out, The Joe Louis Story, School Daze, Do the Right Thing,* and *Jungle Fever.* He was especially good in a small but effective role as a judge in *The Client.*

Davis's wife, Ruby Dee, who played Mrs. Robinson in *The Jackie Robinson Story* and has frequently appeared with her husband in films and on the stage, has a small role as a naysaying neighbor who discourages Green's efforts to attend the all-white school.

The Ernest Green Story is an inspiring movie all young viewers should see. Some of the confrontations between taunting, racist white students and the nine courageous black students might be disturbing, but they represent a fact of life, and the way the black students deal with it is exemplary and heroic. The film provides a lesson in tolerance and understanding.

Escape to Witch Mountain

Category: Adventure. Starring Kim Richards, Ike Eisenmann, Ray Milland, Eddie Albert, Donald Pleasence. Screenplay by Robert Malcolm Young, based on the book by Alexander King. 97 minutes. 1975. Rated G. Buena Vista Home Video.
Director: John Hough.
Suggested Age Group: 6 and older.

The Story

Tia and Tony, two orphans gifted with the powers of telekinesis (they can make objects move by intense concentration and telepathic communication), decide to try to discover their origins. When he hears of their unusual talents, an evil millionaire named Mr. Bolt forges papers and fools the authorities into thinking he's a long-lost relative, installs a special kids' complex for them to play in his mansion, and adopts them.

The children soon find their new life quite agreeable. They tame a previously recalcitrant horse named Thunderhead, bringing marionettes to life with the aid of a harmonica, and cause a motorcycle to drive itself off a cliff. Unbeknownst to them, however, the millionaire's motives are less than altruistic, and he's set up their room with hidden video cameras.

Tia quickly senses that Mr. Bolt is sinister, and discovers his plans to move them to a remote island so he can harness their fantastic powers for his own purposes. Fortunately, accompanied by their black cat Winkie, Tia and Tony manage to escape and join forces with a kindly widower traveling across the country.

As the movie progresses, Tia gets more and more flashes of their earlier life, which only serves to make their urge to discover their origins even more intense.

Background: This is an amiable, endearing movie starring two likable child actors whose characters are blessed with the powers every kid would love to have. They communicate with each other silently, foretell traumatic events before they happen, and visualize distant places they will soon visit. Their adventures, while predictable to adult viewers, will nevertheless delight young viewers.

Three of Hollywood's most venerable character actors provide an appeal for older viewers. Ray Milland, as the evil Aristotle Bolt, won the 1945 Academy Award for Best Actor for *The Lost Weekend,* the first Hollywood movie to deal frankly with alcoholism, and an enduring classic of the genre. He also starred in *It Happens Every Spring, Love Story,* and *Dial M for Murder.* In *Escape to Witch Mountain,* Milland is every child's vision of a cold tycoon who will do anything to achieve his goals. Before his death in 1986, Milland enjoyed a career spanning fifty-seven years.

The late Donald Pleasence, who plays Mr. Doranian, Milland's assistant, was a stage-trained actor who was a prisoner of war during World War II. Perhaps best known for his role in *Halloween,* he also appeared in *The Night of the Generals, The Great Escape,* and *The Greatest Story Ever Told.*

Eddie Albert is probably best known to parents for starring on TV's *Green Acres,* but he has enjoyed a six-decade screen career in films such as *Brother Rat, Roman Holiday, The Heartbreak Kid,* and *Dreamscape.*

Escape to Witch Mountain offers agreeable young characters with the engaging ability to spot danger and the less admirable side of grown-ups' natures. They manage to outwit the adults at every turn and find their own happy ending. What more could any kid want?

Fiddler on the Roof

Category: Musical. Starring Chaim Topol, Norma Crane, Neva Small, Molly Picon, Paul Michael Glaser. Screenplay by Joseph Stein, adapted from his book of the musical, based on stories by Sholem Aleichem. Music by Jerry Bock, lyrics by Sheldon Harnick. 181 minutes. 1971. Rated G. MGM/UA Home Video.
Director: Norman Jewison.
Suggested Age Group: 7 and older.

| The Story | Set in the tiny Russian village of Anatevka around 1905, this is the story of Tevye, a poor milkman who has five loving daughters and a devoted wife. Tevye |

has a special relationship with God, with whom he has numerous conversations and to whom he looks for guidance as life's hardships and wonders befall him.

He is a wise and gentle man who always considers both sides of any issue. Nevertheless, he doesn't have an easy time of it when his family undergoes enormous changes, hand in hand with those of the outside world. One daughter, Tzeitel, has been promised by the village matchmaker to a much older man, but she convinces Tevye to break centuries-old tradition by letting her marry the man she loves, a poor tailor named Motel.

Meanwhile, some of Tevye's other daughters develop their own ideas as well. Hodel falls in love with Perchik, a worldly tutor who has come to the isolated village from the outside world, bringing the warning that life as they know it is going to change drastically. Chava is trying to warn the villagers that their own insulated view of the world is naive and that their days of life as they have always known it are numbered. What's more, Chava is attracted to a Russian soldier, who is not Jewish.

After Tzeitel's wedding is interrupted by a pogrom (a bloody raid by Russian Cossacks), Tevye sees the writing on the wall and decides to leave his beloved village and move his family to America.

Background: Sometime in 1963, my father and I attended a backers' audition for a new Broadway show. The lyricist, Sheldon Harnick, a distant cousin, and his partner, composer Jerry Bock, played some songs in rough form. "Two weeks in the Yiddish theater, maybe, Sheldon," my father said. "But on Broadway? Never." It was, of course, the early version of *Fiddler on the Roof*, perhaps the greatest, most beautiful American musical ever written.

It went on to become an international sensation, with companies playing across America, in Europe, South America, and even Asia. For every culture has its Tevye, a wise man who is making the best of his life, with an abiding love for his family and his maker.

Incredibly, this was not the first version of this classic tale, which tells the story so typical among turn-of-the-century Jewish villages of Eastern Europe. There had also been a Yiddish movie called *Tevye* made in 1939 and adapted from the same stories of Sholem Aleichem that served as the basis for *Fiddler on the Roof*.

Zero Mostel created the role on Broadway in 1964, and this show became one of the longest-running hits in Broadway history, with several revivals; it is likely to be presented again, somewhere, forever. When it came time to shoot the movie, however, Chaim Topol, the Israeli-born actor who'd played Tevye on the stage in London, got the part. On screen, Topol gets the job done, though he lacks Mostel's over-the-top, larger-than-life delivery. Years after the film was released, I asked director Norman Jewison why he didn't cast Mostel in the movie and thus preserve one of the great characterizations for all time.

"Simple," he told me. "Zero was such a talent, but so unpredictable that we couldn't be certain he'd do two takes exactly the same. Every night on Broadway, we'd see him come out, go into the 'If I Were a Rich Man' number, then find someone in the audience and say hello, then go on. We couldn't risk that in the movie."

The movie version opens with the sweeping vistas of Anatevka, leading one critic to compare it to the huge King ranch in Texas. Filmed near Zagreb in what was then Yugoslavia, the location conveys both the poverty and the closeness of the townspeople, existing peacefully with their non-Jewish neighbors and insulated for centuries from the outside world.

The songs and choreography in *Fiddler* are so wonderful that they almost create a dream world, even on the flat, impersonal screen.

Starting off with the rousing "Tradition," "If I Were a Rich Man," "To Life," and the poignant "Sunrise, Sunset," the songs in *Fiddler on the Roof* will stay with you forever.

Although he had completed a few forgettable films before *Fiddler,* Topol was largely unknown here when the movie opened. After all, movies like *Sallah,* a little-seen Israeli movie, or *Before Winter Comes* didn't exactly make him a household word. Nevertheless, he has immortalized the role of Tevye, a simple man simultaneously trying to adapt to a changing world and hold on to his traditions. Topol's other memorable roles came in TV movies such as *The House on Garibaldi Street,* about the capture of Eichmann by Israeli agents in Argentina, and in *The Winds of War* and its sequel, *War and Remembrance.*

Notable among the cast is Neva Small, who as Chava falls in love with a non-Jew and so must be banished from the family by her heartbroken father. Her long red hair stands out in contrast with the appearance of her sisters, and she brings a unique charm to her portrayal.

Paul Michael Glaser, who plays Perchik, the worldly tutor to Tevye's daughters, is best known for his portrayal of detective Dave Starsky from the TV series *Starsky and Hutch* and for the tragic loss of his daughter and wife to AIDS. His wife, Elizabeth, who died at the end of 1994, became a national spokeswoman for AIDS research, and touched the nation with her speech at the 1992 Democratic National Convention. Glaser is now a director who works frequently on television.

Molly Picon, who plays Yenta the matchmaker, was one of the great stars of the Yiddish theater, and she was often referred to as "the Jewish Helen Hayes." Upon hearing this reference, Miss Hayes, known as "the First Lady of the American Theater," referred to herself in turn as the "shiksa [non-Jewish] Molly Picon." Molly Picon died in 1992 at ninety-four, the last of the great stars of the Yiddish theater in America.

Field of Dreams

Category: Drama. Starring Kevin Costner, Amy Madigan, James Earl Jones, Ray Liotta, Burt Lancaster, Timothy Busfield, Frank Whaley. Screenplay by Phil Alden Robinson, based on the book *Shoeless Joe* by W. P. Kinsella. Music by James Horner. 106 minutes. 1989. Rated PG. Warner Bros. Home Video.
Director: Phil Alden Robinson.
Suggested Age Group: 8 and older.

| **The Story** | An Iowa farmer named Ray Kinsella, with a heavily mortgaged farm and a wife and daughter to support, wants nothing more than to avoid the same |

end as his father, a onetime minor-league baseball player who never pursued his dreams. One day Ray hears a mysterious voice in the middle of his cornfield, saying "If you build it, he will come." He can't understand what this means at first, but then, responding to urges he can't explain, Ray clears his land and builds a baseball field, complete with outdoor lights.

Soon the very lifelike spirit of long-ago baseball superstar "Shoeless Joe" Jackson appears, followed by his teammates from the infamous 1919 Chicago White Sox, who threw the World Series and were subsequently banned from baseball for life. Ray then understands his reason for building the ball field—to provide a place for the exiled players to play.

But the voice persists, urging him to seek out the reclusive writer Terence Mann, who'd influenced him when he was a Berkeley radical in the sixties. So he dutifully treks to Boston, finds Mann, and somehow convinces the cantankerous literary legend to attend a Red Sox game, simply in response to the voice which is now telling him to "ease his pain."

Neither man understands the voice or their role in this situation, but both know they must obey their odd impulses. These impulses lead them to tiny Chisholm, Minnesota, to seek out a turn-of-the-century player named "Moonlight" Graham, who played only one half of one inning on the last day of the season, then quit baseball and became a doctor. They discover that the doctor has died, but as Ray and Mann head back to Iowa, they pick up a young hitchhiker, who, it turns out, is the youthful incarnation of "Moonlight." Ray and Mann head back to Iowa. By the time they all return to the ball field, the old White Sox players have been joined by a dozen other old ballplayers, and they are now playing an actual game. Ignoring his brother-in-law's plea to sell his nearly bankrupt farm (his brother-in-law cannot see the spirit ball players), Ray decides to keep his farm.

In a turning point in the film, Ray's young daughter is choking on a hot dog while watching the game, when young "Moonlight" Graham steps outside the ball field. He instantly becomes the elderly "Doc" Graham and saves the choking child. As he disappears into the whispering cornstalks, it's clear that everyone, including Ray's bothersome brother-in-law, can now see the dreamlike spectacle being played on the ball field. Ray gets to meet and have a catch with the spirit of his youthful father and, in one of the most famous final scenes of recent movie history, an endless stream of visitors' cars light up the farm, coming to see baseball's immortals playing under the moon, coming to see the fulfillment of dreams. Even if you know nothing about baseball, this movie will touch you deeply.

Background: This was, for my money, the best movie of the 1980s, an ode to the generational lure of baseball, the one true constant in our nation's history. It is a film about a man approaching middle age, afraid of getting old, and never able to forgive his own father for growing old. To the uninitiated, it might seem nothing more than a sentimental baseball movie. But it's nothing of the sort.

Baseball is used as a metaphor for the link between generations. Ray never got the chance to tell his father he loved him, but when he builds the ball field, he gets another chance. He encounters and is amazed by the spirit of his father as a young minor-league hopeful, years before Ray was even the proverbial twinkle in his eye. And, in an ending guaranteed to bring tears to the eyes of any child who misses a late father, or simply wishes for a stronger bond with a living father, they have that long-delayed catch.

The movie is filled with funny, intimate moments. When, for instance, the right-handed "Shoeless Joe" Jackson (the movie's only major historical mistake; the real Jackson batted left-handed) asks Ray to pitch to him, Kinsella asks "Don't we need a catcher?"

"We don't need a catcher," replies Jackson, coolly. "Not if you get it near the plate."

Later, when Kinsella and Mann stop at the library in Chisholm, they pore over clippings about "Moonlight" Graham, who had died in 1972. After the librarian reads the obituary she had written about him, the great writer Mann opines: "You're a good writer." "So are you," she replies, patting him on the forearm.

For Kevin Costner, *Field of Dreams* capped a decade in which he rose to the top of his profession. After his first screen appearance as a dead body during the opening credits of *The Big Chill*, he made *Bull Durham* (now *that's* a pure baseball movie), the little-seen but cult favorite *Fandango,* the huge hit *The Untouchables,* the epic *Dances with Wolves,* and *JFK.* His career made him the Gary Cooper of his generation.

Ironically, James Earl Jones, who played the reclusive writer Terence Mann, has often told me that he "hates" baseball and, in fact, has never even been to a big league game! Yet he starred in *The Bingo Long Traveling All-Stars & Motor Kings,* and narrated *When It Was a Game,* the superb 1990 HBO baseball documentary, as well as costarring in *Field of Dreams.* He also portrayed a former player in the family baseball movie *The Sandlot.* His majestic presence never overwhelms *Field of Dreams,* but it certainly lends it substance.

This was the penultimate movie for Burt Lancaster, whose career is reviewed under *Rocket Gibraltar.* Even here, at the end of his career and nearly his life, you can still see the body language, the grace, and the screen presence that made him one of the legendary figures in the history of movies.

For children, *Field of Dreams* is a movie that reinforces family ties and reminds them that some dreams can really come true. It has a gentle tone, and while some of the off-color language is unnecessary, young viewers will become enthralled with the idea of a fantasy coming true in a normal, everyday backyard. This is a movie for families to savor like a poignant fairy tale come true.

Flight of the Navigator

Category: Science fiction/adventure. Starring Joey Cramer, Cliff De Young, Veronica Cartwright, Howard Hesseman, Sarah Jessica Parker. Screenplay by Michael Burton and Matt MacManus. 90 minutes. 1986. Rated PG. Buena Vista Home Video.
Director: Randal Kleiser.
Suggested Age Group: 7 and older.

The Story   An ordinary twelve-year-old Ft. Lauderdale boy named David falls into a ditch and hits his head on July 4, 1978. When he awakens, he returns to his home, only to find that his family no longer lives there and everything around him looks different. Eight years have passed, and eventually we learn that he's been whisked away by an alien spacecraft commanded by a wisecracking robot named Max.

David soon finds his family, but to his dismay he discovers his parents and brother have aged, while he's remained twelve. What's more, his brain is emitting strong waves containing thoughts and symbols far more advanced than anything on earth.

Soon a NASA official convinces Joey's parents to allow him to be studied at a secure facility for just forty-eight hours. When he finds himself kept in a locked room, he wants only to escape. When he does get away, David is reunited with Max on the spacecraft and taken for a wild ride, with government helicopters in futile pursuit, before he finally returns home to his family, this time just as he left them in 1978.

Background: This is a fast-paced adventure with no particularly heavy messages. The story simply concerns a boy who wants only to go home and have things set right again.

The young star, Joey Cramer, hasn't had much of a film career beyond this, but he's perfectly suited to the role of the wide-eyed boy who quickly accepts his new friend Max, climbs aboard the spacecraft, and thrills at whisking around at a speed ten times faster than any earthbound aircraft.

"Paul Mall," the name listed for the voice of Max, the robotic commander, is actually a pseudonym for Paul Reubens, just approaching the height of his short-lived career on television and on the big screen as the persona of Pee-wee Herman.

Howard Hesseman, who plays the harried but well-intentioned NASA official who wants to study David's incredible brain activity, gained fame as the star of the popular TV sitcom *WKRP in Cincinnati.* He has turned up in a dozen movies, most of them mediocre outings like *Steelyard Blues* or just plain awful, such as *Dr. Detroit.* He did, however, appear in a nearly unknown but fascinating film about acrophobia called *Inside Out,* which starred Elliott Gould. Here he's well cast in a conventional role.

Director Randal Kleiser's debut behind the lenses was the smash hit movie version of *Grease.* He followed that with the picturesque though unintentionally hilarious *The Blue Lagoon,* but rebounded with *Rich and Famous* and, in 1992, *Honey, I Blew Up the Kids.* His style is straightforward and without particular distinction, but in an unpretentious film like this, that's just what the doctor ordered.

Flight of the Navigator isn't a classic by any means. But it is a movie in which the young protagonist is firmly in control at all times, doing whatever he can to return home to his family as it was when he left. The film is never threatening or overly dependent on special effects. It is a delightful fantasy adventure that will have every young viewer eager to tag along.

Friendly Persuasion

Category: Drama. Starring Gary Cooper, Dorothy McGuire, Anthony Perkins, Marjorie Main. Screenplay by Michael Wilson, from the book *The Friendly Persuasion* by Jessamyn West. Music by Dimitri Tiomkin. 140 minutes. 1956. CBS Fox Home Video.
Director: William Wyler.
Suggested Age Group: 8 and older.

The Story

This is the gentle story of a Quaker family living in Indiana in 1862. The father, Jess Birdwell, and the mother, Eliza, are determined pacifists who refuse to take sides during the Civil War, living as normal a life as possible. Each Sunday on the way to church, for instance, they race their buggy with a neighbor. Life, for the present, seems normal. But all is not calm. Their son, Josh, is considering taking up arms for the Union Army, and a daughter, Mattie, falls in love with the soldier next door. As the war draws closer, Josh decides to join the home guard. While he is away a group of Confederate raiders shows up at the farm. But before they can destroy it, Eliza offers them food. When a soldier grabs the Birdwells' cantankerous goose, visualizing a tasty meal, Eliza, against her deepest convictions, hits him on the head with a broom, then explains that the goose is a family pet.

Meanwhile, when Jess goes looking for his son, he finds his old friend Sam Jordan dying from a sniper's bullet. The war has come at last. The same sniper takes a shot at Jess and misses, but Jess plays dead, and when the sniper approaches, Jess overpowers him, then surprises him by sending him away unharmed. "I'll not harm thee," says the pacifist Quaker.

Finally, Jess encounters his son, Josh, wounded after a fierce battle, and brings him home to recover. Josh remains convinced that entering the war was the right decision. His sister Mattie, meanwhile, is seen riding in her boyfriend, Gard's, buggy, and the Birdwell family, now back together, rides off to their Sunday meeting. Even though the war has come, they have remained together, at peace with themselves and with the changes in their lives, yet still committed to their strong beliefs.

Background: The story behind the making of *Friendly Persuasion* could make a movie in itself. The idea for the film had been kicking around Hollywood for more than a decade. A series of short stories, based on true incidents in the life of Jessamyn West's Quaker family, had caught the eye of Frank Capra, the master of homespun, earthy movies. Paramount bought the rights for Capra, but eventually, as so often happens in Hollywood, it allowed the option to lapse.

Enter another great director, William Wyler. No stranger to such movies himself, Wyler had already copped Oscars for *Mrs. Miniver* and *The Best Years of Our Lives.* But it took seven more years to secure Gary Cooper, Wyler's choice for the role of Jess Birdwell. Cooper had other commitments and had to overcome his reluctance to portray a father for the first time in his career.

Friendly Persuasion is a subtly drawn story of a family wanting only to be left alone with its beliefs, yet forced to cope with the outside world and its problems.

By the time he made *Friendly Persuasion,* Gary Cooper had made eighty-three movies, including his legendary performances in *Pride of the Yankees, Sergeant York, The Westerner, For Whom the Bell Tolls,* and *High Noon.* His career dated back to silent films of the mid-twenties, with frequent appearances as an extra. Then slowly but surely his star rose, until he became the personification of the strong, silent American ideal. Stoicism was his most famous attribute. When, for instance, Cooper was once asked who he thought was better, Da Vinci or Michelangelo, he thought about it a long time, gritted his teeth, then replied, "Depends."

On another occasion, he was handed a script by playwright Clifford Odets for the movie *The General Died at Dawn.* Cooper scanned it, thought a moment, then said, "A lot of words, but I'll learn 'em." This laconic wit was on display during the filming of *Friendly Persuasion* when in one scene, Cooper and McGuire were to melt into each other's arms. Director Wyler watched them clinch, then called "Cut!" He asked Cooper, "Don't you think you're holding Dorothy in your arms just a little too long?"

"Gosh, Willie," replied Cooper, "I don't drink or smoke."

Anthony Perkins, who plays Josh, is, of course, best remembered as Norman Bates for *Psycho* and its less successful, rather hokey sequels. But even though he became somewhat of a caricature of himself toward the end of his career, his films include some impressive performances.

The son of stage and occasional movie actor Osgood Perkins,

Anthony Perkins made his screen debut three years before *Friendly Persuasion* in *The Actress.* The following year he was a compelling if unathletic Jimmy Piersall in *Fear Strikes Out,* about the baseball player driven half mad by his overbearing father. His other movies of note include *The Matchmaker, Desire Under the Elms, The Tin Star,* and *Winter Kills.*

Dimitri Tiomkin, who wrote the music for *Friendly Persuasion,* is one of the greatest composers of movie scores in history. He wrote the title song for *High Noon* and composed the scores for *Giant, It's a Wonderful Life, Duel in the Sun, Red River, Strangers on a Train, Dial M for Murder, The High and the Mighty,* and *Gunfight at the OK Corral.*

Friendly Persuasion is an enduring saga about a close, loving family determined to stick to its convictions. Its message of peace is timeless.

Hans Christian Andersen

Category: Musical. Starring Danny Kaye, Farley Granger, Jean-maire, Roland Petit, Joseph Walsh. Screenplay by Moss Hart, based on a story by Myles Connally. Music by Frank Loesser. Choreography by Roland Petit. 120 minutes. 1952. Samuel Goldwyn Home Video.
Director: Charles Vidor.
Suggested Age Group: 5 and older.

The Story   This is the completely fabricated story of Hans Christian Andersen, a cobbler who lives in the small town of Odense, Denmark, in 1830. His fairy tales enchant the town's children, often making them late for school. Finally, the schoolmaster decrees that either he or the cobbler will have to leave town, since Andersen is interfering with the children's education.

So Andersen heads for Copenhagen with his apprentice and, after again running afoul of the authorities, he learns that the ballet company there happens to be in need of a shoemaker. He falls in love with the ballet's principal dancer, a proud and exotic woman who is married to the harsh director of the company. Her husband continually mistreats her, only to make up with her passionately. Andersen writes a ballet called *The Little Mermaid* as a love letter to the ballerina. Though oblivious to Andersen's feelings, she decides to have his ballet performed.

Now established in his new cobbler's shop in Copenhagen, Andersen takes the time to comfort a lonely little boy whose head had to be shaved due to treatment for an illness. The boy's father, a newspaper publisher, rewards Andersen by offering to publish his fairy tales.

Andersen's ballet is staged as planned, but he is thrown out of a rehearsal when he insists on presenting a pair of ballet shoes to his beloved ballerina. To add insult to injury, he misses the performance when he is accidentally locked in a closet. Despite her marital problems, the ballerina expresses her commitment to her husband, and Andersen, famous but lovesick, returns to his hometown, now free to tell his stories to the children.

Background: Although this film bears almost no resemblance
to the facts about the real Andersen's life, the movie features a
terrific, engaging performance by Danny Kaye, one of the great
stars of the Goldwyn studio, not to mention a number of brilliant songs by Frank Loesser. These assets more than overcome
some of the visual shortcomings of the movie, such as the over-
abundance of interior sets doubling for exterior street scenes.

Hans Christian Andersen had a budget of $4 million, consid-
ered large back then, and was ready to be filmed only after sixteen screenplays had been rejected. *The Little Mermaid* ballet
sequence, which cost $400,000 to stage, runs an interminable
seventeen minutes; still, it is a beautiful spectacle to behold.

Although announced box-office receipts can be as fanciful as
an Andersen fairy tale, the movie reportedly grossed $6 million,
a considerable sum at the time. It followed *The Best Years of Our
Lives* and *Guys and Dolls* on the list of hits for the independent
Goldwyn studio. It was nominated for six Oscars, including Best
Song for "Thumbelina," as well as Scoring, Cinematography and
Art Direction for Color (categories now eliminated), and Cos-
tume Design.

Danny Kaye was considered by some an odd choice for the
title role, as he was associated with wild, off-the-wall portrayals
in films such as *Up in Arms, The Secret Life of Walter Mitty,* and
The Court Jester. But he toned down his delivery and added a
poignancy to the performance audiences hadn't seen before.

Moira Shearer, the British ballerina, was the original choice to
play Doro, the ballet dancer. Coincidentally, she had starred in
the most famous ballet movie of them all, *The Red Shoes,* which
was taken from another Andersen story.

When Shearer became pregnant, Goldwyn replaced her with
Renée Jeanmaire, the star of the Ballet de Paris and wife of
Roland Petit, who choreographed the film and performed the
role of the Prince in *The Little Mermaid* sequence. Jeanmaire's
only subsequent movie appearance of note was in *Anything Goes*
in 1956.

Samuel Goldwyn, who produced *Hans Christian Andersen,*
was probably the most colorful movie mogul of them all. One
of the true pioneers of the industry, he was born Shmuel Gelb-
fisz in Poland and arrived in America penniless in 1895, before
finding work as a glove maker. Eventually he went into the fledg-
ling movie business with other visionaries like Adolph Zukor and
Jesse Lasky.

After founding his own company, Goldwyn fostered the careers of Gary Cooper, David Niven, Will Rogers, Lucille Ball, and Merle Oberon, and hired top writers such as Sinclair Lewis, Ben Hecht, Lillian Hellman, and Sidney Kingsley. Goldwyn's classic films include *The Westerner, Pride of the Yankees, The Best Years of Our Lives, Guys and Dolls,* and *Porgy and Bess.*

It's hard to believe that Frank Loesser, who wrote the songs for *Hans Christian Andersen,* also wrote the songs for *Guys and Dolls,* the vastly different musical about gangsters. Among his other credits are the wonderful Broadway musical *Most Happy Fella, Where's Charley?,* and the Pulitzer Prize–winner *How to Succeed in Business Without Really Trying.*

Loesser wrote twelve songs for this movie, but only eight were used. "Wonderful Copenhagen," "I'm Hans Christian Andersen," and "No Two People" are among the most beautiful ever written directly for the screen.

At the time of its release, *Hans Christian Andersen* did not receive universal acclaim. Some Danes, in fact, were insulted at the choice of Kaye, a light comic prone to exaggeration, to play their national hero. So a goodwill tour of Denmark was organized, and Kaye even made appearances in Andersen's native village. Nevertheless, some Danes remained dissatisfied.

Hans Christian Andersen was one of the last films made under the aegis of Samuel Goldwyn, as the studio cut back production on subsequent films. Danny Kaye went to Paramount, and most of the other stars of the film, except for Farley Granger, would do little further work in movies. Still, this remains an enchanting musical guaranteed to please every generation.

Harry and the Hendersons

Category: Comedy. Starring John Lithgow, Melinda Dillon, Margaret Langrick, Joshua Rudoy, Kevin Peter Hall, David Suchet, Lainie Kazan, Don Ameche, M. Emmet Walsh. 110 minutes. 1987. Rated PG. MCA/Universal Home Video.
Director: William Dear.
Suggested Age Group: 6 and older.

 The Story On an isolated road in a forest near Seattle, George Henderson, his wife, Nancy, and their children, Sarah and Ernie, are driving home from a vacation. Between the thick branches of foliage that surround them, the sun peeks through, momentarily blinding George as he's driving. Suddenly, their station wagon hits a huge, undefined but definitely hairy form, throwing it into the road.

Cautiously approaching the apparently lifeless form, George pokes at it and realizes he's hit what most people refer to as Bigfoot, the mythical creature said to roam the woods of the Pacific Northwest. Thinking they've killed it, the family ties the creature to the top of their car and lugs him home. Of course, he in fact is not dead, and when he awakens, he enters their home.

After some hilarious encounters between the strange, hulking animal and the terrified family, a friendship slowly develops. Since "Harry," as they dub him, is over seven feet tall and weighs several hundred pounds, their home takes a terrible pounding.

The Hendersons decide to try to keep Harry's presence in their home a secret until they figure out how to return him to the wild. In the meantime, Harry, with deep sadness, finds the stuffed heads of game animals George had killed and mounted over the years, and, with great fanfare, buries them in the Hendersons' backyard.

Soon George finds that concealing Harry's existence is next to impossible. Word quickly begins to spread about the strange creature spotted in the suburbs. The sporting-goods store George owns with his father then becomes the mecca for Bigfoot hunters, who gather there to load up for the hunt.

Since this is a children's movie, Harry is returned to the wild, after a furious chase. Eventually, with his trusting nature and outgoing animal charm, he even befriends an evil hunter. As the movie ends, we see other members of his species ("Bigfeet"?) emerge from the woods to follow Harry deeper into the wilderness.

Background: Reminiscent of *E.T.* in its exploration of one family's friendship with an unusual creature, *Harry and the Hendersons* touches upon many family-oriented themes and serves up plenty of laughs for young viewers.

George Henderson is played skillfully by John Lithgow, one of the most versatile actors in films. At 6'4", a candidate to play Harry himself, he's dwarfed by the late Kevin Peter Hall, who, thanks to Academy Award–winning Rick Baker's costume and makeup, was transformed into the towering Harry. Lithgow is one of those rare actors equally adept at comedy or drama. The Harvard graduate and onetime Fulbright fellow is a well-trained stage actor, whose performance on Broadway in *M. Butterfly* was one of the best of recent years.

Melinda Dillon, who plays Nancy Henderson, was an Oscar nominee for *Close Encounters of the Third Kind.* The Arkansas-born, stage-trained actress was also the original Honey in the landmark stage production of *Who's Afraid of Virginia Woolf?* Her other films of note include *Absence of Malice* and *Bound for Glory,* and here she is perfectly cast as the mother who eventually welcomes Harry into her home.

Don Ameche has a delightful cameo role in *Harry and the Hendersons* as Dr. Wallace Wrightwood, a onetime author on the Bigfoot phenomenon who now runs a tacky store filled with Bigfoot memorabilia. In one of the most moving scenes of the film, he sits at the Hendersons' dinner table, explaining how this strange, apelike creature has been his focus for most of his life. All the while, Harry is about to present himself as, without a doubt, the most remarkable friend he'll ever make.

Like that of George Burns before him, Ameche's career was revived late in his life, when his performance in *Cocoon* won him the Oscar for Best Supporting Actor in 1988.

Harry and the Hendersons is a funny and engaging light comedy. By the end of the movie, you may even believe in Bigfoot. If not, you might turn your attention to other things, as does the sinister Bigfoot hunter, Jack Lefleur. "Oh well," he says, after befriending the beast, "there's always the Loch Ness Monster."

Harvey

Category: Comedy. Starring James Stewart, Josephine Hull, Peggy Dow, Charles Drake, Jesse White, Cecil Kellaway. Screenplay by Mary Chase and Oscar Brodney, based on a play by Chase. 104 minutes. 1950. Black and white. MCA/Universal Home Video.
Director: Henry Koster.
Suggested Age Group: 9 and over.

The Story

Elwood P. Dowd, a gentle soul, has two problems: he's an alcoholic, and he has an invisible friend, Harvey, a six-foot rabbit who accompanies him nearly everywhere. This seemingly harmless relationship eventually causes great concern among his family and friends, leading his well-intentioned sister, Veta Louise, to try to have him committed. Instead, it is she who winds up in the institution, albeit temporarily. The rest of *Harvey* sorts out just who belongs where. The movie treats Dowd's drinking benignly, and, while it doesn't address the negative aspects of alcoholism, it also doesn't depict it as a clearly desirable state. Any young viewer who ever had an imaginary friend will marvel at Elwood's charming obliviousness to the skepticism and dismay of everyone around him.

Background: Though at forty-two he might have been a tad too young for the part (Josephine Hull, who plays his sister, was twenty-four years older), James Stewart has always referred to Elwood Dowd as one of his favorite roles, a character he came to know intimately. And no wonder: he'd been a summer replacement for Frank Fay, the originator of the role in the Pulitzer Prize–winning Broadway play, then performed it again in London before being cast in the movie. Twenty years after the film, Stewart returned to Broadway in a *Harvey* revival, with Helen Hayes playing his equally batty sister.

Stewart won an Oscar nomination for Best Actor for *Harvey* that year, though he lost to José Ferrer's titanic portrayal in *Cyrano de Bergerac*. Nevertheless, the nomination was good enough to make *Harvey* one of the high points in Stewart's distinguished career. Ahead lay many classics such as *Rear Window, The Man Who Knew Too Much, Spirit of St. Louis, Vertigo, Anatomy of a Murder,* and *Cheyenne Autumn.* Young viewers watching Stewart's masterful portrayal of one of the great characters in movie history will appreciate a screen immortal at the height of his career.

Josephine Hull, who managed to beat out Celeste Holm for *All About Eve* to win the Best Supporting Actress Oscar, had portrayed Veta Louise on Broadway as well and was no stranger to fast-paced comedy. Her stage credits included *Arsenic and Old Lace* and *The Solid Gold Cadillac.* She was one of several members of the Broadway cast fortunate enough to be cast in the same roles for the movie version.

While it may be true that the movie glosses over the problems of alcoholism and mental instability (hardly the ordinary fare for a children's movie), the overpowering goodness of Dowd's character and the warmth of the story are what makes this a wonderful viewing experience. Stewart is instantly believable as Dowd, and by the end of the movie, viewers young and old can just about catch a glimpse of his unusual friend peeking over his shoulder, helping him through life. We could all use a Harvey in our lives.

Heidi

Category: Drama. Starring Shirley Temple, Jean Hersholt, Arthur Treacher, Mary Nash. Screenplay by Walter Ferris and Julian Josephson, based on Johanna Spyri's classic novel. 88 minutes. 1937. Fox Home Video.
Director: Allan Dwan.
Suggested Age Group: 5 and older.

 The Story Set in the nineteenth-century Swiss Alps, the film features a young orphaned girl named Heidi who is taken by her gruff, unpleasant aunt to live with the girl's grandfather, a hermit who simply wants to be left alone. He doesn't know what to do with the little girl, but slowly, she wins his heart.

Heidi's aunt returns to take her down to live in the village, at the residence of a well-to-do sickly girl. Heidi befriends her but longs to return to her grandfather. When she's told she can never go back to him, her grandfather descends from the mountain to try to find her. Her aunt then steals her away and tries to sell her to Gypsies before the grandfather can find her.

The police are called in but, in a confrontation, at first believe the aunt's story that Heidi belongs in her custody. At the last minute, however, they decide to investigate and discover that Heidi has been telling the truth, that this is her grandfather with whom she wants to live. So they grant Heidi's wishes and she is allowed to remain with him.

Background: Despite a remake in 1968 starring Jennifer Edwards as the lead, Shirley Temple remains the quintessential Heidi. It has become somewhat chic in recent years to look at her movies and shudder at her contrived sweetness. But even the most skeptical viewer can't fail to be moved by her poignant portrayal here. Children and parents alike will find her screen presence and natural performing talent enormously appealing.

In the history of Hollywood, no other star had above-the-title billing at only six years of age. She wasn't a great singer, but she was something to behold when given a song to perform. She danced with Bill "Bojangles" Robinson and Buddy Ebsen, charmed everyone who saw her, and stood atop the list of box-office draws during the Depression.

Incredibly, *Heidi* was the eight-year-old actress's twenty-second film, arriving in theaters just after *Wee Willie Winkie* and before *Ali Baba Goes to Town.* All were released in 1937. She would have several more years of stardom, for still ahead lay *Rebecca of Sunnybrook Farm, Little Miss Broadway,* and *The Bachelor and the Bobby-Soxer.* She began her career in movie shorts called *Baby Burlesks,* then was hired to sing "Baby Take a Bow" in 1934's *Stand Up and Cheer.* Her salary began at $150 a week at Fox, eventually soaring to $100,000 per film, a veritable fortune during the Depression. One estimate placed her earnings at half the assets of the bank where her father was a teller.

Danish-born Jean Hersholt, who plays the antisocial grandfather who comes to adore Heidi, began in movies in 1915's *The Disciple* and later appeared in great films such as *Grand Hotel, Alexander's Ragtime Band, Dinner at Eight,* and *Men in White.* He won two special Oscars for service to the motion picture industry, in particular for his founding of the Motion Picture Relief Fund and his service as president of the Academy of Motion Picture Arts and Sciences. The Jean Hersholt Humanitarian Award was created as a lasting tribute, and is presented periodically to members of the industry who continue his philanthropic vision.

Heidi is sweet, innocent fare to delight children and parents alike. It will instantly convert all those who doubt Shirley Temple's status as the greatest child star of all time.

Homeward Bound: The Incredible Journey

Category: Drama. Starring the voices of Don Ameche, Sally Field, Michael J. Fox. Screenplay by Caroline Thompson, Linda Wolverton, based on the novel *The Incredible Journey* by Sheila Burnford. 84 minutes. 1993. Rated G. Walt Disney Home Video.
Director: DuWayne Dunham.
Suggested Age Group: 4 and older.

The Story When two brothers and their sister are forced to leave their pets at an isolated California farm to begin a new life in San Francisco, the family pets, two dogs and a cat, decide to follow their masters, no matter how far or how treacherous the journey may be.

While their kindly new caretaker is away, the animals break through the backyard fence and head in the direction they think their young masters have gone, unaware that ahead of them lies a difficult and dangerous journey through the rugged Sierra Nevada Mountains.

As you'd expect, they encounter one adventure after another. The Himalayan cat, Sassy, is washed over a waterfall and given up for dead by her friends Shadow, a lovable old golden retriever, and Chance, a precocious young spotted American bulldog. The trio encounters the obligatory bear, a mountain lion Chance calls Arnold Schwarzakitty, and most dangerous of all, a porcupine who deposits some of his barbs in Chance's jowls.

Shadow is the wise and experienced member of the trio; Sassy lives by the adage "Cats rule. Dogs drool," and Chance lives up to his name by jumping headfirst into every adventure. Despite their differences, however, these best friends manage to survive, to save a lost girl in the wilderness, and eventually to reunite with their human family.

Background: This is a wonderful remake of another fine, little-known Disney movie called *The Incredible Journey* that was released in 1963. Narrated by Michael J. Fox, who provides the voice of Chance, *Homeward Bound* is a true feat of animal coordination. The talented Joe Camp, the wrangler for the *Benji* movies, was responsible for handling not only these furry film stars, but also trained "Mike the Dog," the precocious canine from *Down and Out in Beverly Hills.*

Since feline dispositions are unpredictable, ten cats were needed to portray Sassy. The cats were trained to react to remote-controlled buzzers placed on the dog's collars so that they would keep up with their canine costars. Four dogs took turns portraying both Shadow and Chance, and animal makeup colorists made sure the dogs all looked alike.

This was one of the last films in the career of Don Ameche, one of Hollywood's dashing leading men of the forties. Although he only provided the voice of the wise old Shadow, his steady presence lends a feeling of warmth and assurance that this trio will somehow survive adversity. Ameche played D'Artagnan in the 1930 version of *The Three Musketeers,* and later starred in *Moon Over Miami, The Magnificent Dope, Heaven Can Wait,* and *A Wing and a Prayer.* Younger audiences will know him from *Trading Places,* his Oscar-winning performance in *Cocoon,* and *Harry and the Hendersons.*

Sally Field, who provides the appropriately perky voice of Sassy the cat, was born into a show-business family. Her mother was a B-movie actress named Margaret Field, who used to carry little Sally on her hip to acting classes with Charles Laughton. "I don't remember what they talked about," she once said, "but I'm sure some of it rubbed off." Her stepfather was Jock Mahoney, best known for playing Tarzan in two films and the title roles in TV's *The Range Rider* and *Yancy Derringer.*

Sally Field might've been trapped in bubbly sitcoms such as *Gidget* and *The Flying Nun.* But she sought more challenging work in films, as in *Sybil,* the movie about a woman who had sixteen different personalities. Though she costarred with Burt Reynolds in *Smokey and the Bandit,* an inane film which nevertheless grossed some $250 million worldwide, and another huge hit, *The Poseidon Adventure,* it was the title role of a union organizer in *Norma Rae* which won her the first of her two Academy Awards. Four years later, in 1984, she solidified her newfound respect in Hollywood by winning again for *Places in the Heart.*

Her more recent films of note include *Not Without My Daughter,* the true story of an American woman trapped with her daughter inside Iran, *Mrs. Doubtfire,* as Robin Williams' estranged wife, and *Forrest Gump,* as Tom Hanks' mother. It was she, in fact, who first uttered the now-famous words in the film: "Life is like a box of chocolates."

Michael J. Fox is best known for starring in the *Back to the Future* movies, in which he was perfectly cast as wide-eyed time traveler Marty McFly. He became a star on TV as Alex Keaton in *Family Ties,* a role so popular he would often receive five hundred fan letters a week; not bad for an actor who was not even the first choice for the part! Though his recent films have not been box-office hits, Fox's voice is perfectly suited for the care-free pup Chance in *Homeward Bound.*

Homeward Bound: The Incredible Journey is one of the most delightful children's movies of recent years. Parents and children will relate to the unique interplay between the film's animal stars, and recognize and cheer for their underlying determination to return to their family.

Honey, I Shrunk the Kids

Category: Comedy. Starring Rick Moranis, Matt Frewer, Marcia Strassman, Kristine Sutherland, Thomas Brown, Jared Rushton, Amy O'Neill, Robert Oliveri. Screenplay by Ed Naha and Tom Shulman. Includes music by James Horner. 93 minutes. 1989. Rated PG. Walt Disney Home Video.
Director: Joe Johnston.
Suggested Age Group: 5 and older.

The Story   An eccentric inventor named Professor Wayne Szalinski can't get any respect. His wife is fed up with his strange experiments, his colleagues think his latest invention (an electromagnetic shrinking machine) won't work, and his neighbors think he's not playing with a full deck. Nevertheless, he seems just a few tinkers away from getting his invention to work.

It seems every time Wayne tries to reduce an object, the laser accidentally blows it up. But when the next-door neighbor's son accidentally hits a baseball through the window one afternoon, the ball hits the gizmo and somehow corrects its flaws.

In short order, the inventor's two children and the two kids from next door are accidentally caught in the laser beam and reduced to the size of ants, then inadvertently swept out with the trash onto the front lawn. To them, of course, the lawn now becomes a huge landscape where blades of grass are as tall as trees. A furious search for the children ensues, accompanied by wonderful special effects.

The kids must fend off attacks from giant insects, try to survive being accidentally eaten along with the Cheerios at breakfast, avoid being sliced up by a lawnmower, and somehow let their parents know where they are.

What is a simple idea ends up being wonderfully done, making *Honey, I Shrunk the Kids* a fast-moving family adventure of the first order.

Background: This is the perfect vehicle for Rick Moranis, the diminutive Canadian actor who plays inventor Wayne Szalinski.

More than anything, Moranis's screen persona projects an innate goodness and a deep caring for his family and responsibilities, but also a sense of eccentricity. Moranis began working on radio while still in high school, then joined the Second City TV troupe. When SCTV was aired in this country, his off-the-wall "McKenzie Brothers" routine, which he created with partner Dave Thomas, won him a large cult following.

But it was *Ghostbusters* which really launched Moranis's career. Roles in comedies such as *Spaceballs, Parenthood, L.A. Story,* and *Little Giants* followed.

Marcia Strassman, who plays Wayne's wife, Diane, played Gabe Kotter's wife on TV's *Welcome Back, Kotter* in addition to being a regular on the TV show *M*A*S*H* and appearing in the films *Soup for One* and *The Aviator,* among others.

Honey, I Shrunk the Kids was filmed at Churubusco Studios in Mexico City, where it was easier to re-create the desired look of the streets and neighborhoods. A home in San Diego was also used as a model for the professor's slightly rundown house. One scene that takes place on the family lawn required 25,000 gallons of mud, made to order with 10,000 pounds of Mexican dirt and 3,500 pounds of dirt imported from Los Angeles.

Most intriguing was the challenge of creating a swimming pool–sized Cheerios bowl, for which 16,000 gallons of artificial milk were required. Large inner tubes painted light brown were used to simulate the giant "O's" cereal.

The idea of being reduced to the size of an ant and encountering now fierce-looking giant insects, or being sliced apart by a lawnmower, might frighten small viewers. But the special effects in this film, especially the giant Cheerios, will probably fascinate more than frighten. In the end, one of the adults gets to be reduced for a time as well, so the children aren't the only ones subjected to this bizarre experience. The notion that "turnaround is fair play" is probably what kids will love the most!

Hoosiers

Category: Drama. Starring Gene Hackman, Dennis Hopper, Barbara Hershey, Sheb Wooley. Screenplay by Angelo Pizzo. 114 minutes. 1986. Rated PG. Live Home Video.
Director: David Anspaugh.
Suggested Age Group: 10 and older.

The Story In Indiana, where there are only two sports that count (basketball and basketball), high school ball is all-important. In the fall of 1952, Norman Dale, a middle-aged former college basketball coach with a checkered past, comes to the tiny farming community of Hickory to become the high school team's new coach. His methods are unorthodox: he closes team practices to the curious alumni and tolerates no challenge to his authority. In the early games, his temper gets the better of him, and he's thrown out of games for arguing with referees. He becomes so unpopular that the alumni organize a petition calling for his ouster.

In a stroke of luck, the reclusive former star of the team, who'd been sitting out the season, agrees to return only if the coach is allowed to remain. When he comes back, the team begins to win, despite the fact that Dale keeps getting thrown out of games. In another unorthodox move, Dale convinces an alcoholic scout named Shooter to become his assistant, provided he clean up his act. The coach even gets himself tossed out of yet another game to give Shooter a chance to show his own stuff running the club.

Despite the continued skepticism of the townspeople, especially an attractive teacher in the school named Myra Fleener, the team keeps on winning, eventually making it to the state finals. Along the way, Shooter suffers an alcoholic relapse, the coach and Miss Fleener begin to indulge their attraction to one another, and the young players must learn to deal with winning for a change.

Background: Based on a true story, *Hoosiers* gives a wonderful sense of time and place, a world of simple values and townspeople suspicious of outsiders. The movie doesn't assume that every viewer will care about basketball, but it uses the ebb and flow of the game to show how the players find the best in themselves and the coach learns to redeem himself. The camera work by Fred Murphy puts the viewer right into the game, gliding back and forth along the court so you feel like a sixth man on the court. And rather than being sentimentalized or glamorized, the look of the flat, drab farmland community is authentic. Finally, the young actors who portray the players are all unknowns who project stoic, believable screen presences.

Despite all of these great elements of the film, however, *Hoosiers* is primarily a vehicle for its star, Gene Hackman. One of the great actors of the past thirty years, Hackman makes three or four movies a year. But you'd never know it from this picture. Every performance is fresh. Subtly and instantly, he assumes the character of Coach Dale, a man who realizes that his lowly coaching assignment is his last chance to prove himself in the profession he loves.

Among Hackman's best films are *The French Connection,* for which he was the producer's third choice and which won him the Oscar for Best Actor in 1971, *I Never Sang for My Father, The Poseidon Adventure, Superman, Mississippi Burning, The Firm, Unforgiven,* which won him his second Oscar for Best Supporting Actor in 1993, and *Crimson Tide.*

Dennis Hopper, who won an Academy Award nomination for Best Supporting Actor for his role as Shooter, is also a prolific actor. After his screen debut in the now-legendary *Rebel Without a Cause,* Hopper changed his entire outlook on his craft. "I'd always thought I was the best actor I'd ever seen. That is, until I saw James Dean," he recalled.

Whereas most other sports movies about an underdog team are comedies, such as *The Bad News Bears* or *The Mighty Ducks,* there is an undercurrent of wistfulness in *Hoosiers,* combined with the sad realization that for many of these farm boys, the big game could be the most exciting thing in their lives.

Hoosiers is a beautiful, nostalgic depiction of a simpler time and the triumph of the underdog. It's a wonderful sports saga with heart.

How the West Was Won

Category: Historical drama. Starring Debbie Reynolds, Gregory Peck, Henry Fonda, James Stewart, Karl Malden, Carroll Baker, Richard Widmark, Robert Preston, Walter Brennan, Lee J. Cobb, Lee Van Cleef, Carolyn Jones, Eli Wallach, Thelma Ritter, John Wayne, Raymond Massey, Andy Devine, Spencer Tracy. Screenplay by James R. Webb. Includes music by Alfred Newman. 155 minutes. 1963. MGM/UA Home Video.
Directors: John Ford, Henry Hathaway, George Marshall.
Suggested Age Group: 9 and older.

The Story This is, quite simply, the most panoramic, sweeping saga of the history of the West in movie history. Tracing the story of two families, the Prescotts and the Rawlings, it begins at the Erie Canal near Albany, New York, where the Prescott family, headed by Zebulon and his wife, Rebecca, is about to head for points west. After a few days on a barge, they disembark along the canal and meet Linus Rawlings, a lanky mountain man. He agrees to stay the night, but disappears by morning, after capturing the affection of one of the Prescott daughters, Eve.

Down river, Linus is waylaid by a murderous family of crooked merchants at their trading post, stabbed, and left for dead. The next day, when the Prescott family arrives, they too are robbed, but the wounded Linus surprises the bandits and saves the Prescotts from almost certain death. A melee ensues, in which the bandits are done in and the trading post burned down.

Continuing down river on their raft, the Prescotts encounter severe rapids. The daughters, Eve and Lillith, land safely on shore, but Zebulon and Rebecca drown. Eve decides to settle in Ohio, convincing Linus to give up his wandering ways and settle down with her there. Meanwhile, Lillith decides to head back east, but her plans change when she becomes a dance hall performer in St. Louis. She is spotted in the bar by a handsome riverboat gambler named Cleve van Valen, who overhears a lawyer informing her that she's inherited a California gold mine from a rich admirer. Lillith hightails it out of St. Louis on a wagon train and, her gambler friend in tow, arrives in California only to find that the gold mine is worthless.

The story then shifts forward to the Civil War, in which Linus Rawlings is killed at the Battle of Shiloh and his son Zeb saves General Grant from assassination. Zeb returns to his family's Ohio farm when the war is over, only to find that his mother, Eve, has died in his absence. After giving his share of the farm to his brother, he decides to head west, now as a cavalry officer assigned to work for the railroad. His specialty is negotiating with the Arapaho chief, trying to get them to allow the railroad to lay tracks over their sacred ground. Still following Zeb, the overall story now covers the building of the transcontinental railway, where Zeb encounters a tyrannical section boss who refuses to honor treaties with the Arapaho. So after the railroad crew and their family suffer a raid and a buffalo stampede caused by the Arapaho, Zeb quits in disgust, heads west, and becomes a marshal.

He marries and starts a family in the West, intending to settle in Arizona. But as they await the arrival of his now-elderly aunt Lillith, who is coming to live with them on her ranch, he encounters an outlaw named Charlie Gant, whose brother Zeb had killed and who has assembled a gang to hold up a train carrying a fortune in gold.

How the West Was Won reaches its climax in a furious gunfight between Zeb Rawlins and Charlie Gant and his gang aboard a runaway train hurtling across the desert, followed by an uplifting ending that offers hope for the future.

Background: While the sweeping story, narrated by Spencer Tracy, is easy to follow, keeping straight the logistics of how they made the movie is no easy task. For the record, there were thirteen major stars and ten costars, for a film with a budget of $15 million, a considerable sum for 1963. The movie had five sections helmed by three credited directors (Hathaway, Ford, and Marshall) and one uncredited director (Richard Thorpe, who directed the transitional sequences). Shooting began in May 1961 in Paducah, Kentucky, and the film was released a scant eighteen months later.

The wide-screen Cinerama process used on *How the West Was Won* employed three cameras, forcing the actors to be constantly aware of where they stood. This often prevented them from looking directly at the person to whom they were speaking. They also had to steer clear of certain locations in a scene, lest they step across one of the two vertical lines which divided the enormous screen into sections, one for each intersecting camera. But the result is totally absorbing. The movie was shown in theaters with three criss-crossing projectors, and on video, the three sections of the screen are clearly visible, especially in the letterboxed version, which is sometimes shown on TV.

Lillith Rawlings, played by Debbie Reynolds, is the one character who turns up through the various sections of the film, providing a sense of continuity as the story depicts the events that opened up the West. Now perhaps best known to younger filmgoers as the mother of Carrie Fisher, aka Princess Leia Organa in the *Star Wars* trilogy, Debbie Reynolds' films include *Singin' in the Rain, The Unsinkable Molly Brown, Hit the Deck,* and *The Tender Trap.*

George Peppard, who plays Zeb Rawlins, ages convincingly from innocent farm boy and battle-weary survivor of the battle of Shiloh to a cavalry officer and finally a marshal on the dangerous frontier. Peppard's other memorable movies include *Breakfast at Tiffany's, The Blue Max,* and *Battle Beyond the Stars.* He also enjoyed small-screen success on the 1980s TV action series, *The A-Team.*

How the West Was Won will provide young viewers with an entertaining overview of this nation's expansion westward. Though of course the movie covers events superficially, it still offers a sense of history and destiny, while also telling the story of three generations and more, heading ever west.

Inherit the Wind

Category: Historical drama. Starring Spencer Tracy, Fredric March, Gene Kelly, Claude Akins, Harry Morgan, Dick York, Florence Eldridge, Elliott Reid, Donna Anderson. Screenplay by Nathan E. Douglas and Harold Jacob Smith, based on the play by Jerome Lawrence and Robert E. Lee. 127 minutes. 1960. Black and white. MGM/UA Home Video.
Director: Stanley Kramer.
Suggested Age Group: 11 and older.

The Story

In 1924, a high school teacher in rural Dayton, Tennessee, a town described as "the Buckle of the Bible Belt," was thrown into jail and put on trial for teaching Darwin's theory of evolution. Thus began one of the great trials in American history. Clarence Darrow, the most famous defense attorney of this century, was pitted against William Jennings Bryan, the three-time presidential candidate and religious fundamentalist, who prosecuted the teacher in question, John T. Scopes.

The so-called Monkey Trial attracted media from all over the country, and *Inherit the Wind* dramatized this groundbreaking trial, conveying the hysteria that rocked the small town and threatened to shatter the lives of its inhabitants. The film's cynical but homespun defense attorney, here called Henry Drummond, uses every trick and weapon at his command to prepare the most effective defense for his client, called Bertram Cates.

In the film's climactic scene, Drummond puts his principal opponent, called Matthew Harrison Brady, on the stand. He mercilessly grills his old friend, insisting that the individual power of the human mind "has more sanctity than all the shouted hosannas and holy, holies." "The Bible is a good book, but it is not the only book," Drummond proclaims. In contrast, his opponent's views are so dogmatic that he even quotes a biblical scholar's belief that the Lord began the Creation on 4,004 BC at 9 AM. "Is that Eastern Standard time? Or Rocky Mountain time?" asks Drummond skeptically. "It wasn't Daylight Savings time, because the Lord didn't make the sun until the Fourth Day." In Drummond's view of the world, an idea is a greater monument than a cathedral.

"Progress has never been a bargain; sometimes you have to pay for it," explains Drummond. He further reasons that Darwin had taken us to a hilltop from which we could see our origins, but in order to have clear vision, we have to abandon our faith.

In the end, the judge finds Cates guilty of violating the law against teaching anything but Creationism, but fines him only $100, which Drummond proclaims he will appeal. As for the price of human progress, Drummond had, in fact, won his point at the cost of destroying his old friend Brady, who, after succumbing to the heat of the courtroom and the stress of the trial, died soon afterward.

Background: "He that troubles his own house shall inherit the wind." So says the book of Proverbs, from which this film's title comes. One of the finest courtroom dramas ever made, it features two titanic performances from the principal players, both of whom were near the end of their magnificent careers. The sparring between the agnostic Chicago lawyer Drummond and the Bible-thumping orator Brady from Weeping Water, Nebraska, also provides some of the best theater ever captured on film. Indeed, *Inherit the Wind* is in some respects a filmed play, but with none of the usual staginess when that style of acting is transferred to a big screen.

Set mostly in the courtroom, the clash of ideas gives the viewer a good sense of both sides of the debate, and at various moments, both seem convincing and powerful in vastly different ways. The movie also conveys authentically the feeling of small-town life, which is steeped in unwavering faith but which provides only a limited perspective on the world.

The role of Henry Drummond was one of the last performances of Spencer Tracy's career. At sixty, Tracy had at first been reluctant to take the part. His health was declining (he would die just seven years later) and he wanted to retire. But director Stanley Kramer convinced Tracy to do the film by telling him Tracy's old friends Fredric March and March's actress wife, Florence Eldridge, had also been cast.

This was also one of the last great performances in the career of Ernest Frederick McIntyre Bickel, better known as Fredric March. March starred in scores of plays, and by the time he made

Inherit the Wind, he had just completed *Middle of the Night*. He would then do the inconsequential *The Young Doctors* before turning his attentions to the riveting *Seven Days in May*. March's greatest films included the original *A Star Is Born, Dr. Jekyll and Mr. Hyde* (later, coincidentally, remade by Tracy as well). *The Best Years of Our Lives,* and *Anthony Adverse.*

There is also a small but memorable performance by Gene Kelly, one of movies' greatest musical stars, in a dramatic role as E. K. Hornbeck, a cynical reporter for the Baltimore *Sun,* a character based on the famed acerbic writer H. L. Mencken.

Harry Morgan, the stone-faced judge, is one of movies' most recognizable character actors. He was Henry Fonda's sidekick in *The Ox Bow Incident* and appeared in another classic cowboy film, *High Noon,* and *How the West Was Won.* TV audiences know him from *Dragnet* as Jack Webb's partner and from *M*A*S*H.*

Inherit the Wind is a typically noble work from director Stanley Kramer, whose credits as producer and director include *Champion, The Defiant Ones, On the Beach,* and *Judgment at Nuremberg.* He has been occasionally accused of producing only "message" films that are sanctimonious and heavy-handed. In this case, however, Kramer simply took a good play and improved upon it for the screen.

Young viewers will find this movie inspiring, provocative, and superbly acted. It will also introduce them to the older Spencer Tracy and to Fredric March, two towering screen actors of earlier generations. These reasons alone make seeing this wonderful movie worthwhile.

In Search of the Castaways

Category: Adventure. Starring Maurice Chevalier, Hayley Mills, Wilfred Hyde-White, George Sanders, Michael Anderson, Jr., Keith Hamshire. Screenplay by Lowell S. Hawley, based on the novel *Captain Grant's Children* by Jules Verne. 100 minutes. 1962. Buena Vista Home Video.
Director: Robert Stevenson.
Suggested Age Group: 7 and older.

The Story Together with their friend, a colorful French professor, two determined children track down their missing sea captain father. Accompanied by the owner of the ship the captain had been commanding, the band of adventurers travels to two continents in their search for him, as they face danger from floods, fires, wild animals, volcanoes, earthquakes, and untrustworthy seamen and merchants. In the end, though, it's all worth it, because the children manage to find their father.

Background: The driving force behind the story is the children's unbending commitment to find their father. They will allow nothing to get in their way, though everything imaginable comes between them and their objective, in a continuous series of delightful and thrilling challenges.

Some of the adventure sequences, in particular the one featuring an erupting volcano, were obviously filmed with trick photography, and some younger viewers will find them unsophisticated when compared to today's computer-enhanced special effects. Nonetheless, they'll be completely swept up as the castaways evade a jaguar and alligators, survive an earthquake, and struggle onward in their globetrotting search for the captain. And unlike some of today's blockbusters, the film emphasizes derring-do over danger, so it's unlikely to induce any post-viewing nightmares.

The story moves from South America to Australia and eventually to New Zealand, where the castaways are temporarily waylaid by a gun runner, who is a former member of their father's crew. Hayley Mills and Keith Hamshire seem able to handle any crisis. In this film, they're the real heroes.

Maurice Chevalier, who plays the children's friend Professor Pangel, was the quintessential Frenchman. He enjoyed a long, distinguished career in music halls, on the legitimate stage, and in movies. "Thank Heaven For Little Girls" from *Gigi* was his signature song, and his screen career, which began in 1908, included *The Merry Widow, Can-Can,* and *Fanny.*

Hayley Mills, who plays the missing captain's daughter, was a top child star when this movie was made, having received a special Oscar two years before for *Pollyanna.* This was her fifth movie, following her appearance in *Whistle Down the Wind* and before *Summer Magic.* Her father is the great actor Sir John Mills, and her older sister is actress Juliet Mills, best known as the nanny from the sixties television series *Nanny and the Professor.* More recently, Hayley Mills' appearances include a role on the TV show *Saved by the Bell.*

Had *In Search of the Castaways* been made a decade or two later, high-tech special effects might've given it an entirely different look. But the occasional interior shots and matte backgrounds dropped in behind scenes to create the appearance of exterior shots were common then, and they ultimately give the film a quaint visual appeal. More important, the film is just plain fun for parents and children alike.

I Remember Mama

Category: Drama. Starring Irene Dunne, Barbara Bel Geddes, Oscar Homolka, Philip Dorn, Sir Cedric Hardwicke, Edgar Bergen, Rudy Vallee, Barbara O'Neil, Ellen Corby. Screenplay by DeWitt Bodeen, based on the play by John Van Druten, adapted from the novel *Mama's Bank Account* by Kathryn Forbes. 134 minutes. 1948. Black and white. Turner Home Video.
Director: George Stevens.
Suggested Age Group: 7 and over.

The Story   Nostalgic recollections about a first and second generation of Norwegian immigrants in 1910 San Francisco form the basis for this enormously heart-warming story. Mama, the center of the household, watches every penny her carpenter husband manages to bring in. They have three daughters and a son, and some of them long to go to high school. Meanwhile, their shy aunt is thinking of marrying an undertaker, and a nosy, domineering uncle who comes to visit turns the house upside-down. As part of the action, the youngest daughter undergoes surgery, the oldest daughter aspires to be a writer, and the uncle eventually dies.

These events are recounted to us by the oldest daughter, Katrin, who succeeds in becoming a writer, as she looks back on her days growing up with her devoted family.

Background: This is one of the most tender family dramas ever made. The movie eventually spawned a TV series of the same name, with Peggy Wood as Mama, Judson Laird as Papa, Dick Van Patten as Nels, and future feminist movement leader Robin Morgan as Dagmar.

Though Greta Garbo had supposedly been the first choice for the role of Mama, Irene Dunne, an actress largely unappreciated by today's moviegoers, got the role and subsequently an Oscar nomination for her performance, one of five the movie garnered. By the time she landed this role, she was already a major Hollywood star. Her films, including *Cimarron, Show Boat, Theodora*

Goes Wild, The Awful Truth, Penny Serenade, A Guy Named Joe, and *The White Cliffs of Dover,* were all popular. Two of her other movies, *Anna and the King of Siam* and *Life with Father,* based on Broadway plays, were also hits, and her last screen appearance was in 1952's *It Grows on Trees.* Dunne later served as an alternate delegate to the United Nations General Assembly, the result of her years of stumping for the Republican party.

Barbara Bel Geddes, who portrays the narrator and eldest daughter Katrin, is best known to younger viewers as Ellie Ewing on *Dallas,* the popular TV series of the 1970s and early 1980s. Primarily a Broadway actress, her other films of note include *Blood on the Moon, Panic in the Streets,* and *The Five Pennies.*

Edgar Bergen, the ventriloquist father of Candice Bergen, has a surprising number of films on his résumé, but in his role as the undertaker and suitor to Ellen Corby, one of Katrin's aunts, he performs without his usual sidekick, dummy Charlie McCarthy. His other movies include *Charlie McCarthy, Detective; Stage Door Cantee;* and *The Muppet Movie,* made just before his death in 1978. Jim Henson, the late master Muppeteer, was influenced by Bergen and dedicated that movie to Bergen's memory.

George Stevens, who directed *I Remember Mama* with a loving hand, is best remembered for sprawling action movies such as *Gunga Din, Shane,* and the movies which won him Oscars, *A Place in the Sun* and *Giant.* But he also demonstrated his versatility with *The Greatest Story Ever Told,* as well as intimate films such as this one and *The Diary of Anne Frank.* Stevens is also responsible for directing Katharine Hepburn early in her career in *Alice Adams,* one of movies' great performances, and *Woman of the Year,* the first Tracy-Hepburn movie. A onetime cameraman for pioneer producer-director Hal Roach, Stevens worked on Laurel-and-Hardy comedy shorts and also directed *Swing Time,* one of the most popular Astaire-Rogers musicals. His namesake son is the director and producer of such landmark documentaries as *John F. Kennedy: Years of Lightning, Day of Drums* and *George Stevens: A Filmmaker's Journey.*

To be sure, *I Remember Mama,* featuring a sick child who recovers, a dying pet that isn't dying at all, and a poor family that really isn't that poor, is somewhat emotionally manipulative. But because it's executed with integrity and includes some timeless performances, you'll find yourself not minding it at all, but loving every member of the family. Most of all, of course, Mama.

Islands in the Stream

Category: Drama. Starring George C. Scott, David Hemmings, Hart Bochner, Claire Bloom, Susan Tyrell, Gilbert Roland. Screenplay by Denne Bart Petitclerc, based on the novel by Ernest Hemingway. 105 minutes. 1977. Rated PG. Paramount Home Video.
Director: Franklin J. Schaffner.
Suggested Age Group: 11 and over.

The Story It's May 1940, just after the fall of France. Tom Hudson is a sculptor living alone in the Bahamas, well settled into his expatriate life, working on his metal sculptures and reflecting on life. Tom has many friends on the island, including Willy, an assistant, and Eddy, a local fishing buddy who has a drinking problem. Tom also has a lady friend named Lil.

But the idyllic, isolated life is fleeting. War is literally lapping at the shores of the island every night, and the flashes of light from explosions aboard torpedo ships can be seen on the horizon, the victims of roving wolf packs of German U-boats.

Islands in the Stream is divided into three parts, respectively called "The Boys," "The Woman," and "The Journey." In the first section, Tom's three sons (by two different ex-wives) arrive for a visit. He hasn't seen them in several years, and at first their reunion goes a bit uneasily. In particular, Tom's middle son, Davey, warms to his father slowly, still unable to deal with his parents' divorce and his long separation from him.

When all the boys go fishing, his eldest son, Tom, makes a narrow escape from the jaws of a hammerhead shark, thanks to Tom's friend Eddy's talent at wielding an automatic rifle. Davey then takes on a huge fish and finally lands him with Tom's help, an experience which eases their strained relationship.

Still, the outside world encroaches. When a young sailor's body washes up on the shore after his ship is blown up by the Germans, Tom tells his father he plans to enlist in the Canadian Air Force as soon as he graduates from college. Eventually, the boys return to Miami with a deep new love and understanding of their father, forged by their hard-earned rapprochement.

"The Woman," set a few months later, concerns Tom's first ex-wife, who comes for a short visit to tell him she's decided to get married again. She also hides a deep, dark secret, which she finally reveals to Tom but which breaks his heart.

"The Journey," the film's final chapter, addresses Tom's desire to return to Florida to move his life in a new direction. He and Eddy decide to use Tom's small cabin cruiser to ferry Jewish refugees from the island to Cuba, where they can then find transportation to America. En route, however, their small boat encounters the Cuban coast guard with disastrous results. Yet in an inexplicable way, Tom's life now seems finally complete and he realizes that everything he's always suspected about the meaning of life, in one way or another, is true.

Background: *Islands in the Stream* was adapted from an unfinished novel by Ernest Hemingway completed by his journalist widow, Mary. Its absorbing mood is established from the opening credits, and it goes on to focus on lead character Tom, played superbly by George C. Scott, who is a barrel-chested, moody artist with several ex-wives, living and working in the Caribbean.

This is one of Scott's best but least appreciated performances. He expresses, at one time or another, happiness, wistfulness, regret, melancholia, and finally, a peace with himself and his life. Well known for criticizing the Oscars as a "meaningless, self-serving meat parade," Scott was given the award anyway for *Patton* (also directed by Franklin Schaffner), ironically a role rejected by Robert Mitchum, Rod Steiger, Lee Marvin, and Burt Lancaster.

Scott's screen debut came in *The Hanging Tree*, which was followed by the riveting *Anatomy of a Murder*, one of the best courtroom dramas ever filmed. His other movies of note include *The Hustler, Dr. Strangelove, They Might Be Giants, Hospital*, and *Movie Movie*. At heart, however, Scott is a stage actor, and he displayed his fine theatrical skills on Broadway in *The Andersonville Trial; The Sly Fox*, a version of *Volpone;* and a production of *Death of a Salesman*. He was also well cast in a delightful but short-lived TV series in 1987 in the title role of *Mr. President*.

Claire Bloom, who plays Audrey, Tom's first wife, is a classically trained English actress whose work has been mostly in the theater. Her movies of note include *Limelight*, one of Chaplin's final films; *Look Back in Anger; Richard III; Alexander the Great;* and Woody Allen's *Crimes and Misdemeanors*.

Islands in the Stream is a heartwarming, tender movie about lives which have taken some misdirections, but which are also touched by abiding love.

It Happens Every Spring

Category: Comedy. Starring Ray Milland, Jean Peters, Paul Douglas, Ed Begley, Ted de Corsia. Screenplay by Valentine Davies, from a story by Shirley W. Smith and Valentine Smith. 87 minutes. 1949. Black and white. 20th Century–Fox Home Video.
Director: Lloyd Bacon.
Suggested Age Group: 6 and older.

 Vernon Simpson, a shy professor of organic chemistry at the University of Michigan, loves baseball so much that he turns on his radio during classes to keep abreast of games. Trying to devise a bug repellent for trees, he accidentally discovers a chemical in his lab that repels any kind of wood it comes in contact with. Soon Vernon realizes that if he were to spray this substance on a baseball, it would cause the ball to avoid contact with wooden bats.

In order to get enough money to marry his girlfriend (who also happens to be one of his students!) he takes leave of his job and heads for St. Louis for a tryout with the Cardinals. Using an alias, he quickly makes the team and becomes their star pitcher, thanks to the chemical he secretly smears on the baseball before his delivery. Eventually, of course, he returns to campus and his life.

Background: *It Happens Every Spring* premiered in Ann Arbor, Michigan, the home of Professor Shirley Smith, whose article on baseball in the *University of Michigan Quarterly* was the basis for the movie. The film's baseball sequences are dated, almost quaint. The professor, for instance, demands a mere $1,000 a game, which today is just a bit above the major-league minimum, but which in those days was an unheard-of sum. Furthermore, the uniforms are baggy and the team logo looks phony. At one point, the team owner tries to call Simpson over to meet a friend in the middle of the game, something which, of course, would never really happen.

Ike Danning, a former major leaguer, who played all of two

games for the 1928 St. Louis Browns, trained Ray Milland for the role of Simpson. Nevertheless, the Welsh-born Milland never looks convincing throwing a ball, and the camera quickly cuts away when he begins his windup. Despite these visual glitches, however, the film is charming and light.

Ray Milland was the recipient of the Best Actor Oscar for 1945's riveting *The Lost Weekend,* the first movie to deal with alcoholism as a disease. By 1949, he'd starred in the classic *Beau Geste, The Major and the Minor, The Big Clock,* and *Star Spangled Rhythm;* he would later go on to the Hitchcock masterpiece *Dial M for Murder* and later *Love Story.*

Jean Peters, who played Milland's girlfriend, Deborah Green-leaf, made her screen debut in *Captain from Castile* opposite Tyrone Power; her other memorable films include *Apache* and *A Man Called Peter.* But she is perhaps best known for having been married from 1956–71 to one of the century's richest and certainly most mysterious and eccentric men, Howard Hughes.

It Happens Every Spring is wholesome entertainment, best viewed at the start of the baseball season, even in these days when the innocence of the game is long gone. It's slight but amusing, and even though Simpson essentially pulls off a stunt using dishonest means, his motives are honorable. The movie asks you to accept its premise without overwhelming you with it, and its charm is enduring.

Ivanhoe

Category: Adventure. Starring Robert Taylor, Joan Fontaine,
Elizabeth Taylor, George Sanders, Emlyn Williams, Finlay Currie.
Screenplay by Noel Langley, adapted by Aenas Mackenzie from the
novel by Sir Walter Scott. Music by Miklos Rozsa. 106 minutes.
1952. MGM/UA Home Video.
Director: Richard Thorpe.
Suggested Age Group: 11 and over.

The Story

In the twelfth century, a wandering Saxon knight,
Wilfred of Ivanhoe, is en route home to England
after the Third Crusade. He has been searching for
the missing King Richard the Lionhearted, who never returned
to England from the Crusades. While in Austria, he hears a response to a song he sings from a castle tower. Sure enough, the
king is being held prisoner inside and tosses a note bearing the
royal seal down to Ivanhoe, which explains that he is being held
for ransom by King Leopold of Austria.

Ivanhoe returns home to raise the ransom and eventually
comes to suspect that Richard's brother John, who has usurped
the throne in Richard's absence, is in league with Norman knights
to keep Richard prisoner. Ivanhoe, accompanied by a band of
Norman knights, then arrives at the home of his father, from
whom he is estranged.

His father, Sir Cedric, had wanted Ivanhoe to remain in England and fight the Normans rather than accompany Richard on
the Crusade. Although he remains unforgiving of his long-absent
son, Ivanhoe nevertheless shares a warm reunion with his devoted love, Rowena, who is Sir Cedric's ward and has been awaiting Ivanhoe's return. Rowena warns him of the Norman plot to
keep John on Richard's throne.

With a newly acquired squire named Wamba, Ivanhoe raises
enough money for an entrance fee to compete against Norman
knights at a jousting contest. He also turns to a prominent Jewish man, Isaac of York, to raise money to ransom Richard. Ivanhoe finds himself attracted to Isaac's beautiful daughter, Rebecca,

despite his feelings for Rowena. And though Rebecca feels the same way about him, the difference in their religions dooms any possibility of a relationship.

Prince John learns of the plan to ransom his brother and has Ivanhoe and his friends arrested and taken to Torquilstone Castle. But never fear. Ivanhoe is rescued by Locksley, aka Robin Hood and his men. Meanwhile, Sir Brian de Bois-Guilbert, a Norman knight in love with Rebecca, uses her as a shield to escape from the castle. He takes Rebecca to Prince John, who, ignoring Bois-Guilbert's feelings for her, orders her tried and burned at the stake unless she can obtain the ransom destined to free Richard.

The ransom is sent to Austria nevertheless, and when Rebecca is condemned, Ivanhoe arrives and claims the right to defend her in a challenge against Sir Brian. A classic battle ensues between Ivanhoe and Sir Brian, which ends just when King Richard, freed by the ransom, arrives with his men. Isaac and his daughter Rowena are then guaranteed safe passage abroad, and Ivanhoe returns to Rowena. Richard is installed on the throne once again, with good triumphing over evil.

Background: Every child should see at least one movie about knighthood and the Middle Ages, and *Ivanhoe* is the best. *Ivanhoe* was filmed entirely on location in England, and the setting's authenticity lends power to the film's ability to take the viewer back eight centuries.

The screenplay is reasonably faithful to Sir Walter Scott's 1819 novel. Parents should know that there are several fight scenes, and that the climactic battle features Ivanhoe and De Bois-Guilbert slugging it out with an ax and a broadsword, among other weapons. While there is no on-screen bloodshed, the film provides a real sense of adventure and a realistic re-creation of the Middle Ages. Indeed, the costumes and sets were the result of careful research done at the British Museum. The castle took some two years to complete and was used for later films as well.

Robert Taylor, who played the title role, was never considered a great actor, but his good looks served him well in leading roles. Here he is surprisingly restrained, playing many scenes with his face covered to conceal his identity. His appearance in *The Magnificent Obsession* with Irene Dunne made him a star, followed by *Camille, A Yank at Oxford,* and *Waterloo Bridge.* Later, Taylor turned to television, starring in *The Detectives.* He was married to screen legend Barbara Stanwyck from 1939 to 1952.

Joan Fontaine, who plays Rowena, was born Joan de Beauvoir de Havilland in Tokyo, sixteen months after her sister, Olivia de Havilland. No other sisters ever achieved the same level of stardom during Hollywood's Golden Era as did the de Havilland sisters. Joan Fontaine adopted her stepfather's surname upon arriving in Hollywood, so as not to be confused with sister Olivia. Her most acclaimed films include *Suspicion,* for which she won the Oscar as Best Actress of 1941, *Rebecca,* for which she recieved an Oscar nomination the year before, *Jane Eyre,* and *Tender Is the Night.*

Undoubtedly the most interesting performance in *Ivanhoe* was given by George Sanders, who portrayed the sinister but still elegant Norman knight Sir Brian de Bois-Guilbert. He falls in love with Rebecca, played by Elizabeth Taylor, and realizing the situation is hopeless, he conveys a genuine sense of sadness in his portrayal. So although you dislike him, you can see that a better man exists beneath the armor and the Norman airs.

George Sanders played the quintessential suave "other man" in many movies of that era. Though he had an elegant English accent, he was actually born in St. Petersburg, Russia, in 1906. He had spent time working in the textile business before being drawn to acting, first on the London stage and eventually in Hollywood. His timing couldn't have been better, for during the war he landed many roles as Nazis and other villainous types. He won an Oscar for Best Supporting Actor in 1950 as the acerbic critic in *All About Eve,* a role perfectly suited to Sanders' delivery and demeanor. He is also the only man who married two Gabors; Zsa Zsa, his second wife, and her sister Magda, his fourth and last wife. Sanders' 1960 autobiography was called *Memoirs of a Professional Cad.*

Ivanhoe is a throwback to a wonderful, prolific time in movie history: an age of epics, biblical films, swashbuckling adventures, Westerns, and tales from the Middle Ages. But a film like *Ivanhoe,* richly filmed in Technicolor hues and combining authentic costumes with a thrilling story, is perfect entertainment for young audiences of any generation. The mythology of knights, their ladies, the Crusades, Robin Hood, King Richard the Lionhearted, and the brave Ivanhoe provide a compelling look back into history that adventure-minded kids will love.

The Jackie Robinson Story

Category: Drama. Starring Jackie Robinson, Ruby Dee, Minor
Watson, Louise Beavers. Screenplay by Lawrence Taylor and Arthur
Mann, story by Louis Pollock. 76 minutes. 1950. Black and white.
MGM/UA Home Video.
Director: Alfred E. Green.
Suggested Age Group: 7 and older.

The Story   This is the true story of the first African-American major leaguer of the twentieth century. Jack Roosevelt Robinson, a tremendous athlete at UCLA in both football and baseball, later joined the army and went on to play in the so-called Negro leagues, back when major-league baseball still barred black players.

Early in the movie, we see Jackie as a rookie on a road trip in the South. When the bus stops at a diner, Jackie, the youngest player on the team, is chosen to request food and the use of the bathroom for his teammates. But the white man behind the counter tells him the kitchen is closed and the rest room is out of order. Robinson endures this indignity silently.

Robinson is scouted by the Brooklyn Dodgers' Clyde Sukeforth, a former major leaguer. The young infielder is given a "can't miss" label, and brought to the attention of Branch Rickey, another ex-ballplayer, then general manager of the Dodgers. Rickey summons Robinson to his office on Montague Street in Brooklyn to see what kind of man he is.

Rickey explains that if Jackie were signed to a contract to play for the Dodgers' top farm team, he would have to have the courage not to respond to the inevitable racial taunting. When Rickey asks what he would do if someone slapped him on the cheek, Robinson replies: "I have another cheek." Rickey knows then that he has his man.

Jackie goes on to tear up the International League in 1946, playing for Montreal, starting with a four-hit, two–home run performance in his first game. But after the game, three burly thugs surround him outside the ballpark. Still, he controls himself and finds himself escorted away by his teammates. Later, however, some of Robinson's teammates circulate a petition stating they don't want to be on the same team with Robinson, and they're called on to the carpet by Rickey.

"Would you have the courage to strip to the waist and tell Robinson to his face, here behind closed doors, that he can't play on the same team as you, tell him he can't earn his living as a ballplayer?" asks a furious Rickey to one of the petition signers.

"I just didn't think," replies the player. "That, sir, is why your teammates call you 'Ironhead,'" snaps the cigar-smoking Rickey.

The next season, 1947, Jackie Robinson made history as the starting first baseman for the Brooklyn Dodgers. Playing a position to which he was unaccustomed, he quickly learned the intricacies of first base and let his brilliant play do his talking. Through it all, he endured continuous abuse, with booing, racial epithets, and even death threats. "I've got to set them on their ear," Robinson tells his wife. "I've got to be the best ballplayer they've ever seen." Jackie Robinson gave the fans an eyeful, then went on to be enshrined in baseball's Hall of Fame as one of the dominant players of his era.

Background: Jackie Robinson portrayed himself with the same self-effacing dignity and grace with which he conducted himself throughout his life. Originally released by little Eagle Lion films, a B studio in the 1950s, *The Jackie Robinson Story* is a tale of grace under fire, of a man summoned to right a terrible wrong, and whose legacy has endured for sixty years.

As baseball movies go, this one has a primitive, slightly grainy look to it. Nevertheless, the baseball sequences have an authentic late-forties look, and Robinson acquits himself surprisingly well for a nonactor faced with the added challenge of portraying himself. Baseball purists will quickly notice that the names of the other Dodgers have been changed, probably in an attempt to spare them some shame for their racist attitudes. Today no doubt the real names would've been used.

In the tradition of most baseball movies, there are frequent cuts to the play-by-play announcer, some of them hokey. For example, he intones with sincerity, "In baseball, it's not who you are, but how you play the game," a line which today would surely draw snickers. But given the time and place, the line seems somehow appropriate. The baseball-rhubarbs arguments between players and umpires appear staged, but the look of Ebbets Field, today a long-demolished shrine, is authentic, as are the baggy uniforms of the day.

Ruby Dee, who plays Jackie's wife, Rachel, debuted on Broadway in *Anna Lucasta* in 1946, the same year that Jackie Robinson played with Montreal. Her other films of note include *Go Man Go!, Purlie Victorious,* and, more recently, *Do the Right Thing* and *Just Cause.*

For veteran character actor Minor Watson, who plays the gravel-voiced Branch Rickey, *The Jackie Robinson Story* came late in his career, which began with 1914's *No. 28* and included *Dead End, Boys Town, They Died with Their Boots On,* and *Yankee Doodle Dandy.*

For a low-budget, minor studio release such as *The Jackie Robinson Story,* the producers were lucky to land a director as experienced as Alfred E. Green. He directed Bette Davis in her first Oscar-winning performance in 1935's *Dangerous* and made dozens of other movies, including *The Jolson Story, The Gracie Allen Murder Case, The Eddie Cantor Story,* and *Top Banana.* His entry into films is reported to have been in 1912, when he acted in jungle dramas. Though mostly a prolific B movie director, he elicited a convincing performance from his slightly nervous title player here.

Children should grow up knowing the contribution Jackie Robinson made to America, as well as the difficulties he faced in making that contribution. This movie is the best, most authentic means by which to learn about one of the most exciting players in baseball history.

Jim Thorpe—All-American

Category: Drama. Starring Burt Lancaster, Charles Bickford, Phyllis Thaxter. Screenplay by Douglas Morrow and Everett Freeman. Includes music by Max Steiner. 107 minutes. 1951. Black and white. Warner Bros. Home Video.
Director: Michael Curtiz.
Suggested Age Group: 9 and older.

The Story

This is the stirring biography of Jim Thorpe, voted greatest athlete of the first half of the twentieth century. It traces his beginnings from a Sac and Fox Indian reservation in Oklahoma, and his days at the Carlisle Indian School in Pennsylvania just after the turn of the century, to his extraordinary later life and career.

At Carlisle, Thorpe comes under the tutelage of Pop Warner, the legendary football coach and pioneer, and the film shows Thorpe's experiences playing football and baseball as well as his trip to the Olympics. Then, as a result of his accepting a small sum for expenses while playing in semi-pro ball, Thorpe unfairly loses his Olympic medals and records. Despite his setbacks, he meets a girl at Carlisle and later marries her, then continues his athletic career in baseball and the early days of professional football.

This is a straightforward, well-acted biography that will introduce new viewers to two heroes: Jim Thorpe, a great athlete and proud Native American, and Burt Lancaster, one of the greatest of Hollywood's stars.

Background: This story was several years in the making. Thorpe wanted Spencer Tracy to play him, but producer Dore Schary suggested that Anthony Quinn would be better suited for the role. Unfortunately, Thorpe's response was, "Quinn? That Mexican?"

Eventually, Burt Lancaster got the part. It was his fourteenth film; by then he'd made a stunning debut in *The Killers,* and starred in *I Walk Alone, All My Sons,* and *Sorry, Wrong Number.* Even greater movies such as *Seven Days in May, The Train, Birdman of Alcatraz,* and an Oscar-winning performance for *Elmer Gantry* would follow.

In *Jim Thorpe—All-American,* Lancaster was at his athletic best. The onetime acrobat and NYU basketball star performed his own stunts on the gridiron and in track events, one of the few actors who look believable in such a role. He handles the track events, especially the pole vault, with effortless grace, and his gestures seem perfectly suited to the character.

Some of the dialogue is corny by today's standards, but it gives the movie an endearing quality. Just before a big game, for instance, Coach Warner tells his team that their opponents have a two-time All-American in their backfield—as if they wouldn't have known that long before. But that's how they made movies back then, concentrating more on characterization.

The football sequences re-creating the formative years of the game when the field was actually a grid—hence the word gridiron—do look authentic, however. Warner tells us that a touchdown was five points and a field goal four. The ball was rounder then, and dropkicking, now a lost art, was an important part of the game. Lancaster looks thoroughly convincing at every aspect of the game, running back kickoffs and plowing through the line. This authentic movie hero looks like he's having the time of his life.

Jim Thorpe—All-American is narrated by Charles Bickford, recounting all the details of Thorpe's illustrious athletic career at a testimonial dinner. Bickford was one of the most authoritative actors of his generation. His booming voice and imposing presence can be enjoyed in movies such as *Anna Christie, The Plainsman, A Star is Born,* and *The Big Country.*

Phyllis Thaxter, who plays Thorpe's wife, had a notable screen career. By the time she'd made *Jim Thorpe—All-American,* she'd appeared in *Thirty Seconds Over Tokyo* and *Sea of Grass.* Subsequent movies included *The World of Henry Orient* and *Superman.*

The screenplay by Douglas Morrow and Everett Freeman, taken from a book cowritten by Thorpe, changes the facts somewhat, skipping two of Thorpe's marriages and his six children. Freeman also adapted the James Thurber story "The Secret Life of Walter Mitty" for the screen.

It was said that Jim Thorpe's favorite sports were hunting and fishing. "Unfortunately," said the greatest athlete of the first half of the century, "no records are kept in those sports."

But *Jim Thorpe—All-American,* which depicts the manner in which he copes with prejudice, the aimlessness that consumed him after he was unjustly stripped of his medals, his bout with the bottle, and his ultimate comeback from the depths, is a stirring, inspiring saga.

The Journey of Natty Gann

Category: Drama. Starring Meredith Salenger, Ray Wise, Lainie Kazan, John Cusack. Screenplay by Jeanne Rosenberg. 101 minutes. 1985. Rated PG. Buena Vista Home Video.
Director: Jeremy Paul Kagan.
Suggested Age Group: 8 and older.

The Story   The setting is Chicago in the depths of the Depression. Sol Gann is a laborer, but like everyone else, he finds getting steady work difficult. It doesn't help that he is also a union organizer who has developed a reputation as a troublemaker. Anxious to act when he hears of an opportunity to work as a logger in Washington state, he has only a few hours to get his affairs in order and hop the bus heading west.

Sol can't locate Natty, his independently minded twelve-year-old daughter, in time for her to accompany him, so he arranges to leave her in the temporary care of Connie, the desk clerk and manager at the hotel where they live.

When Natty returns, she learns of her new situation by overhearing a conversation Connie has with the authorities about Natty's predicament. To avoid being placed in an orphanage, she leaves town, determined to find her father.

Thus begins her adventure, as the movie takes us on a tour of Depression-era America. Natty rides the rails, hitches bus rides, and generally does whatever she can to keep traveling. Along the way, Natty meets Harry, a worldly young hobo who shows her the ropes and accompanies her on part of her trip. He gives her her first kiss just before they split up.

More important, Natty acquires a dog she names Wolf, who becomes her constant companion and guardian. Their friendship evolves gradually. First, spotting him in a backroom dogfight, she opens the back door to provide his means of escape, only to find him following her on her trip.

Never giving up, Natty finally finds the logging camp where her father was last known to be working. Believing Natty had been killed in a train accident, her father, no longer caring if he lives or dies, volunteers for hazardous jobs in a special camp where explosives are used. Just as Natty arrives, an accident occurs, and we fear Sol has been killed. But in fact, he is spared, so we're able to witness their hard-won and tender reunion.

Background: *The Journey of Natty Gann* is an exciting and touching look at a desperate girl caught in a perilous situation, fueled only by her determination to find her father. Meredith Salenger showed great promise in the title role, but her subsequent films *Dream a Little Dream, The Kiss,* and *A Night in the Life of Jimmy Reardon* amounted to very little.

John Cusack, who plays Harry, the hobo, has gone on to many other feature film roles and today is, together with his sister Joan, one of the busiest young actors in films. *The Journey of Natty Gann* is a wonderful adventure, with a strong daughter-father bond at its core. It is never overly sentimental or grim, despite its setting in the Depression, but a powerful depiction of a young woman's courage and commitment in the face of great hardship and sacrifice.

The Jungle Book

Category: Adventure. Starring Jason Scott Lee, Cary Elwes, Lena
Headey, Sam Neill, John Cleese. Screenplay by Stephen Sommers
and Ronald Yanover, based on characters from *The Jungle Book* by
Rudyard Kipling. 108 minutes. 1994. Rated PG. Buena Vista Home
Video.
Director: Stephen Sommers.
Suggested Age Group: 8 and older.

The Story   Not to be confused with either the 1942 original or
the 1967 Disney animated adaptation, this is a live-
action sequel to the classic Kipling story, set during
the British colonial rule of India in the late nineteenth century.

The movie opens with a caravan of soldiers, porters, and two
children. One is a little English girl named Kitty, the daughter of
the unit's commanding officer, and the other is Mowgli, the young
son of one of the Indian guides.

A dreaded, legendary tiger is on the prowl, determined to de-
vour anyone responsible for violating the laws of the jungle. As
the natives predicted, it soon brings the destruction of the caravan's camp. In the confusion and pandemonium, Mowgli's father is killed, and Mowgli himself is separated from the rest of
the caravan, given up for lost.

Years pass, and in the next scene, we see a group of young
Englishwomen as they approach the edge of the dense jungle,
fascinated by its beauty and mystery. One of them ventures
across a forbidden bridge, only to be confronted by a wild-look-
ing young man who saves her from a menacing bear. As it turns
out, the beast is a friend of the young man, who happens to be
the same Mowgli who was separated from the caravan long ago
and raised by the animals of the forest.

Mowgli is captured by the soldiers and taken to the city, where
his identity is soon revealed. Of course, the young woman who'd
ventured into the forest is the grown-up Kitty, Mowgli's childhood playmate. Although she is about to be engaged to a stuffy
lieutenant, Kitty is quickly drawn to Mowgli. With the help of the

garrison's doctor, she begins teaching Mowgli English and the ways of civilization.

Of course this doesn't sit well with her fiancé, and when he learns that Mowgli knows the location of a legendary lost treasure city, he conspires to have Mowgli lead him and his friends there. Thus begins an adventure involving danger, wild animals, gorgeous scenery, and romance.

Background: *The Jungle Book* is a rousing old tale, updated and given fresh life and energy by its charismatic star, Jason Scott Lee, the Hawaiian-born actor who rose to fame in 1993 playing Bruce Lee in the highly enjoyable *Dragon: The Bruce Lee Story.*

Lee began with a small comedy appearance in *Born in East L.A.,* and appeared in *Back to the Future Part II.* He was also superb as Avik, an Eskimo villager in the underappreciated romantic saga *Map of the Human Heart,* a sweeping 1993 epic set in Alaska and England during World War II. Here he combines athleticism and charisma to create a compassionate Mowgli, who wins Kitty's heart with his bravery and honesty.

Lena Headey, who plays Kitty, reached a wide audience as the young housemaid in *The Remains of the Day* in 1993. She also appeared that same year in the delightful movie *The Summer House,* holding her own with venerable grand dames Lady Joan Plowright and Jeanne Moreau. She is an enchanting leading lady who convincingly conveys Kitty's emotional dilemma.

Sam Neill plays Kitty's father, stuffy Major Brydon, who is determined to see her marry a "proper" young man, namely the lieutenant who has courted her. In the end, however, he reluctantly accepts her decision on the matter. For the New Zealand–born Neill, *The Jungle Book* followed his appearances in *The Piano* and *Jurassic Park,* adding to a résumé which includes *The Omen, Plenty, A Cry in the Dark,* and *The Hunt for Red October.* He has been honored with an O.B.E. (Order of the British Empire) for his service to acting.

Cary Elwes, who plays the duplicitous Captain Boone, made a big impact in his screen debut in 1984's *Another Country.* That film was followed by the memorable costume drama *Lady Jane* and then the movie which made him a Hollywood actor, 1987's costume fable *The Princess Bride.* Among his other credits are *Glory, Days of Thunder, Hot Shots!, Bram Stoker's Dracula, The Crush,* and the title role in Mel Brooks' spoof *Robin Hood: Men in Tights.*

Monty Python alumnus John Cleese has a surprisingly small but effective role in *The Jungle Book* as Doctor Plumford, who, along with Kitty, helps Mowgli learn English and later treats Mowgli's friend, a brown bear, who's been wounded. Cleese's movie roster includes *And Now for Something Completely Different, Monty Python and the Holy Grail,* all in the Monty Python series, as well as *Mary Shelley's Frankenstein* and *A Fish Called Wanda.*

Parents should be advised that there is considerable violence in *The Jungle Book.* One soldier is sucked under by a pond of quicksand and dies a slow death, another man is smothered by cascading bags of salt, and Mowgli is continually forced to defend himself against villainous attacks from soldiers and thugs. Nevertheless, these scenes don't tend to be frightening or gory, so most children will be able to view them without being scared. Ultimately, it's the wonderful characterizations, exotic locations, and nonstop adventure that will hold their attention and have them cheering for Mowgli's eventual triumph.

The King and I

Category: Musical. Starring Yul Brynner, Deborah Kerr, Rita Moreno, Carlos Rivas. Screenplay by Ernest Lehman, based on the musical by Oscar Hammerstein II, from the book *Anna and the King of Siam* by Margaret Landon. Music by Richard Rodgers, lyrics by Oscar Hammerstein II. Choreography by Jerome Robbins. Cinematography by Leon Shamroy. 133 minutes. 1956. Rated G. Fox Home Video.
Director: Walter Lang.
Suggested Age Group: 5 and older.

The Story   This is the true story of Anna, a widowed English governess and teacher who, along with her young son, moves to Siam in 1862 to tutor the large family (sixty-seven children in all) of the king. The relationship between the governess and the king fluctuates from mutual admiration to animosity, as the king finds Anna's Western ways curious and she finds his pomposity insufferable. A subplot involves a furtive affair between Tuptim, a gift to the king who is to become one of his wives, and Lun Tha, her lover. Their defiance of ancient customs is abetted by Anna, who recalls her strong love for her own late husband.

Over time, Anna and the king overlook their differences, and a strong bond between them develops. In the end, the king is stricken with a fatal disease and, just before dying, passes the throne to his eldest son.

Background: Every schoolchild above the age of eight has probably either acted in or seen a production of *The King and I,* one of the most enduring, magnificent musicals in the history of the American theater. This true story was taken from the diary of Anna Leonowens called *The English Governess at the Siamese Court,* and was transferred from stage to the screen, starring Deborah Kerr. It lost none of its elegance and sweep, winning Oscars for Best Actor, Art and Set Direction, Sound, Adapted Score, and Costume Design.

Although four of the songs from the Broadway production ("My Lord and Master," "Shall I Tell You What I Think of You?," "I Have Dreamed," and "Western People Funny") were excised from the movie, the songs which remain are as strong a selling point as the masterful performances, beginning with "I Whistle a Happy Tune." "The March of the Siamese Children" is an instrumental familiar to most, and "Getting to Know You" is probably sung on the first day of kindergartens everywhere. Other notable tunes include "Hello, Young Lovers," one of Rodgers and Hammerstein's most enduring love songs, and "Shall We Dance?," a rousing accompaniment to the climactic ballroom sequence.

The King and I was based on a play that opened on Broadway at the St. James Theater, March 29, 1951, and ran for 1,246 performances. The original musical had been based on the Margaret Landon book, which had inspired a 1946 nonmusical black-and-white film drama with Rex Harrison and Irene Dunne. Landon's book, in turn, was based on Anna Leonowens' diaries. The star of the Broadway show, Gertrude Lawrence, had originally sought out Cole Porter to write a musical version, before Rodgers and Hammerstein took on the project. Gertrude Lawrence died suddenly in September 1952, and when the film version was being cast, the producers needed an established star for the part of Anna.

By the time she portrayed the courageous, strong-willed Anna, Deborah Kerr had already established herself on screen with films such as *Major Barbara; Black Narcissus; Edward, My Son;* and *The Prisoner of Zenda.* In *From Here to Eternity,* her adulterous love scene on the beach with Burt Lancaster, in which she uttered lines like "I never knew it could be like this," belied her screen image as a cool, elegant presence and shocked audiences of the time. It also firmly established her as a star. She would be nominated for six Oscars, including one for *The King and I,* before finally being presented with a special statuette in 1994. Her other movies of note include *Heaven Knows, Mr. Allison; Separate Tables; The Sundowners;* and *The Chalk Garden.*

Lassie

Category: Drama. Starring Thomas Guiry, Helen Slater, Jon Tenney, Frederic Forrest, Richard Farnsworth, Lassie. Screenplay by Matthew Jacobs and Elizabeth Anderson. 91 minutes. 1994. Rated PG. Paramount Home Video.
Director: Daniel Petrie.
Suggested Age Group: 5 and older.

 This is the most recent chronicle of Lassie's adventures. The story concerns a father, his new wife, and his son and daughter, who leave their home in Baltimore to move to the dilapidated farmhouse in which the children's mother spent her childhood.

While driving to their new home, they come upon an accident in which a truck driver hauling a load of sheep was killed. The driver's herding dog spots the children and follows them to a nearby diner, and they decide to adopt the dog then and there. They name the dog Lassie.

The daughter is delighted with the family's new home, but the teenaged son, Matt, misses life in the big city. Only his friendship with Lassie begins to bring him out of his depression over the death of his mother and softens his refusal to accept his stepmother as a member of the family.

As it turns out, the family's next-door neighbors, the biggest sheepherders in the state, don't like the idea of people moving in, because it means they must share valuable grazing land. The sheep rancher's two sons are bullies who make the new residents' lives miserable. Only Lassie can help her new owners.

Throughout the movie, the children are constantly reminded of their late mother by entries in her diary, recalled images, and songs she used to sing to them. Since the issue of grief is central to the film, young viewers may pose questions about death, and parents may want to prepare themselves for such discussions. There is a brief fight scene in the movie but Lassie soon comes to the rescue. Matt's healing process, furthermore, leads to his bonding with his stepmother. And later, Lassie saves the life of one of the bullying neighbor boys, so all is forgiven.

Background: The promotional material for this film touts the box-office take of $9.5 million in 1994, but in fact that figure represents a financial failure, the movie's modest budget notwithstanding. It just shows that no matter how good, wholesome, or endearing a movie might be, audiences sometimes ignore it, don't hear about it, or would simply rather flock to see the latest blockbuster action-adventure film, and wait for a quality film to find its home on video.

Jon Tenney plays Steve Turner, the father who uproots his life to move to rural Virginia. His skillful delivery and presence are well-suited for the loving father with an uncertain future, eager to make a new life for his family. Tenney's credits include *Beverly Hills Cop III, Tombstone, Guilty by Suspicion,* and *Free Willie 2.*

Helen Slater, who plays the children's stepmother, may be best known as *Supergirl,* but she has also appeared in more important films. In *City Slickers,* for instance, she plays the lone female on an otherwise all-guys cattle drive. Her other credits include *The Secret of My Success, Ruthless People,* and *The Legend of Billie Jean.*

Veteran actor Frederic Forrest plays the wealthy sheep rancher next door who will stop at nothing to destroy the competition. His extensive résumé includes *Apocalypse Now, The Conversation, The Rose,* for which he was nominated for an Oscar for Best Supporting Actor, *The Stone Boy,* and his debut in 1972, *When the Legends Die.*

Richard Farnsworth has the most varied credits of anyone in the movie. The veteran actor, who plays the children's maternal grandfather, Len Collins, spent most of his career in movies as a stuntman. He often doubled for Roy Rogers and Gary Cooper, and made his breakthrough appearance in *The Grey Fox* in 1983. His other films include *The Natural, Comes a Horseman,* and *Tom Horn.* Coincidentally, he performed stunts for both *Lassie* TV series.

The latest *Lassie* continues a long line of dogs (all male, as a matter of fact) who have delighted audiences for generations. He is the eighth in the line of the famous collies, and his trainer is Robert Weatherwax, son of the first Lassie trainer, Rudd Weatherwax.

What makes this *Lassie* exceptional is that it combines the warmth of the original movies with a contemporary setting. And the gorgeous Shenandoah Valley provides a magnificent backdrop for this absorbing story.

Although it begins with tragedy, this film version of *Lassie* has suspense, villains who ultimately find redemption, a young character who makes a transformation, and the happiest ending imaginable.

Lean on Me

Category: Drama. Starring Morgan Freeman, Robert Guillaume, Beverly Todd, Lynne Thigpen. Screenplay by Michael Schiffer. 109 minutes. 1989. Rated PG. Warner Bros. Home Video.
Director: John G. Avildsen.
Suggested Age Group: 11 and older.

The Story   This film tells the true story of Joe Clark, a onetime teacher at Eastside High in Paterson, New Jersey, who'd left the school amid controversy several years before for another teaching assignment. Because the school's basic reading skill levels fall far short of legal requirements, the state threatens to take over the school if test scores don't improve. Beyond this crisis, vandals and drug dealers have taken over the school, and the administration is at wit's end. So, against their better judgment, the mayor and the school board convince Clark to return to Eastside High as its principal and institute drastic academic reforms.

And that he does, immediately expelling known drug dealers and troublemakers, putting locks and chains on the doors to keep out undesirables, firing teachers he deems incompetent, and demanding that students learn the school song and be prepared to sing it on demand.

"Discipline is not the enemy of enthusiasm" he declares to a group of teachers. His unorthodox methods include using a bullhorn and carrying a baseball bat to reclaim the school from the lawless thugs who have made teaching and learning all but impossible.

Naturally, Clark's stern disciplinary methods do not always win him friends. One parent activist who is outraged by his harsh and unpredictable style conspires with the mayor to have Clark removed, citing the chains he put on the doors as a dangerous violation of the fire law and an example of his incompetence.

Clark will not be deterred, however. When the practice scores for the reading exam come back alarmingly low, he clamps down even more. But just when it seems he is getting things turned around, he is arrested for violating the fire law. Fortunately, he finds vindication when his students, who had previously shown very little school support, rally behind him. Finally, just when it looks like he will lose his battle to his political enemies, the actual reading test scores come back above the minimum reading level requirements.

"What's that in your locker?" Clark demands of one of his students. Pointing to his schoolbooks, the student replies: "My future." We recognize that in the end, Joe Clark has succeeded in convincing his charges that education is all-important.

Background: *Lean on Me* is one of the most inspiring stories of recent years, a film about self-respect, dignity, and love of learning. The story moves quickly, focusing on a character who is sometimes downright obnoxious, who even oversteps his bounds from time to time, but who is clearly a man on a mission.

After watching his fiery performance as Joe Clark in *Lean on Me,* it's hard to believe this is the same Morgan Freeman who played Easy Reader on the PBS TV series *The Electric Company.* But it shouldn't come as a surprise, as the Memphis-born actor has shown an incredible range in his two decades of work.

Freeman's most famous role to date is as Hoke Colburn, the chauffeur in 1989's *Driving Miss Daisy.* He was also superb as the longtime convict in *The Shawshank Redemption,* which earned him an Oscar nomination in 1994, and more recently he appeared in *Outbreak.* Other movies on his impressive list include *Brubaker, Clean and Sober, Robin Hood: Prince of Thieves,* and *Unforgiven.*

Lynne Thigpen, who plays the fiery leader of the group opposing Principal Clark's unorthodox methods, is a veteran character actress best known to TV audiences as the host of the inventive children's geography show *Where in the World is Carmen San Diego?* She also appeared in *Article 99,* a riveting movie about tensions at a veteran's hospital.

Director John G. Avildsen shot to the top and won the Oscar for Best Director for *Rocky,* returning to helm *Rocky V* fourteen years later. In between, he directed Jack Lemmon in his Oscarwinning performance in *Save the Tiger,* the hugely successful *Karate Kid* and its two sequels, and *The Power of One,* a stirring true story about boxing and apartheid in South Africa.

Lean on Me is the inspiring, absorbing story of a charismatic leader who is the last hope for many of the students in his school.

Emphasizing the importance of dedication and self-esteem, it is a film that will stir many young viewers. There are some realistic scenes of roughness and a few utterances of raw language, but these should not be unfamiliar to school-age children.

Little Women

Category: Drama. Starring Winona Ryder, Susan Sarandon, Trini Alvarado, Samantha Mathis, Kirsten Dunst, Claire Danes, Gabriel Byrne, Christian Bale, Eric Stoltz. Screenplay by Robin Swicord, based on the book by Louisa May Alcott. 118 minutes. 1994. Rated PG. Walt Disney Home Video.
Director: Gillian Armstrong.
Suggested Age Group: 9 and older.

The Story   This is the famous story of the four March sisters and their coming of age in Concord, Massachusetts, during the Civil War. They experience love and loss, and passionately discuss life, literature, and values. Their mother, Marmee, is kind, intelligent, and nurturing, and she above all understands that her daughters all have different needs. One daughter, Jo, is an aspiring writer; another, Beth, is a sickly but talented musician; a third, Amy, is a spoiled child but a promising painter; and the eldest, Meg, is content to be a wife and mother. Somehow, they manage to survive the war and to help their less fortunate neighbors along the way, all the while awaiting the return of their father, an army chaplain off at the front.

The story jumps ahead a few years when Jo goes to New York to escape an awkward situation with her old friend and neighbor, Laurie, who has asked her to marry him. In New York, Jo meets an older professor who falls in love with her. Meanwhile, her sisters pursue their own passions as they are pursued by various suitors. Their lives progress and evolve, through happy times and sad, all along the way deeply involving and moving the audience.

Background: Including a 1978 TV version, this is the fifth time this classic story has been filmed, and it is probably the best of the lot. When Louisa May Alcott was asked to write a story for young readers, she had her doubts. She simply didn't believe she was up to the task. Of course, the October 1868 edition of the novel was a sellout, and it was followed by four more editions. To date, it has been translated into thirty languages.

The first celluloid version of the story was a silent film in 1918, now almost impossible to find. More famous is the 1933 version (available on video) directed by George Cukor (the so-called "women's director"), which featured Katharine Hepburn, Joan Bennett, Paul Lukas, Frances Dee, and the best character actress of the thirties, Edna May Oliver.

A slightly longer version was made in 1949 with Mervyn LeRoy behind the lenses, directing June Allyson, Elizabeth Taylor, Margaret O'Brien, and Janet Leigh. In 1978, Meredith Baxter Birney, Susan Dey, Robert Young, Greer Garson, Dorothy McGuire, and William Shatner starred in a TV version. But this latest version of 1994, as it turns out, is in fact the most relevant and absorbing of the bunch, a rare achievement for a story being interpreted for the fifth time.

This is the fifteenth film in the career of Winona Ryder, one of today's brightest stars. Her father was a friend of and archivist for Timothy Leary, the sixties LSD proponent, who is, in fact, her godfather. After she trained on the stage in San Francisco, her movie debut came in 1986 in the likable coming-of-age movie *Lucas* (also cataloged in this book). She quickly followed that project with *Beetlejuice, Heathers, Edward Scissorhands, Dracula,* and *Reality Bites.* She earned an Oscar nomination for Best Supporting Actress for her performance in *The Age of Innocence* and followed that project with another period piece, *Little Women,* this time earning a Best Actress nomination.

Susan Sarandon, who plays Marmee, was an Oscar nominee for *Lorenzo's Oil,* her third nomination following those for *Thelma & Louise* and *Atlantic City.* She won yet another nomination for *The Client* in 1994. The prolific, talented actress followed *Little Women* with *Ready to Wear, Safe Passage,* and *Dead Man Walking.* Her other films of note include *Bull Durham, The Witches of Eastwick, The Front Page,* and the cult favorite *The Rocky Horror Picture Show.* She has defied conventional casting and all the odds to become one of the busiest over-forty leading actresses in films.

Trini Alvarado, who plays Meg, began as a flamenco dancer with her parents' performing troupe. She also starred on Broadway before her movie debut in *Rich Kids.* This isn't her first role as a daughter: she played Diane Keaton's daughter in another Gillian Armstrong–directed film, *Mrs. Soffel,* and Bette Midler's daughter in *Stella.* She also played Babe Ruth's long-suffering wife in *The Babe* and Anjelica Huston's daughter in *The Perez Family.*

Gabriel Byrne, the Irish actor who plays Jo's eventual suitor, Professor Fritz Bhaer, was once an archaeologist and a Spanish teacher. He made his screen debut in *Excalibur*, and later starred in *Miller's Crossing*, a cult favorite. He also produced and starred in *Into the West*, a rather somber movie mistakenly aimed at a young audience. At one time married to actress Ellen Barkin, who costarred with him in *Into the West*, he followed *Little Women* with *Trial by Jury*, *The Usual Suspects*, *Dead Man*, and *Buffalo Girls*.

Samantha Mathis, who plays Amy at age sixteen, is a rising young star whose credits include *Pump Up the Volume*, *This Is My Life*, and *The Music of Chance*. She also provided one of the principal voices in the delightful animated movie, *FernGully . . . The Last Rainforest*, and more recently appeared in *Jack and Sara* and *How to Make an American Quilt*.

Kirsten Dunst, who portrays Amy at twelve, was the precocious but frightening young bloodsucker in *Interview with the Vampire*. Her credits include the feature film *Greedy*, and she appeared on the long-running TV series *Sisters*.

Claire Danes, who plays Beth, made her movie debut in *Little Women*. Best known for her starring role on the short-lived but widely acclaimed TV series *My So Called Life*, she also appeared in *Home for the Holidays*, directed by Jodie Foster.

Christian Bale, who plays Laurie, starred in *Swing Kids*, *Newsies*, and *Henry V*, though perhaps most notably in *Empire of the Sun*, as the young protagonist.

Eric Stoltz, another suitor, made his mark in *Mask, Fast Times at Ridgemont High, Memphis Belle*, and *The Waterdance*. He is probably the only well-known actor born in American Samoa.

Director Gillian Armstrong caused an international sensation with her first full-length feature, *My Brilliant Career*, in 1978. It was such a critical success that it was an act almost impossible to follow, until she made *Little Women* fourteen years later. Her other films include *Starstruck, Mrs. Soffel*, and *High Tide*.

The studio feared that this version of *Little Women* might scare away male viewers. But it turned up on many critics' ten-best lists, regardless of the critic's gender, for its compassionate performances, its masterfully drawn characters, and its genuine sense of family. When, for instance, one of the sisters finally succumbs to disease, rose petals are scattered across her empty bed and over the dolls with which she loved to play. It is a scene to bring tears to the eyes of any viewer.

Little Women was filmed near Vancouver, British Columbia, and the film's costumes, sets, and lush score by *Fried Green Tomatoes* composer Thomas Newman combine to make a deeply moving experience.

Lost Horizon

Category: Drama. Starring Ronald Colman, Sam Jaffe, Jane Wyatt,
H. B. Warner, Thomas Mitchell, Edward Everett Horton, Isabel Jew-
ell, John Howard, Margo. Screenplay by Robert Riskin, based on the
book by James Hilton. Includes music by Dimitri Tiomkin. 132 minutes. 1937. Black and white. Columbia Home Video.
Director: Frank Capra.
Suggested Age Group: 10 and older.

 If you've ever dreamed of a more perfect world,
where care and strife don't exist and where you can
live almost forever, then this is the movie for you.

A famous diplomat named Conway is in a remote part of
China to rescue British subjects caught in a local civil war. He
herds them onto a waiting plane, but during the flight, they realize they're headed in the wrong direction. When the passengers
knock on the cockpit window, they see an unfamiliar pilot wav-
ing a gun, ordering them to sit down. Conway temporarily accepts his fate, more out of intellectual curiosity than anything
else, but his nervous brother, George, and the others in the
group are understandably terrified. The plane lands at a remote
tribal outpost for refueling, and a huge band of fierce tribesmen
keep the hostages huddled inside the plane. It all begins to seem
as if there is some sort of mysterious plan.

On the second leg of their flight the plane runs out of gas and
crashes, killing the pilot. All the passengers survive, but are then
left in a howling snowstorm in the uncharted mountains of the
Himalayas. As Conway bravely starts to set out for help, a caravan
of porters arrives, headed by one who speaks perfect English. He
leads the bewildered and frightened passengers to a protected
valley called Shangri-La, which turns out to be a Utopian society
protected from the elements, where inhabitants can live virtually
forever.

Eventually, as the wonders of Shangri-La unfold, Conway is
summoned to meet the aged High Lama, the leader of this enchanted place, who tells him he wants Conway to become the

new Lama. Conway also meets a beautiful woman he'd like to get to know better. Meanwhile, however, Conway's brother and the others (a swindler, a paleontologist, and a frightened, sickly woman) don't believe any of what's happened to them, so, led by Conway's cynical brother, they arrange to leave Shangri-La to return to civilization.

Conway reluctantly agrees, knowing he will probably never see Shangri-La or the beautiful woman again. George sets out to return to England, but after witnessing one of the women from Shangri-La turn into a horrifying old hag, he dies. It's then clear that Shangri-La does indeed have magical powers, but outside its shelter, its inhabitants revert to their real ages.

Conway makes it back to London, but his thoughts are still in Shangri-La. Driven by his heart and mind, he makes his way back, presumably to live there forever.

Background: When *Lost Horizon* was about to be released, it was played for test audiences, who didn't respond well to its original 132-minute running time. In particular, they disliked an opening sequence about a revolution in a fictitious Asian country. Consequently, director Frank Capra removed most of it and reportedly burned the negatives. Additionally, about eight more minutes from the rest of the film were also trimmed. Over the years, that valuable footage was also lost, though there was always hope it would somehow be recovered.

Decades later, a worldwide effort was made to restore the movie, and prints on video now include some of the missing footage. Some scenes survived only in the form of recovered sound track, so still photos have been inserted, infusing the film with an eerie look that's somehow in keeping with the strange story.

A Best Picture nominee, *Lost Horizon* came out during the depths of the Depression, when audiences longed for an ideal world free of strife, as depicted in Shangri-La.

Ronald Colman was perfectly cast as Conway, the dashing international figure, with his trademark elegant speaking manner and charisma. He was one of the few stars able to make the difficult leap from stardom in silent films, such as *Stella Dallas* and *Beau Geste* (in which he had the title role), to talking pictures.

By the time he starred in *Lost Horizon,* he'd already made *The Man Who Broke the Bank at Monte Carlo* and the better known *A Tale of Two Cities. Lost Horizon, If I Were King,* and *Random Har-*

vest solidified his stardom. He also starred in *The Prisoner of Zenda* and *A Double Life*. His performance in the latter earned him an Oscar for Best Actor.

Sam Jaffe was just forty-six when he played the High Lama in *Lost Horizon*, but thanks to lighting and his far-off stare, he radiates the appearance of the 200-year-old priest he's portraying. Audiences will also remember him in the title role of the original *Gunga Din* two years later, and younger audiences followed him to TV when he played Dr. Zorba in *Ben Casey*. Considering his half-century as an actor, he made relatively few films, but his impressive résumé includes *Gentleman's Agreement, The Asphalt Jungle,* and *Ben-Hur*.

John Howard, who plays Colman's disbelieving brother, George, was mostly an actor in B pictures. He did, however, play Katharine Hepburn's fiancé in *The Philadelphia Story* three years later. And in 1954 he appeared in *The High and the Mighty,* the finest airplane disaster movie of them all.

Jane Wyatt, who plays the beautiful woman Conway meets in Shangri-La, never became a major film star, though her movies included *Great Expectations, Our Very Own,* and more recently *Star Trek 4: The Journey Home*. If she looks familiar, however, it's probably because you remember her as Robert Young's wife on the TV series *Father Knows Best*.

Margo, the exotic Mexican actress whose face changes horrifyingly to reveal her true age once she leaves Shangri-La, was the niece of Xavier Cugat and sang with his band in nightclubs. The late actress was trained by Rita Hayworth's father, Eduardo Cansino, but would appear in only fourteen films. Best known among them are *Viva Zapata* and *I'll Cry Tomorrow*. She was the wife of Eddie Albert and the mother of another actor, Edward Albert.

James Hilton took only six weeks to write the novel *Lost Horizon,* but screenwriter Robert Riskin and Capra needed nearly two years to adapt it for the screen. *Shangri-La* was actually filmed on an elaborate set located in Burbank, California, which, if you listen to any number of standup comics' routines, is anything but the ideal place in which to live! The $2 million budget for the movie represented half the expense of Columbia's entire lineup of films for that year. Colman was paid $162,500 for his work in the film, about what one of today's top stars might receive for a lunch break. Presumably as part of that contract, he later recorded a six-part adaptation on 78 rpm records.

One of the pivotal roles in the movie is portrayed by H. B. Warner, who earned an Oscar nomination for Best Supporting Actor. As Chang, the High Lama's principal assistant, he adds a degree of mystery and dignity to the proceedings. His erect bearing and elegant presence was no accident. The son of Charles Warner, a British stage actor, he gave up the study of medicine to enter films in 1914. He portrayed Christ in Cecil B. DeMille's *King of Kings* in 1927 and also appeared in *Kidnapped, Bulldog Drummond, The Corsican Brothers, Sunset Boulevard,* and *The Ten Commandments.*

Lost Horizon had a profound effect on its audience that lasted long after its initial release. For example, when, early in 1942, General James Doolittle led a daring raid on Tokyo to give post–Pearl Harbor America a morale boost, President Roosevelt was asked the location from which the bombers had taken off. With a twinkle in his eye, FDR replied "Shangri-La." Shortly after that unexpected bit of priceless publicity, the movie was re-released, retitled *Lost Horizon of Shangri-La.*

The mood of *Lost Horizon* will stay with you long after you see it. Though it has some hokey thirties special effects and miniatures, and the snowstorm was actually filmed in a Los Angeles cold storage warehouse with ice chips doubling for snowflakes, the tone and the message of the film—that there can be a Utopia somewhere in this bleak world—is hauntingly beautiful and incandescent.

At one point in their unforgettable first meeting, the High Lama, who knows he will soon die, hasn't yet told Conway he wants him to succeed him as the new High Lama. Instead, he simply tells Conway that Shangri-La is based on one principle: "Be kind." The film's lingering message is that it's a cold, hard world out there, a world in which that simple message is continually ignored. If only we could follow it, the world would be free of its strife, and we might all live in harmony forever.

Lucas

Category: Drama. Starring Corey Haim, Kerri Green, Charlie Sheen, Winona Ryder, Courtney Thorne-Smith, Thomas E. Hodges, Garret M. Brown. Screenplay by David Seltzer. 100 minutes. 1986. Rated PG-13. Fox Home Video.
Director: David Seltzer.
Suggested Age Group: 11 and older.

The Story

Lucas is an undersized but intelligent fourteen-year-old high school student who loves insects and whose best friends play in the school band. He meets and befriends an attractive sixteen-year-old newcomer to the school named Maggie, and for a while, he is her only friend. Gradually, though, she fits into her new social setting, goes out for the cheerleading squad, and catches the eye of the football team's star receiver.

Lucas is understandably shaken by Maggie's rise to the popular ranks, meanwhile ignoring the attentions of Rina, a shy member of the school marching band. Finally, after being humiliated one too many times at a school pep rally, Lucas takes drastic measures. Citing some vague civil rights law as his justification, he joins the football team and begs the coach to let him participate in scrimmages, just so he can impress Maggie.

Though Cappie the football star quickly befriends Lucas and helps defend him from other bullies on the team, Lucas comes to realize that Cappie is rapidly becoming attracted to Maggie.

But the school principal puts a stop to it, demanding to see Lucas's parents. Then, when the team falls behind in the big game, Lucas defies the principal's edict, suits up, and begs the coach to be put in for a few plays. In disgust, the coach agrees, and when the quarterback, who'd ignored Lucas on the previous play, spots him open on a pass play, he tosses a bomb to Lucas.

Eventually, Lucas' emotional situation gets resolved when he realizes that Rina has loved him all along and also finds a lasting friendship with Maggie is just beginning.

Background: This is a thoughtful, often delightful and poignant coming-of-age movie that is sensitive to teenagers' often-delicate emotional concerns. It depicts a real boy at a crossroads in his life, handling new challenges and evolving relationships. Unlike scores of other "youth" movies, the only stereotypes are a bullying football player and a jealous girlfriend. And even these characters are used only as plot devices, not to address the film's central theme.

Corey Haim, the Toronto-born title player, had appeared in *Firstborn, Secret Admirer, Silver Bullet,* and *Murphy's Romance,* but this was his most important role. And though he's gone on to make other films, such as *The Lost Boys,* none of them proved to be either as emotionally sensitive or as substantial.

Charlie Sheen, who plays Cappie, is today one of the best-known young American leading men. Born Carlos Irwin Estevez, the son of actor Martin Sheen and younger brother of actor Emilio Estevez, he made his lead acting debut in the hit movie *Red Dawn* in 1984. *Lucas* was just his third film, made just before a funny cameo in *Ferris Bueller's Day Off.* He was yet to make his memorable appearance in *Wall Street* and two effective slapstick comedies, *Hot Shots!* and its sequel, *Hot Shots! Part Deux.* The onetime professional baseball hopeful also used his athletic skills playing the game in *Eight Men Out* and the two *Major League* comedies.

Winona Ryder, today one of the biggest stars in films, made her debut in *Lucas* in the role of Rina. The actress (whose career is also discussed in the entry on *Little Women*) is perfectly cast here as a shy girl, whose love for Lucas is obvious. After the little-seen *Squaredance,* she became a star in the eccentric and popular *Beetlejuice,* and rose to superstardom in subsequent films such as *Heathers, Edward Scissorhands, Dracula,* and *Reality Bites.*

Anyone who saw *Lucas* during its run in theaters will remember it as a sensitive, intelligent look at teenage life. Fully capturing the essence of a boy losing his innocence about life, it provides a poignant viewing experience.

The Man in the Moon

Category: Drama. Starring Reese Witherspoon, Sam Waterston, Tess Harper, Jason London, Emily Warfield, Bentley Mitchum. Written by Jenny Wingfield. 99 minutes. 1991. Rated PG-13. MGM/UA Home Video.
Director: Robert Mulligan.
Suggested Age Group: 12 and over.

The Story In rural Louisiana in 1957, a fourteen-year-old girl named Danny is just discovering the wonders of life. She has a close relationship with her older sister, dances to Elvis songs, and still remembers the days when she believed that problems can be solved by confiding to the Man in the Moon. When Cort, a handsome older boy who used to live near the family years before, moves in next door, she quickly develops a crush on him.

One night, Danny sneaks down to the water hole for a rendezvous with the boy, only to face disappointment and then tragedy when her pregnant mother, searching for her, is injured and taken to the hospital.

More problems lie ahead, when Cort meets her older sister, Maureen, and quickly rechannels his affection. Understandably, Danny becomes jealous of Maureen and must learn to accept the loss of the boy's attention as a fact of life. Eventually these situations pale when a real tragedy strikes, and Danny must learn to stand by Maureen and go on with her life.

Background: This is an earthy, heartfelt, coming-of-age story in which a young woman faces some difficult choices in her life and makes some wondrous discoveries. Reese Witherspoon makes an impressive screen debut as the adolescent quickly entering womanhood and forced to deal with some emotions she has never experienced before.

In one scene, for instance, Danny is seen nearly immersed in the nearby water hole, fully expecting to be kissed by Cort, when he realizes she's probably too young for him and backs away. Her reaction is perfectly nuanced, mixing astonishment with the sense of dignity she tries to maintain. When, later in the film, Danny really does get her first kiss, her facial expression reflects a delight so precious, it's as if she'd just tasted a delicious new candy for the first time.

Young Danny is also struggling with her evolving relationship with her father, who is somewhat overprotective of her older sister and uses an outward firmness to mask his abiding love for his family. In one scene, however, after she has misbehaved and placed her mother in grave danger, the father beats Danny with a belt. This scene is brief and off-camera, made more powerful by suggestion clearly in keeping with the father's character.

For his part, Sam Waterston turns in his usual dignified performance as the father. True, his upper-crust Yale background might make the task of portraying a convincing farmer more of a challenge. But his familiar crisp style and his choice to perform the role without an accent lend the portrayal an admirable earnestness. As with any good actor, it is impossible to see his craft, only the results.

Waterston's training on the New York stage performing the classics is evident in every role he tackles. By the time he starred in *The Man in the Moon,* he'd already made many memorable movies, including *The Great Gatsby, Capricorn One,* and *Interiors.* He won an Oscar nomination for Best Actor for his performance in *The Killing Fields,* and went on to appear in two critically acclaimed TV series, *I'll Fly Away* and *Law and Order.*

Tess Harper, who plays Danny's mother, has often portrayed southern characters, which is no surprise, since she was born in Mammoth Springs, Arkansas. She won an Oscar nomination for Best Supporting Actress for *Crimes of the Heart* in 1986. Her other films of note include *Tender Mercies, Silkwood,* and the intriguing mystery *Flashpoint.*

Director Robert Mulligan has a long dossier of fine films to his credit, many of which deal with strong personal relationships among young people. The son of a New York policeman, and a onetime director in the era of live TV dramas, Mulligan made his directorial film debut in 1957 with *Fear Strikes Out.* His other films of note include *To Kill a Mockingbird; Love with the Proper Stranger; Baby, the Rain Must Fall; Up the Down Staircase;* and *Summer of '42.*

The Man in the Moon's most powerful scene involves the death of one of the principal characters in a farming accident. It is as good taste dictates, depicted briefly and subtly, with emotions kept in check and dialogue at a minimum.

The movie also contains one sexual encounter between Cort and Maureen, but it is tender and tasteful, perfectly suitable for most children twelve and older.

This is a beautiful, somewhat haunting film, a throwback to another time and place, when strong emotions were understated. Temporal setting aside, however, it is a perfect film for viewers just coming of age themselves.

The Man Who Never Was

Category: Drama. Starring Clifton Webb, Gloria Grahame, Robert Flemyng, Josephine Griffin, Stephen Boyd. Screenplay by Nigel Balchin, based on the book by Ewen Montagu. 103 minutes. 1956. Fox Home Video.

Director: Ronald Neame.

Suggested Age Group: 12 and older.

 In 1943, with the Allies beginning to turn the tide of war, it was only a matter of time before an invasion of Europe would come. But the question was, where and when? One of the most important would be the invasion of Sicily, which would establish a firm foothold on the Continent.

The Germans knew this strategy too, of course, but wondered where and when the invasion would begin. *The Man Who Never Was* is the story of the elaborate ruse, concocted by British naval officer Ewen Montagu, which ultimately fooled the Germans into thinking an invasion would come in Greece rather than Sicily.

The ruse was dubbed "Operation Mincemeat"; the phrase "the man who never was" refers specifically to a corpse, chosen carefully by Commander Montagu and his staff, which is given a nonexistent identity, fake documents, and personal items, then dropped from a submarine off the shores of Huelva in neutral Spain. The plan is that the Germans would find the body, inspect the phony documents, and be misled as to the date and location of the invasion.

But first Montagu has to find just the right type of body. His team decided that "Major William Martin," a fictitious young courier for the Royal Marines, would have to be the identity attached to the body the Germans would find at sea, presumably lost in a plane crash. After some difficulty, they find a suitable body. Montagu convinces the dead man's grieving father that even though he can't reveal why his son's body is needed, he could be proud that his son would be doing "a great service for England." Once the body washes up on the Spanish coast, the

Germans obtain the information in the documents and put them back in "Major Martin's" briefcase. Even so, Montagu suspects that the Germans didn't swallow all the bait. He is proven right, as they send an Irish-born espionage agent named "O'Reilly" to London, who goes around checking up on "Major Martin." He checks on his bank records, his tailor, his men's club, even his girlfriend.

As a slight complication, Scotland Yard has also picked up the presence of the spy and they almost close in on him to make an arrest. Fortunately, Montagu overtakes the pursuing agents and convinces them to permit O'Reilly to leave England. After all, he hasn't hurt anyone, argues Montagu, and if he were captured after transmitting his findings to Berlin, the enemy would know it was all a ploy. The spy is then permitted to leave England, presumably to be dealt with after the war.

Background: *The Man Who Never Was* is a thoroughly absorbing true spy story, but with none of the phony devices that make other cloak-and-dagger yarns seem contrived. It features an unconventional middle-aged hero, and does a wonderful job of evoking the sights and sounds of wartime London. It is a rare espionage movie that relies on subtle tension. While the ostensible focus of the story is on a body that washes up on shore, in fact the real excitement comes from the mind games played between the British and German intelligence agents. Somewhat sophisticated young viewers will quickly be drawn into the film's powerful sense of time, atmosphere, and mood.

After the war, the real Ewen Montagu came across captured Nazi documents written after the Allied invasion of Sicily. The Nazi ambassador in Madrid, responding to an angry inquiry from Berlin about the Reich's having been duped by "the man who never was," still insisted in his reply that the documents found on the body were genuine.

To portray a real man elevated to greatness because of a brilliant idea, Clifton Webb could not have been a better choice. Although he had a crisp, aristocratic British accent, Webb was actually born Webb Parmallee Hollenbeck in Indianapolis in 1891. He began as a child performer in a 1902 production of *Huckleberry Finn*, after which he became a dancer and appeared in light comedies, and performed with the Boston Opera Company. He made his screen debut in 1920 in a silent film with the intriguing title *Polly with a Past*.

Often cast as an effete snob, Webb was one of those few leading men who became a star later in his career, well into middle age, in fact. His best-known role was as the columnist Waldo Lydecker in 1944's *Laura,* his first talking picture and his first screen appearance in twenty years. The now-famous part had almost gone to another actor, Laird Cregar, but Otto Preminger, an old friend of Webb's, took over the picture from director Rouben Mamoulian and ended up hiring his friend.

Clifton Webb was also memorable in his starring roles in *The Razor's Edge, Cheaper by the Dozen,* and *The Remarkable Mr. Pennypacker,* as well as his cantankerous babysitter Mr. Belvedere in the comedy *Sitting Pretty,* which won him an Oscar nomination and led to several sequels.

Stephen Boyd, who plays the Irish-born German spy, was a handsome leading man of the sixties. His appearance as O'Reilly, the smiling but sinister spy sent to London to investigate "Major Martin," was only his second film role, following his debut in something called *An Alligator Named Daisy.* Three years later, he would become a star playing Messala, Charlton Heston's rival in *Ben-Hur,* the movie which won more Oscars than any other in movie history. Eventually, however, Boyd's career fizzled, and he was forced to make a number of low-budget films in Spain.

One of the most effective scenes in *The Man Who Never Was* shows Montagu and an assistant attending a comedy show in a London theater. Although surrounded by laughing patrons, they remain silent, obviously preoccupied with the plot they have just hatched to fool the Germans. From that scene, the shot then dissolves (a device not often used in today's films) into a shot showing the coastline, continuing the story.

The Man Who Never Was isn't a well-known movie, but older children and their parents will find it fascinating. Better yet, the story is entirely true.

Meet Me in St. Louis

Category: Musical. Starring Judy Garland, Margaret O'Brien, Lucille Bremer, Tom Drake, Mary Astor, Leon Ames, Marjorie Main. Screenplay by Irving Brecher and Fred F. Finklehoffe, based on a book by Sally Benson. 113 minutes. 1944. MGM Home Video.
Director: Vincente Minnelli.
Suggested Age Group: 6 and older.

The Story Set in St. Louis six months before 1903's World's Fair, the film concerns a lawyer and his daughters, who live at 5135 Kensington Avenue in a large, warm Victorian house. The film is divided into four seasons, all leading up to the eagerly awaited fair. As we get to know the family, we learn that the eldest girl has a boyfriend in New York. Her younger sister has her eye on the proverbial boy next door, and the youngest is simply an adorable child who goes by the nickname "Tootie."

Life seems perfect in that innocent time, but then the father suddenly accepts a job in New York. This change will mean a complete upheaval for the entire family, so the children do whatever they can to convince their father to turn the job down and stay in St. Louis. Soon, however, they accept his decision and try to prepare themselves for the adjustment to their lives. But of course in the end, the family winds up staying put after all, much to everyone's delight, and they attend the World's Fair at last.

Background: *Meet Me in St. Louis,* made during the heyday of the MGM musical, was the first Technicolor movie directed by Vincente Minnelli. He'd directed Broadway musicals in the mid-thirties, and by the time he helmed *Meet Me in St. Louis,* he'd already directed *Cabin in the Sky* as well as musical numbers for *Strike Up the Band* and *Babes on Broadway,* both with Judy Garland, whom he would marry the year after completing this movie.

The pair would also work together in *The Pirate* and *The Clock,* and Minnelli would direct other classics like *An American in Paris, The Band Wagon, Father of the Bride,* and *Lust for Life.*

But many feel his most important creation came in collaboration with Miss Garland: their daughter, Liza Minnelli.

As for the star of this film, there really never was a performer quite like Judy Garland, who was just twenty when the film was released. She'd become a huge star when MGM couldn't arrange to borrow Shirley Temple from Fox and then wisely decided to cast her instead in *The Wizard of Oz* in 1939. By 1944, she'd reached that bothersome "in between" age for an actress, and had to be cajoled into playing the role of Esther, the second daughter, in *Meet Me in St. Louis.*

Despite her ease with any song she sang, Judy Garland's only musical training came when she chanced to get a job in a synagogue choir. It gave her that tender cantorial throb she used so effectively the rest of her life. Her other memorable films include *Easter Parade, Girl Crazy, The Harvey Girls, The Pirate,* and *A Star Is Born.*

Leon Ames, who plays the father in *Meet Me in St. Louis,* made scores of movies, including *Little Women, Tora! Tora! Tora!,* and 1986's *Peggy Sue Got Married.* He also appeared in *Thirty Seconds Over Tokyo,* as well as on TV in *Life With Father.*

Mary Astor, who plays the stoic mother, is best known for her role in the 1941 classic *The Maltese Falcon.* Her other films of note include *Dodsworth, The Prisoner of Zenda, The Hurricane, The Palm Beach Story, Midnight,* and *Hush . . . Hush, Sweet Charlotte.* In all, she appeared in more than 100 films.

Margaret O'Brien, who played the youngest daughter, Tootie, won a special Oscar for her portrayal. Regarded as one of the best child actresses of all time, she appeared in the 1949 version of *Little Women* and made a few other movies before her career faded. This is her finest role.

The screenplay for *Meet Me in St. Louis* was written by Irving Brecher and Fred F. Finklehoffe. Brecher had written *At the Circus,* one of the Marx brothers' last films; *DuBarry Was a Lady*; and *Best Foot Forward.* Finklehoffe's credits include *Strike Up the Band* with Judy Garland in 1940.

Meet Me in St. Louis was just what wartime audiences craved: a carefree look at a more innocent time in America, with wonderful songs, beautiful costumes, and an optimistic outlook on life. Its idealistic, sanitized look at life is part of its enduring appeal, and half a century later, it remains a wonderful example of why, in its day, MGM was the greatest studio of all.

The Miracle Worker

Category: Drama. Starring Anne Bancroft, Patty Duke, Victor Jory, Inga Swenson, Andrew Prine, Beah Richards. Screenplay by William Gibson, based on his Broadway play. 107 minutes. 1962. Black and white. MGM/UA Home Video.
Director: Arthur Penn.
Suggested Age Group: 7 and older.

The Story This film tells the true story of the early life of Helen Keller, who soon after her birth in 1880 in Tuscumbia, Alabama, fell ill with rheumatic fever, leaving her blind and deaf. The movie begins in 1887, when Helen has already been spoiled by her parents and has settled into a routine of being treated with little more dignity or understanding than a troublesome pet.

Her frustrated parents consider institutionalizing her, but as a last, desperate attempt, they summon a stern Boston teacher, Annie Sullivan, to try to get through to the little girl and teach her to communicate. The first few weeks are extremely difficult, both for young Helen and her new teacher. Finally, the teacher realizes that any progress she hoped to make with Helen would be next to impossible if they continue to live in the household. So she demands to keep Helen to herself in a nearby guest house for two weeks, tricking Helen into thinking they are by themselves, far from home.

Thus begins the intense bonding process between these two strong personalities. "She has a mind like a mousetrap," Sullivan says to the impatient Kellers, who want quick results and don't have the discipline to separate themselves from their daughter for very long.

In the end, after one last temper tantrum at Helen's homecoming party, the lonely little girl makes a breakthrough, at last associating tangible objects with letters spelled out with the fingers. As she spells out "W-A-T-E-R" on Annie's palm, then awaits the rush of water from the pump outside the house, Annie Sullivan and the Keller family realize a true miracle has occurred.

Background: Helen Keller was one of the great ladies of the world. After her childhood in Alabama, she went to Radcliffe, from which she was graduated *cum laude,* lectured throughout the world, and wrote the books *The World I Live In, The Story of My Life,* and *Let Us Have Faith.* She traveled the world lecturing, accompanied first by Ms. Sullivan, until her death in 1936, then by her secretary, Polly Thompson, and finally by a companion, Mrs. Winifred Corbelly. She would receive every conceivable honor over the course of her lifetime. She died in 1968.

Helen Keller and Anne Bancroft, who plays Annie Sullivan, actually met at Miss Keller's eightieth birthday party in June 1960, during the Broadway run of *The Miracle Worker.* When they shook hands, Miss Keller said "It feels just like Teacher's!"

From the moment she comes on to the screen, Anne Bancroft takes over *The Miracle Worker,* giving one of the most powerful performances of her career. She instantly becomes the nearly blind but determined teacher, who takes control of her difficult young charge and stands up to the interfering Kellers. Helen's father is especially intrusive and is distrustful of her. His lingering bitterness about the South's loss in the Civil War leads him to resent this Yankee who thinks she can succeed where they have failed. He doesn't realize that years of coddling and indulging Helen have done her far more harm than good.

Born Anna Maria Louise Italiano in the Bronx, trained as a dancer, Anne Bancroft broke into TV during the golden age of live performances, and made her screen debut in *Don't Bother to Knock,* with Marilyn Monroe and Richard Widmark. She might've gone on to enjoy a successful, if little-noticed career in B movies, like *Treasure of the Golden Condor, The Kid from Left Field, Gorilla at Large,* and *Demetrius and the Gladiators.* But she wisely escaped from that tempting lure of continuous movie employment and returned to New York where, opposite Henry Fonda, she won the Tony Award in 1958 for *Two for the Seesaw.* Then she won another Tony for *The Miracle Worker* on Broadway, and, newly elevated to the list of actresses for A movies, eased in to the movie role. Again the role served her well, earning her the Best Actress Oscar for 1962, competing against Bette Davis and Katharine Hepburn, among others. Not bad for a kid from the Bronx!

In 1967, she beat out Jeanne Moreau, Lauren Bacall, and even Doris Day for the part of Mrs. Robinson in *The Graduate.* Her sultry portrayal, as an unhappy woman having a torrid but loveless affair with the disaffected son of her husband's business partner, became one of the most famous parts in movie history. Her other film roles of note include *Young Winston, The Prisoner of Second Avenue, The Elephant Man, Garbo Talks,* and *84 Charing Cross Road.*

When Anne Bancroft and Patty Duke played their respective roles in the Broadway production of *The Miracle Worker,* Bancroft learned sign language, then taught it to her young costar. They would talk to one another in sign during rehearsals, which prompted another member of the cast to say, "Look at them, talking with their fingers. Behind our backs and in front of our faces."

When her fiancé Mel Brooks brought her home for the first time to meet his mother, he introduced his beloved as "Anna Maria Italiano." His mother then excused herself from the room, and, to show her displeasure at her Jewish son marrying out of the faith, calmly placed her head in the oven.

Patty Duke became a star with *The Miracle Worker,* but the powerful role forever typecast her. Born Anna Marie Duke in New York, she became, at sixteen, the youngest person up to that time ever to win an Oscar for Best Supporting Actress. She later had her own TV show in the mid-sixties, but she never again found the stardom she enjoyed as a young actress. Ironically, aside from work as an extra in *I'll Cry Tomorrow* in 1955 and *Somebody Up There Likes Me* the following year, *The Miracle Worker* is, to date, her only important film.

Victor Jory, who plays Helen's stern father, is best remembered for his role as the carpetbagger in *Gone With the Wind.* Probably the only well-known actor born in Alaska, he appeared in dozens of movies, including *A Midsummer Night's Dream, The Adventures of Tom Sawyer, Each Dawn I Die,* and *The Fugitive Kind.*

Philadelphia-born Arthur Penn, who directed *The Miracle Worker,* was a floor director on TV in the fifties on *The Colgate Comedy Hour.* He learned his craft directing live dramas on TV, and he directed Anne Bancroft in *Two for the Seesaw* and *The Miracle Worker* on Broadway. In the film version of *The Miracle Worker,* the understanding between star and director is obvious.

One of Penn's most intriguing movies, which pops up on late-night TV occasionally, is *The Chase,* featuring Marlon Brando as a small-town sheriff tracking an escaped convict, played by a young Robert Redford. But it was his next movie, *Bonnie and Clyde,* that finally earned Penn a permanent place among top directors. The movie was a huge success and propelled Warren

Beatty and Faye Dunaway to stardom. It was the first major movie in which people who are shot actually bleed the way they do in real life. The gunshots, furthermore, were also recorded at the decibel level of real firearms, adding to the verisimilitude.

Arthur Penn is one of the most versatile of filmmakers, but not one who is prone to jumping into one project after another. Among his other projects are *Alice's Restaurant* and *Little Big Man.*

In *The Miracle Worker,* the moment when young Helen Keller at last understands the relationship between her signing language and the objects the words represent opens up the outside world to her. One of the most powerful, dramatic moments of recent cinema, its poignancy is due in no small part to Penn's extensive experience directing on the stage, where there are no retakes.

The Miracle Worker takes many chances. It has just a touch of staginess about it, evoking the play. There are also several lengthy sequences during which nothing is said. Instead, Penn simply shows long, furious fights between student and teacher; chairs are thrown, tablecloths ripped off, dishes cast asunder. Even without dialogue, these scenes are realistic and compelling.

This film provides a wonderful opportunity for young viewers to see a courageous child learning difficult lessons about life and the world around her. It will inspire them to learn more about Helen Keller, one of this century's most remarkable women, whose boundless courage was nothing short of awesome.

Mister Roberts

Category: Comedy. Starring Henry Fonda, James Cagney, Jack
Lemmon, William Powell, Betsy Palmer, Ward Bond, Phillip Carey,
Ken Curtis, Nick Adams, Harry Carey, Jr. Screenplay by Frank S.
Nugent and Joshua Logan, based on the play by Logan and Thomas
Heggen, from the novel by Heggen. Music by Franz Waxman. 123
minutes. 1955. Warner Bros. Home Video.
Directors: John Ford, Mervyn LeRoy.
Suggested Age Group: 10 and older.

The Story The time is the last months of World War II. The
place the Pacific, in the backwater area of the conflict, where a navy supply vessel, the *Reluctant*,
continually supplies the combat ships on an endless voyage between "Tedium" and "Apathy," with side trips to "Monotony," as
they call their uninteresting, frequently-visited supply dropoffs.
Some of its crew members, in particular Lieutenant Roberts, long
for a taste of combat. The captain runs a tight ship, sticking to the
book of petty rules of conduct. For instance, he insists that his
crewmen always wear their shirts, no matter how sweltering the
heat. Devotedly caring for a prized potted palm tree which has to
be watered constantly, it's obvious the captain has an intense dislike for Roberts, a popular, easygoing officer the enlisted men
adore.

Other officers include a wise old doctor and a young, brash,
skirt-chasing Ensign Pulver, who spends most of his time in his
bunk. But some female nurses are smuggled aboard, and Pulver
later sets off some fulminate of mercury in the laundry room,
spreading soap suds all over the lower deck. Meanwhile, repeat-
edly denied permission by the captain to transfer to a combat
vessel, Roberts finally takes matters into his own hands.

To celebrate V-E Day, the end of the war in Europe, Roberts
tosses the captain's palm tree over the side. "Whooo did it?" demands the captain in a confrontation with the "smart college
boy," as he calls Roberts. One of the highlights of the movie, this
scene is both outrageously funny and sad. Of course, the captain

immediately requisitions a new plant to replace the one he lost.

Roberts is eventually given his transfer to a combat vessel during the final days of the war. Soon after, his old crew mates receive a letter informing them that Roberts was killed in a freak accident during a lull in the fighting. This devastating news spurs the newly emboldened Pulver to toss the captain's new plant overboard and confront him, just as Mr. Roberts had done so often.

Background: Though Jack Lemmon won a Best Supporting Actor Oscar for his portrayal of Ensign Pulver, the movie really belongs to Henry Fonda for his cool, almost detached performance in the role he originally created on Broadway.

This was Fonda's forty-second movie, coming between *Jigsaw* and the epic *War and Peace*. He'd been away from films for six years, including time on Broadway for the stage version of *Mister Roberts*. Oddly, though it has become one of Fonda's greatest roles, originally Warner Bros. wanted William Holden to take the part, then offered it to Marlon Brando, who accepted. Fonda, who'd been away from movies for so long, was no longer considered big at the box office. But director John Ford insisted on Fonda, not imagining that during the filming of the movie they would nearly come to blows during a dispute. Ford then took ill and Mervyn LeRoy finished up.

This was James Cagney's fifty-third movie. He would make eight more, retire, and make a last comeback in 1981's *Ragtime*. Cagney, who hadn't made a comedy since *The Bride Came C.O.D.* in 1941, said he based his characterization of the captain on a Massachusetts bank president he knew, imbuing it with much more humor than had been the case in the Broadway version.

Mister Roberts was Jack Lemmon's fourth movie, following his debut in *It Should Happen to You*. His previous films included the movie with, arguably, the worst title in film history: *Phffft!*

One of the most memorable aspects of Lemmon's characterization of Ensign Pulver was his constant whistling of the old thirties song "If I Could Be with You." He dubbed himself in postproduction, after early screenings led audiences to say the film was too theatrical and the pacing needed to be picked up.

When he saw *Mister Roberts,* Joshua Logan, who directed the Broadway version and cowrote the screenplay, asked Lemmon: "Where on earth were you eight years ago when I was casting the play?" "I'll tell you where I was," said Lemmon. "I was outside the theater, trying to see you to get a bit role."

Lemmon was in good company, for Logan had also turned down another young actor. "You look too skinny to be believable as a sailor," he said to the auditioning hopeful. "But I was at Pearl Harbor and had a ship shot out under me at Guadalcanal," said the young actor. "I was even awarded some battle stars."

"You could've used a few more pounds," Logan responded to the young actor, Jason Robards, Jr., who would later become a two-time Oscar-winner and one of America's most accomplished actors of the stage and screen.

Mister Roberts was the last film in the distinguished career of William Powell, who plays the ship's doctor. One of the screen's most suave, elegant stars, his most famous character was sophisticated sleuth Nick Charles in the popular *The Thin Man* series. He also created the character of private eye Philo Vance and starred in movies like *My Man Godfrey, Manhattan Melodrama,* and *Life With Father.*

Mister Roberts is a funny, engaging comedy young audiences will like. The risqué elements from the Broadway version have been cut, making it first-rate family entertainment.

Mr. Smith Goes to Washington

Category: Drama. Starring James Stewart, Jean Arthur, Thomas
Mitchell, Claude Rains, Edward Arnold, Harry Carey, Eugene Pallette. Screenplay by Sidney Buchman, based on Lewis R. Foster's
story "The Gentleman from Montana." Music by Dimitri Tiomkin.
129 minutes. 1939. Black and white. Columbia Home Video.
Director: Frank Capra.
Suggested Age Group: 11 and older.

> **The Story** When a U.S. Senator dies, his colleague from his
state, Senator Payne, seeks a temporary replace-
ment to fill out the term. Since Payne is involved in
an illegal land deal involving the construction of a dam, legisla-
tion he hopes to ram through the Senate, he decides to choose a
simple, naive man for the seat, the son of an old friend.

Jefferson Smith seems the perfect choice for the job. A total innocent, he heads the Boy Rangers, a scouting organization. When
he arrives, wide-eyed, in Washington, he takes a tour of the Lincoln Memorial and other sites around town. At his office on Capitol Hill, Smith meets his acerbic secretary, Saunders, and a
cynical reporter, who know the ins and outs of Washington. They
realize they have a know-nothing patsy on their hands, just waiting to be chewed up and spit out by sinister political forces.

But Smith is no innocent. He soon learns of the illegal land
scheme and meets with Jim Taylor, the corrupt politician who is
pulling the strings on the deal. Idealistically, Smith decides to
fight him. But he is framed on the Senate floor, wrongfully accused of owning land on which he hopes to raise money for a
camp for the Boy Rangers. Seemingly beaten, Smith prepares to
leave Washington in disgrace, until Saunders finds him once
again at the Lincoln Memorial, and inspires him to fight on.

On the Senate floor the next day, Jefferson Smith faces expul-
sion by his colleagues. But after the Vice President, presiding
over the Senate, calls on him, he refuses to yield the floor and
begins to fight back. Looking up to Saunders for cues on parlia-
mentary rules, he angrily denies any corruption and states his

case to his colleagues. Other senators leave the floor in protest, and he makes his speech before a nearly empty chamber still dutifully presided over by the Vice President. The news of this battle spreads across the country, and support begins to turn in Smith's favor.

Meanwhile, Taylor harnesses his own machine to discredit Smith, while other senators begin to have doubts about the controversial bill and return to the floor, still held by the rapidly fading Smith, who is forced by the Senate rules to stay on his feet and keep talking.

Smith knows that if he yields the floor his goose is cooked, so he reads from the Declaration of Independence and begins to spout platitudes, but his voice and stamina begin to falter.

To protect his hometown interest, the unscrupulous Taylor manages to suppress the newspapers back home so they won't cover the filibuster, until Smith's Boy Ranger newspaper prints its own edition and distributes it all over the state. The rival groups clash. Opposition to the political machine builds until children start getting hurt by professional goons.

Finally, Senator Payne, Smith's onetime mentor and now his enemy, displays fifty thousand letters demanding Smith yield the floor. We then see an anguished close-up of Smith, about to give up the good fight, but then, encouraged by a slight smile from the Vice President, he goes on, declaring his cause to be "just another lost cause worth fighting for." Physically and mentally drained, Smith faints.

Just outside the Senate floor, Senator Payne, at last realizing the error of his ways, tries to shoot himself, then storms back onto the floor, proclaiming that everything Smith has said is true and instantly sending the gallery and Senate into pandemonium.

In the end, Mr. Smith and all he stands for have triumphed.

Background: Although the 1939 Oscar went to Robert Donat for *Goodbye, Mr. Chips,* Jimmy Stewart's portrayal of Jefferson Smith has, over the years, become far more famous, an enduring character who has inspired three generations of moviegoers.

Incredibly, Stewart was not Capra's first choice for the role! The success of *Mr. Deeds Goes to Town* led the director to offer the role to Gary Cooper, but when he was unavailable, Stewart, who had just completed *It's a Wonderful World,* made this, his twentieth role, one of his greatest.

Capra faithfully re-created the Senate chamber to a degree

which has never been matched since. The movie, which would mark the end of Capra's glory years at Columbia, opened in Washington before a crowd of leading political figures of the day. Its scathing depiction of a corrupt Senate led to understandably mixed reviews, but across the country audiences flocked to see it anyway.

Jean Arthur, who plays Saunders, is best known for this movie, and for her role as the homesteading wife and mother in *Shane*. Born Gladys Georgianna Greene in New York in 1905, her debut came in a 1923 film called *Cameo Kirby,* directed by John Ford. By the time she made *Mr. Smith,* she had costarred in numerous silent films as well as *The Whole Town's Talking* and *Mr. Deeds Goes to Town.*

Claude Rains, who was nominated for an Oscar for portraying the corrupt Senator Payne, also starred in *The Prince and the Pauper* and *The Adventures of Robin Hood,* and of course *Casablanca.*

In any other year, *Mr. Smith Goes to Washington* would have been a certain Oscar winner. But 1939 was the greatest year in movie history, with more classics and great performances than in any other. Rules were different then, as well, and ten pictures contended for the Oscar. *Mr. Smith* was competing with the likes of *Ninotchka, Of Mice and Men, Dark Victory, Stagecoach,* and a trio of all-time classics, *The Wizard of Oz, Wuthering Heights,* and the winner, a little something called *Gone With the Wind.*

This is one of Frank Capra's best morality stories, though also one of his most cynical. Corruption is shown not as the exception but the rule, violated, as it were, only by the naive Mr. Smith, who strives to live by the ideals set forth by the nation's forefathers. No matter how many times one sees it, *Mr. Smith Goes to Washington* remains a stirring ode to patriotism and the triumph of good over evil, to be enjoyed by every generation.

Mutiny on the Bounty

Category: Drama. Starring Clark Gable, Charles Laughton, Franchot Tone. Screenplay by Talbot Jennings, Jules Furthman, and Carey Wilson, based on the novels *Mutiny on the Bounty* and *Men Against the Sea* by Charles Nordhoff and James Norman Hall. 132 minutes. 1935. Black and white. MGM/UA Home Video.
Director: Frank Lloyd.
Suggested Age Group: 9 and older.

The Story   In December 1787, discipline was the watchword of the British navy, and ships' captains were quick to use the lash on rule-breakers. As the movie begins, several seamen are ordered to report for duty on the HMS *Bounty,* for a two-year scientific mission to the South Seas to gather exotic trees. Some of the recruits are fresh out of jail, while others are forced to leave their families on the spot. As he accompanies them to the ship, First Officer Fletcher Christian (Clark Gable) expresses his regret at the unpleasant recruiting orders he's been forced to carry out.

But leaving their homes and families is just the beginning of the men's problems, for the *Bounty* is commanded by a disciplinarian named Captain William Bligh (Charles Laughton), who soon sets sail from Portsmouth Harbor on what will be a long, star-crossed journey. Early in the voyage, Bligh orders the flogging of a seaman who'd broken a rule, even though the sailor has died. Christian realizes there will likely be trouble ahead between Bligh and the men.

Christian, a fair-minded officer, is aware that Bligh is a great seaman, but is troubled by the captain's harsh treatment of his men. Midshipman Roger Byam (Franchot Tone) is Christian's best friend and next in command. As the *Bounty* sails down the Atlantic to Cape Horn, Christian grows restless and increasingly defiant of Bligh's cruel treatment of the crew.

Bligh feeds his starving men rancid meat and orders Christian to sign a fraudulent record book. When he learns that Christian has disobeyed his orders, Bligh summons him on deck before the entire crew. Finally, Christian reluctantly signs the book, while demanding an investigation by a court of inquiry. As Bligh calls him a "mutinous dog," the island of Tahiti is sighted. The *Bounty* drops anchor in the harbor and Bligh renews his friendship with the Tahitian king, while denying Christian shore leave.

The *Bounty* spends several restful months in Tahiti, where every crew member seems to have a scantily clothed native woman on his arm. After finally getting his shore leave at the behest of the king, Christian is nevertheless soon recalled to the ship by Bligh, just so the captain can reassert his power. The ship's precious exotic plants in tow, the *Bounty* sets sail, but under Bligh's orders to cut the crew's water rations to allow more water for the plants.

As the voyage continues, Bligh summons a sick, elderly officer on deck for punishment, but the seaman collapses and dies. This is one act too many for Christian, who then leads most of the crewmen in mutiny and takes the ship. Bligh and eighteen sailors loyal to him are tossed into a small lifeboat and cast adrift 3,500 miles from the nearest port of call.

In one of the most memorable moments in movie history, Bligh, drifting away in the lifeboat, stands and waves his fist, yelling up at Christian. "You think you're sending me to my doom, Mr. Christian? Well, you're wrong!"

Bligh miraculously keeps his word and sails his men to safety after forty days adrift. When at last they spot land, he says in a parched voice "We've beaten the sea itself!"

Meanwhile, Christian, now in command of the *Bounty*, declares, "From now on, they'll spell 'mutiny' with my name." They return to Tahiti and after many months there, on Christmas morning, Byam, who took no part in the mutiny, makes peace with Christian. They spot a British warship entering the harbor, obviously sent to find them, and Byam and the other men who'd opposed the mutiny remain behind to be picked up, while Christian and his men flee on the *Bounty*.

Upon boarding the warship, Byam is astonished to see that it is Bligh himself who is in command, and before he can protest his innocence, he is taken below in irons.

Back in England, Byam and the others are court-martialed and condemned to death, but Byam gives a powerful speech calling for greater understanding between officers and men. This earns him a reprieve and a return to duty. The court commends

Bligh for his great seamanship but then snubs him for his brutal methods.

Just as Byam says he would give anything to know what became of his friend, Christian and his mutineers have finally found the uncharted island they'll call home—far-off Pitcairn Island in the South Pacific. To reaffirm this commitment, they burn the *Bounty* in the harbor to conceal their presence, and discourage any men from trying to return to England.

Background: Unlike the characters in the movie, the real-life men of the *Bounty* met unfortunate fates. Some died at the hands of natives or as a result of quarrels with one another. When a British ship landed on the island in 1812, only one *Bounty* crewman, John Adams, survived. He was allowed to live out his life in whatever peace was left to him.

History shows that Bligh was actually not snubbed by the Naval court at all. He was in fact promoted to admiral and wound up governor of New South Wales, Australia, where, obviously still set in his ways, he was then the subject of a second mutiny. He died in 1817 and is buried in London.

Captain Bligh's own log and a 1932 best-selling book about the mutiny were both used as a basis for the screenplay, but this book was not, in fact, the first version of the story. In 1932, an unknown actor named Errol Flynn starred in an obscure semidocumentary film called *In the Wake of the Bounty,* which included shots filmed on Pitcairn Island, where descendants of Christian and his men still live today. It even included some underwater footage of the wreckage of the real *Bounty.*

In the scene in which Bligh and his men are tossed into the lifeboat, Charles Laughton actually manages to make the sadistic Bligh almost sympathetic. Love him or hate him, Bligh's determination to lead the men to a port, and to make their ten days' rations last long enough for survival, is nothing short of heroic.

This is the best of the three famous versions of *Mutiny on the Bounty.* The 1962 remake with Marlon Brando and Trevor Howard and the 1984 version, *The Bounty,* with Mel Gibson and Sir Anthony Hopkins, while admirable, can't come close to the original, which was shot in a large tank on the MGM back lot and on Catalina Island off the coast of Los Angeles.

Clark Gable had initially resisted the role of Fletcher Christian, fearing his appearance in a costume drama. But he was perfect in the part. He began his career as an extra in silent films, then made the transition to talking pictures with his famous performance in *It Happened One Night,* for which he won the Oscar as Best Actor in 1934. Though he'd been rejected for the lead in the classic gangster movie *Little Caesar* in 1931 because his ears were too big, *It Happened One Night* helped make him Hollywood's number-one romantic star, dubbed him "The King," and earned him $4,000 a week, a salary fit for a king during the Depression.

Of course, Gable acted like a king, too. In all his long years in Hollywood, the star of movies like *Gone With the Wind, Command Decision,* and *Mogambo* was never once the subject of a disparaging word.

Charles Laughton actually gives the most powerful performance in the movie as Captain Bligh. Having played the title roles in *Island of Dr. Moreau* and *The Private Life of Henry VIII,* he also appeared in *The Hunchback of Notre Dame, Witness for the Prosecution,* and *Spartacus.*

Alfred Hitchcock was once asked to list the most difficult things to photograph, and he replied, "Children, dogs, trains, and Charles Laughton."

In preparation for *Mutiny on the Bounty,* Laughton went to Gieves', the ancient firm of military and naval tailors in London, to ask what sort of uniforms Bligh might've worn. "Just a moment," said the salesman, who then produced a dusty book containing the original order for Captain Bligh's uniforms, complete with his measurements, dated 1784.

Franchot Tone, who played Midshipman Byam, won the part only after Robert Montgomery, a much bigger star at the time, rejected it. Nevertheless, Tone earned an Oscar nomination as Best Actor, even though the role of Byam is a supporting part, because in 1935, the Supporting Actor category didn't yet exist. His other films of note include *The Lives of a Bengal Lancer, Dangerous, Star Spangled Rhythm, Five Graves to Cairo,* and *Advise and Consent.*

Mutiny on the Bounty won the Oscar for Best Picture, and back in those days, it had to beat out eleven other entries! No wonder. The plot is so strong and the performances so powerful that this movie will stay with you long afterward. Parents should be cautioned that the film has several scenes of men being flogged and cast in irons, but it is shot in the typical thirties style, with no bloodshed or gore.

Mutiny on the Bounty has an indomitable spirit and brilliant performances. Herbert Stothart's rousing score helps make this one of the most exciting adventures in movie history, a film every young viewer will love.

My Fair Lady

Category: Musical. Starring Audrey Hepburn, Rex Harrison, Stanley Holloway, Wilfred Hyde-White, Theodore Bikel. Screenplay by Alan Jay Lerner, from the Lerner and Frederick Loewe Broadway musical, based on the play *Pygmalion* by George Bernard Shaw. Music by Frederick Loewe, lyrics by Alan Jay Lerner. 170 minutes. 1964. Warner Bros. Home Video.
Director: George Cukor.
Suggested Age Group: 6 and older.

The Story   A snobbish London linguist sets out to prove he can transform any woman (no matter what her station) into a lady. He does, they eventually become attracted to each other, and the story ends. Sounds simple, right? But that basic idea by George Bernard Shaw became *Pygmalion* in 1912, one of his greatest plays, from which several movies were made. Of course, it became even more popular when a musical version became one of the biggest hits in Broadway history and, in its film version, won eight Academy Awards.

Set in Edwardian England, the story begins when Professor Henry Higgins, a somewhat cantankerous linguist, meets a Cockney flower girl one day at a street market. He simultaneously meets Colonel Pickering, author of a book called *Spoken Sanskrit,* who quickly becomes a colleague in his experiment.

Upon hearing the flower girl, Eliza Doolittle, mangle the King's English with her heavy Cockney accent, Higgins complains that the English can't teach their children how to speak properly. Nevertheless, he insists he can turn such an uneducated person into a lady by improving her speech and teaching her social graces and bearing, and he invites Pickering to move in with him and witness his unusual experiment taking shape.

For her part, Eliza also dreams of being a lady, as she expresses in the song "Wouldn't It Be Loverly." Eventually, she does decide to go to Higgins' house to take him up on his offer. Higgins begins his tutoring, realizing that such an undertaking is far from simple. Even so, he is persistent and demanding, ultimately driving Eliza into a rage.

Despite their conflicts, however, Higgins succeeds in separating Eliza from her lower-class Cockney accent. In one of the film's most famous scenes, he is triumphant over her newly cultivated ability to enunciate the sentence "The rain in Spain stays mainly in the plain." "I think she's got it! By Jove, she's got it!" he exclaims as they burst into song.

Later, still savoring her victory, Eliza sings "I Could Have Danced All Night," having clearly softened her position toward Professor Higgins. Soon after, Higgins decides to take her to the Ascot races, a gathering place of the upper crust of British society, to see if he can pass her off as a member of the aristocracy.

At Ascot, one of the film's most visually appealing sequences, Eliza does well, making only a few gaffes, including one startling one. She also catches the eye of young dandy Freddy Eynsford-Hill, who, obviously smitten, later wanders past Higgins' house singing "On the Street Where You Live." At her next outing, an embassy ball, Eliza also manages to fool Zoltan Karpathy, another linguistic expert and former student of Professor Higgins, who boasts he can spot any impostor.

Later, Higgins and Pickering congratulate each other with the rousing song "You Did It!" inadvertently relegating Eliza to the subject of an experiment. Dejected by Higgins' lack of interest in her as a woman, she encounters the moping Freddy outside the house and, aware of his feelings for her, asks him to demonstrate his affection by singing to him "Show Me."

Eventually, she goes back to her old haunts at the flower garden, where she finds her father preparing for his wedding and singing "Get Me to the Church on Time."

When Eliza returns to Higgins' home, he is dumbfounded by her emotions. He asks the musical question: "Why Can't a Woman Be More Like a Man?" When Eliza counters by telling him that the finer things in life will go on "Without You," he informs her that, although not quite in love with her, he's nevertheless "Grown Accustomed to Her Face." After this increasingly tender exchange, it's clear that Higgins and Eliza are destined to stay together.

Background: Children will instantly fall in love with this enchanting movie, with its gorgeous sets and costumes, appealing characters, radiant performances, and, above all, its collection of beautiful songs which have become standards.

The story behind *My Fair Lady* is even more interesting than the movie itself. In this movie musical based on the George Bernard Shaw play his story has been kept intact. Although Shaw ignored the audience's desire to see Higgins and Eliza Doolittle fall in love (he even tacked on an epilogue in which she married the wimpy Freddy!) Alan Jay Lerner gave the audience what they wanted when he adapted *My Fair Lady* for Broadway. In all likelihood, Shaw would probably have hated the idea of *My Fair Lady*. As a matter of fact, late in 1948, Shaw responded with a strong rebuke to a request for permission to perform *Pygmalion* as a musical.

After Shaw's death in 1950, Rodgers and Hammerstein rejected the prospect of turning *Pygmalion* into a musical. Subsequently, Alan Jay Lerner and Frederick Loewe accepted the challenge of adapting it. Their original title, incidentally, was to be *Lady Liza*. They worked on it for three months, then tabled the project for a lengthy respite. Finally, they returned to it, creating a masterpiece.

When Rex Harrison was offered the role of Professor Higgins, he was reluctant to do a musical. He insisted that certain parts of Shaw's original dialogue be retained, as he'd had considerable experience in Shavian theater. After three weeks of indecision, he finally agreed to play Professor Higgins, thus creating one of the most famous musical characters of all time, even though he couldn't sing a note!

Harrison mastered a technique he called "talking on pitch," so that here and there he seems about to carry a tune, when in fact he's never actually singing. The key was that he remained consistent in his nonspeaking style. Of all the performers in the movie version, Harrison was the only one whose songs were recorded live, through a microphone concealed beneath the knot of his tie (something the restorers of the original print, Jim Katz and Bob Harris, discovered nearly thirty years later). So, when you hear Professor Higgins say "I'll make a duchess out of this dragtailed guttersnipe," the words are just as Harrison said them that very day on the set. Of course this early feat of electronic wizardry was not accomplished without some initial setbacks, particularly because the primitive wireless microphone had a nasty habit of picking up radio transmissions from taxis outside the studio.

On Broadway, the original choice for Eliza Doolittle had been Texas-born Mary Martin, a major Broadway star who was unavailable at the time. So the producers took a chance and signed twenty-year-old Julie Andrews who, despite her young age, wasn't a complete unknown, having starred on Broadway in the 1954 hit *The Boy Friend.*

Because of the show's long Broadway run, it wasn't until 1963 that Jack L. Warner bought the movie rights, paying the considerable sum of $5.5 million, a record for that time. Of course, acquiring the rights was one thing, but casting the movie quite another. Names like Cary Grant and even Frank Sinatra were bandied about to play Higgins, and the retired Jimmy Cagney was offered the part of Alfred P. Doolittle, Eliza's feisty father. But Cagney, who might very well have stolen the movie from its principal players, rejected the offer, and Stanley Holloway, who'd played the part successfully on Broadway, ended up with the movie part as well.

As for the role of Professor Higgins, Cary Grant stated the obvious when he said that Harrison owned the part and no one else need be considered. In fact, he added, if the studio did not give Harrison the part, Grant would never work there again!

After veteran movie character actor Wilfred Hyde-White was signed to play Colonel Pickering, the only surprise in the casting of the film came with its lead player. It had been assumed that Warner would hire Julie Andrews, but, though he admired her stage performance, he chose the safer route and cast an established (if nonsinging) movie star, Audrey Hepburn. She was so strong a name, in fact, that she was given billing above the title.

Marni Nixon, who'd provided Deborah Kerr's singing voice in *The King and I* and Natalie Wood's in *West Side Story,* again stepped in to do the job for Miss Hepburn. Her contract even stipulated that she was prohibited from making this fact public. For her part, when Audrey Hepburn was told that her own voice would not be used in the film, she staged a one-day walkout before returning to the set. Years later, the restorers of the original negatives of the movie discovered several scenes which had been filmed using Audrey Hepburn's voice, which they restored with surprisingly rewarding results.

Ironically enough, even though Julie Andrews didn't get the coveted film role of Eliza Doolittle, she did win the Best Actress Oscar that year for her performance in *Mary Poppins.* Hepburn's performance wasn't even nominated, though the movie did, in fact, win for Best Picture and Best Director.

Although she didn't garner an Oscar for this role, Audrey Hepburn, then a rail-thin thirty-five, was one of the most radiant actresses of her time. She grew up in occupied Holland studying ballet, then turned to acting and got a bit part in a movie called *Nederland in 7 Lessen* in 1948, as well as parts in British movies such as *One Wild Goat, Laughter in Paradise,* and the comedy classic *The Lavender Hill Mob.*

As luck would have it, Colette, the writer, was looking for a lead for the Broadway version of her novel *Gigi* when she spotted Hepburn in a small movie called *Monte Carlo Baby.* En route to Broadway, the young actress stopped off in London to do a screen test for Paramount, and again was spotted, this time by director William Wyler. After a successful run on Broadway in *Gigi,* she landed the starring role opposite Gregory Peck in Wyler's *Roman Holiday,* for which she won the Oscar. That auspicious starring debut would be followed by nominations for *Sabrina, The Nun's Story, Breakfast at Tiffany's,* and *Wait Until Dark.*

My Fair Lady was Hepburn's thirteenth American film, following other memorable roles in *Funny Face,* with Fred Astaire, and the romantic thriller *Charade,* one of the most stylish thrillers of the sixties. Her other films of note include *War and Peace, The Unforgiven, Two for the Road,* and *The Children's Hour.*

Rex Harrison, the perfect choice for the role of Henry Higgins, debuted onstage at sixteen at the Liverpool Repertory in 1924. That began a long stage and film career in England and on Broadway. By the time he'd won worldwide acclaim for *My Fair Lady,* Harrison's film résumé included Shaw's *Major Barbara,* filmed in between German air attacks on London in 1941, *The Ghost and Mrs. Muir,* and the overblown 1963 flop *Cleopatra,* playing Julius Caesar.

Oddly, his only film of note after *My Fair Lady* would be another costly failure (and another musical), ironically called *Dr. Dolittle.*

Lyricist Alan Lerner met composer Frederick Loewe at the Lamb's Club, an actor's club in New York in 1942; they formed one of the most brilliant musical teams in history. By the time they'd written *My Fair Lady,* they'd completed *Brigadoon* and *Gigi* and would later collaborate on *Camelot* and *Paint Your Wagon.*

George Cukor, the director of *My Fair Lady,* was by 1964 already a legendary filmmaker, referred to as "the women's director" for his sensitive, intelligent work with some of the great actresses of Hollywood's golden era. Consider Ethel Barrymore, Jeanne Eagels, and Laurette Taylor on the stage. Or Katharine Hepburn in *A Bill of Divorcement, The Philadelphia Story, Adam's*

Rib, and *Pat and Mike.* Cukor also directed Greta Garbo's last film, *Two-Faced Woman,* in 1941. There was Ingrid Bergman in *Gaslight* and Judy Holliday in *Born Yesterday.* He also directed Judy Garland in *A Star Is Born,* another of the greatest musicals of all time, and Marilyn Monroe in *Let's Make Love.*

When it came time to restore the prints of *My Fair Lady,* in conjunction with the thirtieth anniversary of its release, Jim Katz and Bob Harris, who'd also restored *Lawrence of Arabia,* found the negatives in shockingly bad condition. Some $600,000 and months later, they'd painstakingly cleaned up scratches and eliminated mysterious dots and smudges on the frames, often with the aid of computers. They also remixed the sound digitally, using modern techniques, and restored the hues to their original, majestic color. Their efforts to produce the rereleased version as audiences first saw it will allow many more generations to enjoy this classic film as it was intended to be enjoyed.

My Favorite Year

Category: Comedy. Starring Peter O'Toole, Mark Linn-Baker, Joe Bologna, Lainie Kazan, Bill Macy, Anne DeSalvo, Lou Jacobi, Adolph Green, Cameron Mitchell. Screenplay by Norman Steinberg. 92 minutes. 1982. Rated PG. MGM/UA Home Video.
Director: Richard Benjamin.
Suggested Age Group: 13 and older.

 In the golden age of television, 1954 was a great year. Audiences were in love with the still relatively new medium, and comedy was king. Narrated with a loving nostalgic style by a then-youthful TV comedy writer working for the top-rated comedy show, *My Favorite Year* introduces us to the show's short-tempered star, King Kaiser, who is constantly surrounded by fawning assistants who live in fear of his mercurial temper. But Kaiser is about to meet his match in the person of Alan Swann, a boozy swashbuckling movie star, a character clearly based on Errol Flynn.

Swann, the show's guest star, arrives half-drunk, but insists he's just fine. "If I were truly plastered, could I do this?" he asks, promptly performing a somersault and winding up flat on his back, out cold, and atop the meeting table of the show's writers.

Meanwhile, the young writer, Benji Stone, is charged with the unenviable task of keeping Swann dry until the big night. In the meantime, a gruff mobster has dropped by the studio with some of his thugs to express his discontent at Kaiser's obvious impersonation of him in some comedy bits.

Benji decides to take control of the situation and invites Swann to his mother's home in Brooklyn for dinner. His mother, Belle, is now married to a former Korean boxer, and their family dinner, also attended by Benji's uncle Morty, is nothing short of hysterical. They put on airs and pump Swann with embarrassing questions, but in the process, they also delight him. Swann, a bachelor with an estranged daughter at a Connecticut boarding school, is obviously a man with troubles of his own, but he thrills Benji's family with his presence.

The night of the show finally arrives, but despite his movie experience, Swann is paralyzed with last-minute stage fright at the prospect of appearing live on nationwide television. When the gangster's thugs return and start a melee in the middle of the telecast, Swann, dressed in his swashbuckling costume, swings down from the rafters and leads the actors and writers to victory.

Background: *My Favorite Year* is a heartwarming, endearing look back at an innocent age. Peter O'Toole, who won one of his many Oscar nominations for the role of Alan Swann, dominates the movie without overwhelming it, giving one of his finest and most memorable performances.

It is widely believed that O'Toole made his screen debut in the title role of *Lawrence of Arabia* in 1962, for which he was also nominated for an Oscar. But that was actually his fourth movie, after his real debut in *The Savage Innocents* in 1960. After Albert Finney rejected the part of T. E. Lawrence, O'Toole grabbed the plum role and instantly became a screen immortal. His other films of note include *The Night of the Generals, Casino Royale, Becket, The Lion in Winter, Murphy's War, The Stunt Man, The Last Emperor,* and *King Ralph.*

Joseph Bologna, who plays King Kaiser, is a Brooklyn-born actor whose films of note include *Lovers and Other Strangers, Chapter Two,* and *Coup De Ville.*

Adolph Green, who portrays harried producer Leo Silver, is one of the giants of the Broadway musical theater. In collaboration with Betty Comden, he wrote the screenplay for *Singin' in the Rain,* and *The Bandwagon,* as well as the book and lyrics for *Bells Are Ringin',* the lyrics for *Do Re Mi* and *On the Town,* among many others.

If Lou Jacobi, who plays Benji's Uncle Morty, looks familiar, he should. The character actor, who asks Swann an embarrassing question at the dinner table, has a long career in films and on TV. His screen credits include *Irma la Douce, The Diary of Anne Frank, Little Murders, Roseland,* and *Arthur.*

Mark Linn-Baker, who is excellent as Benji, is best known for the TV series *Perfect Strangers.*

Lainie Kazan, who plays Benji's mother, Belle, is primarily a singer but has made occasional screen appearances, in *The Journey of Natty Gann, Beaches,* and *Harry and the Hendersons.*

Richard Benjamin, who directed *My Favorite Year,* is also an actor. He starred as Neil in *Goodbye, Columbus,* one of the best movies of the sixties. Married to actress Paula Prentiss, he also starred in *Diary of a Mad Housewife, The Marriage of a Young Stockbroker,* and *Love at First Bite.* His directing credits include *Racing with the Moon, Little Nikita, Mermaids,* and *Made in America.*

My Favorite Year is a funny, nostalgic look at the heyday of live television programming. O'Toole's Errol Flynn sendup is one of the best performances of the eighties, and the warm but frantic action is enough to keep even the most distracted young teen entertained.

My Girl

Category: Drama. Starring Dan Aykroyd, Jamie Lee Curtis, Anna Chlumsky, Macaulay Culkin, Richard Masur, Griffin Dunne. Screenplay by Laurice Elehwany. 102 minutes. 1991. Rated PG. Columbia Home Video.
Director: Howard Zieff.
Suggested Age Group: 9 and older.

The Story It's 1972 in the quiet town of Madison, Pennsylvania, the setting for this touching movie about Harry Sultenfuss, a widower who happens to be the town undertaker and his eleven-year-old daughter, Vada, who has grown up in their basement mortuary. Vada deals with her father's unusual profession by paying frequent visits to her family doctor, complaining of some ill-defined and nonexistent ailment.

One day a perky cosmetologist, Shelly De Voto, arrives pulling a house trailer. Responding to an ad Harry had placed in the paper, Shelly soon realizes that the clients she will be making up are all dead. She's a trouper, though, and soon adjusts to the situation.

Soon Shelly's growing attraction to the mortician is obvious to young Vada, who spends her spare time with her friend Thomas J., a quiet, introspective neighbor. Meanwhile, she has a crush on a teacher and enrolls in his summer adult writing course to be near him. Little does she know that he is already engaged.

When her friend Thomas J. is stung by a bee and dies after a severe allergic reaction, young Vada learns to deal with rather than avoid the subject of death. She can then continue on with her life, while still remembering her good friend.

Background: If you have never seen *My Girl,* its subject matter may be something you might want to consider carefully. But rest assured. This is a gentle, very absorbing story held together by a terrific performance by young Anna Chlumsky. You never see her acting, which is an unusual quality to find in a young actress. Although she hadn't appeared previously in any other films, she did go on to star in this film's sequel *My Girl 2,* in which her character goes to California on her own to learn more about the life of her late mother.

Dan Aykroyd, who plays her father, Harry, shot to fame as one of the original "Not Ready for Prime Time Players" on *Saturday Night Live,* back when it was the hottest, most provocative program on television. Who, for instance, will ever forget his sendup of Julia Child, or his role as the father, Beldar, in the Coneheads? He played dozens of characters honed, no doubt, from his years as a member of the *SNL* troupe. Aykroyd was so much a part of the early success of *Saturday Night Live,* it's hard to believe that he only appeared during the first five seasons.

Since departing from the show, his films have ranged from the awful *Dr. Detroit* and the routine *Dragnet* and *Caddyshack II* to the highly entertaining *Ghostbusters, The Blues Brothers, Sneakers,* and *Driving Miss Daisy,* for which he was nominated for an Oscar for Best Supporting Actor.

Jamie Lee Curtis, who plays Shelly, was born into the business, the daughter of Tony Curtis and Janet Leigh. After the surprise hit *Halloween,* she starred in such films as *The Fog, Prom Night,* and *Terror Train.* Gradually, however, she escaped the horror genre to carve out a respectable career in *Trading Places, Amazing Grace and Chuck,* and especially *A Fish Called Wanda.* More recently, she played Arnold Schwarzenegger's wife in *True Lies,* managing to demonstrate her acting skills amidst the expected mayhem and thrills. She also costarred in *My Girl 2* in 1994.

Macaulay Culkin, who plays Thomas J., made his debut in *Rocket Gibraltar,* then shot to fame in *Home Alone.* Other films include *Uncle Buck, The Good Son,* a tedious film version of *The Nutcracker,* and the cartoon flop *The Pagemaster,* before he played the title role in *Richie Rich.* He is the highest-paid child star in movie history.

My Girl is a gentle, engaging comedy. While it relies on an odd premise for its humor, it is ultimately a heartwarming study of a girl at a pivotal time in her life.

National Velvet

Category: Drama. Starring Elizabeth Taylor, Mickey Rooney, Anne Revere, Angela Lansbury, Jackie "Butch" Jenkins. Screenplay by Theodore Reeves and Helen Deutsch, from the novel by Enid Bagnold. 125 minutes. 1944. MGM/UA Home Video.
Director: Clarence Brown.
Suggested Age Group: 7 and older.

The Story Set in England in the late 1920s, "a long time ago in a spinning world," the story concerns a young schoolgirl, her horse named The Pie, a young jockey, and their determination to win the Grand National steeplechase race. Velvet, the young girl, will let nothing get in the way of her dreams. When she meets an itinerant jockey with a troubled past, he helps her train the Pie and she enlists him to lead her to victory. She then decides to ride her horse herself, disguising the fact that she's female, but when they win, she's disqualified.

Background: *National Velvet* was made when MGM ruled the roost during the heyday of MGM, where there were "more stars than there are in Heaven," as the glittering studio boasted at the time. Elizabeth Taylor gave one of her most radiant performances in this film, early in her career, and Mickey Rooney, who plays the jockey and trainer, was at the time one of the top stars in films. They head a magnificent cast in a movie that still has a magical glow about it, undiminished by half a century.

Any young viewer, girl or boy, will adore this movie, which includes an eight-minute re-creation of the Grand National race, as thrilling a horse race as has ever been filmed.

By 1944, twelve-year-old Elizabeth Taylor was already established as a young MGM star in this, her fifth film. She made her debut in *There's One Born Every Minute* two years before. *Lassie Come Home* and *Jane Eyre* were also already on her résumé, and ahead lay several dozen movies and a career the world has followed with great interest ever since (to say nothing of her frequent illnesses and seven husbands!).

Mickey Rooney was one of the biggest child actors in movie history. Born Joe Yule, Jr., he was just twenty-four when he costarred in *National Velvet,* but by then had already been acting for seventeen years, after his debut in 1927's *Orchids and Ermine.* Seven years before *National Velvet,* he had become a huge star in the *Andy Hardy* movies, as well as in other films such as *Boys Town* and *The Adventures of Huckleberry Finn.*

A special Oscar followed, as did films including *The Bridges at Toko-Ri, Pete's Dragon,* and *The Black Stallion.* His career was revived on the Broadway stage with the smash hit *Sugar Babies* in 1979, a year after he'd announced his retirement. His is one of the most enduring careers in movie history.

Mickey Rooney's eight wives, including Ava Gardner, whom he divorced the year before *National Velvet* (one more marriage than Miss Taylor, if you count Richard Burton only once), left him bankrupt.

Anne Revere, who plays Velvet's saintly mother, won a Best Supporting Actress Oscar for her efforts in this film, edging out, among others, Angela Lansbury, who played her elder daughter in this film, but who was nominated that year for another movie, *The Picture of Dorian Gray.* Ms. Revere had been nominated for *The Song of Bernadette,* and three years later would be so honored again for *Gentleman's Agreement* before the horrors of the blacklisting era would nearly wreck her career. She triumphed, however, winning the 1970 Tony Award on Broadway for *Toys in the Attic.*

Veteran character actor and director Donald Crisp, who plays Velvet's gentle but sometimes acerbic father, made dozens of screen appearances in a career which began in 1914 when he was a member of D. W. Griffith's stock company. He portrayed Ulysses S. Grant in Griffith's *The Birth of a Nation* in 1915 and was Don Sebastian to Douglas Fairbanks' Zorro in *Don Q, Son of Zorro* in 1925. He won a Best Supporting Actor awad in 1941's *How Green Was My Valley.* His other films include the original *Wuthering Heights, Jezebel, Lassie Come Home, The Long Gray Line,* and *Pollyanna.* His final film was 1963's *Spencer's Mountain.*

Fans of TV's *Murder, She Wrote* will, of course, recognize the somewhat ungainly-looking Angela Lansbury, who plays Velvet's older sister. The London-born daughter of Irish actress Moyna MacGill, she was aboard one of the last ships to leave for America during the German blitz, thanks to the help of her godfather, Peter Ustinov. Her first screen role, *Gaslight,* made the same year as *National Velvet,* won her an Oscar nomination, and the follow-ing year she was honored again for *The Picture of Dorian Gray.* She also appeared in the memorable *The Harvey Girls* with Judy Garland.

Though she has not played many starring roles on the big screen, audiences would never forget her in *The Manchurian Candidate,* for which she was nominated in 1962 as Best Sup-porting Actress. She played the evil mother of Laurence Harvey, just seven years her junior. Director John Frankenheimer threat-ened to quit rather than give in to his coproducer's and star Frank Sinatra's attempts to cast Lucille Ball in the role.

Angela Lansbury is one of those rare stars who has enjoyed three separate careers, starring in film, on TV, and on Broadway in shows such as *A Taste of Honey, Anyone Can Whistle, Mame,* and *Sweeney Todd.* Four Tony awards adorn her mantelpiece.

National Velvet provides a nostalgic look at another time and place, where the innocent, pure love of a young girl for her horse is a thing of sheer beauty. It will warm the heart of everyone who sees it, and if you can't get enough of it, then rent the adequate but by no means necessary sequel, *International Velvet,* made in 1978, featuring Nanette Newman, Tatum O'Neal, and Sir Anthony Hopkins.

Some parents might find *National Velvet* terribly dated and an idealized look at childhood, but young viewers will still feel its magic.

Never Cry Wolf

Category: Drama. Starring Charles Martin Smith, Brian Dennehy, Zachary Ittimangnaq. Screenplay based on the novel by Farley Mowat. 105 minutes. 1983. Rated PG. Buena Vista Home Video.
Director: Carroll Ballard.
Suggested Age Group: 10 and older.

> ### The Story
A young, idealistic biologist named Tyler flies to a remote area of the Arctic to spend a winter studying wolves, who have been blamed for the disappearance of caribou in the region. *Never Cry Wolf* is told through Tyler's narration as he gradually adjusts to the harsh environment and slowly wins the toleration, if not the outright trust, of a pack of wolves.

Each wolf assumes its own particular personality, as the scientist takes notes, makes entries in his journal, befriends some local Eskimos, and becomes more attached to the wolves and their plight. He also names each wolf according to the traits he perceives in each. Rosie, a gruff bush pilot, flies Smith into the wilderness, then runs into him again the following spring. Rosie's plans to develop the region pose a threat to the wolves' habitat, and the movie's message of protecting their environment becomes the ultimate impetus of *Never Cry Wolf.*

The film offers gorgeous vistas, an overwhelming sense of loneliness, and insight into how wolves live in the wild. A caribou stampede, with Tyler running in the middle, is a precursor to a similar scene from *Dances with Wolves,* although in this movie Tyler, getting even closer to nature, is naked.

Never Cry Wolf depicts a dedicated scientist's voyage of self-discovery, during which he gains an understanding of the almost mystical, misunderstood animals. In one scene, he uses his scientist's knowledge and common sense to establish his terrain by marking a circle with his own urine. Then, by deliberately making lots of noise, he establishes his presence among the wolves and shows them he has arrived with some idea of how to cope in his new environment.

Background: This is a movie which easily might have been pious and ponderous, but the screen adaptation of Farley Mowat's book makes for a riveting adventure. Charles Martin Smith, whose films include *The Untouchables, The Buddy Holly Story, American Graffiti,* and the underappreciated Western *The Culpepper Cattle Company,* here is given a rare chance for a character actor to star in what is essentially a one-character work.

Brian Dennehy, who appears as Rosie, the bush pilot, near the beginning and just before the end of *Never Cry Wolf,* is one of Hollywood's most prolific actors. Indeed, one wonders how he managed to appear here, since by the time he made this film he'd been making two or three movies a year.

Younger viewers will love one scene in particular when, his food supply nearly exhausted, Tyler resorts to an Arctic delicacy, fried field mouse! This scene is presented in a humorous way, so as to evoke squeals of perverse delight from children, and it provides a funny respite from the low-key tone of most of the movie.

There is a slow section of the film, when Tyler meets some Native Americans and is introduced to a bit of mysticism. But this is a thoughtful film of many moods, and its characters enjoy a perfect and idyllic symbiosis with their world.

A Night at the Opera

Category: Comedy. Starring Groucho, Chico, and Harpo Marx,
Siegfried Rumann, Margaret Dumont, Kitty Carlisle, Allan Jones,
Walter Woolf King. Produced by Irving Thalberg. Screenplay by
George S. Kaufman, Morrie Ryskind, Al Boasberg, Bert Kalmar,
and Harry Ruby, based on a story by James Kevin McGuinness.
92 minutes. 1935. Black and white. MGM/UA Home Video.
Director: Sam Wood.
Suggested Age Group: 9 and older.

The Story   To describe the nuttiness afoot in this film in a conventional narrative would be impossible; with the
Marx brothers on the loose, anything goes. Nevertheless, the general premise for their hijinks is a story in which
Groucho is a ne'er-do-well producer named Otis B. Driftwood.
He's hoping to get $200,000 from a rich woman named Mrs. Clay-
pool to back an opera he wants to produce in New York. At the
same time, she hopes financing the opera will move her into high
society.

Meanwhile, another, more legitimate opera impresario named
Lassparri catches Mrs. Claypool's ear and talks some sense into
her, at least temporarily. He hires his own star for the opera, a
self-centered pompous snob, while Driftwood, still lurking
around Mrs. Fluffy Claypool, tries to enlist a younger, more amiable singer named Baroni who'd like a chance to sing more than
anything.

Eventually, everyone, including Forelo, Driftwood's new manager, piles onto an ocean liner headed for New York. Driftwood's
room is a tiny closet-sized box, into which he, Forelo, Harpo, and
a dozen other people are gradually crammed in on top of one
another in one of the movie's funniest and most famous scenes.
The young singer who is Driftwood's protégé is also along, just to
be near the soprano star of the opera, the woman he loves.

In New York, Driftwood and Co., in their havoc-wreaking state,
run into a detective named Henderson, who says he's a "plain-
clothes man." "You look more like an *old* clothes man to me,"

replies Driftwood. A trio of famous Russian aviators turns up, for no apparent reason other than as an obvious comedic device. The three have matching beards, which of course Groucho, Chico, and Harpo snip off, and everyone winds up at a City Hall ceremony honoring the "aviators," with the boys hilarious in their disguises.

Finally the opera is performed, but Henderson is still after Groucho, Chico, and Harpo, who take this opportunity to cavort across the scenery. This so unnerves the temperamental star of the opera that he is unable to continue, and Driftwood's protégé is given the chance to sing at last.

Background: For young viewers, this film provides the chance to witness the funniest trio of actors in the history of the movies: Groucho, spewing lines with double entendres and non sequiturs; Chico, with that awful Italian accent, playing the piano in his unique style; and silent Harpo, performing brilliantly on the instrument whose name he bore, all the while staying just a step or two ahead of the police, who are in hot pursuit.

More than anything, *A Night at the Opera* offers a chance to enjoy Groucho's impeccable comic timing. You instantly get the idea that Driftwood is a man who doesn't know where his next dime is coming from, yet who somehow manages to smoke expensive cigars and cavort with a rich dowager. He constantly keeps the audience off balance with quips and asides, the perfect meshing of a comic and a comedian. (Groucho was both; to use Ed Wynn's classic definition, he not only said funny things, but he also said things funny.)

This was not the first time that the Marx brothers had worked with writer George S. Kaufman. He'd written *The Coconuts,* the Broadway play, which later became their first movie in 1929. During the run of the play, the brothers frequently ad-libbed the dialogue. Backstage one night, Kaufman quipped: "Excuse me. I thought I heard one of my original lines onstage."

Julius, Leonard, and Adolph Marx (aka Chico, Harpo, and Groucho) were never better together. Chico was so named because of his constant womanizing; Harpo, of course, for his mastery of that difficult instrument; Groucho, because of his disposition; Zeppo after a popular monkey act in vaudeville; and Gummo—who never appeared in movies—because of his penchant for wearing gum-soled shoes.

Harpo never spoke onstage or in films, resorting for expression to whistles, frantic gestures, and an occasional honking of a horn. His world-famous persona came about quite by accident, when their uncle, a vaudevillian named Al Shean, wrote a stage routine for the brothers and accidentally forgot to write dialogue for Harpo. "Just let him go on," he said. "He'll think of something to do."

By the time the Marx brothers made *A Night at the Opera,* Herbert, aka Zeppo, had left the act to become an agent. Milton, aka Gummo, was in the act only briefly. The brothers were by then a well-timed act, with experience on Broadway and in vaudeville before they went on to Hollywood.

Following their smash Broadway debut in 1924's *I'll Say She Is,* the Marx brothers starred in the plays *The Coconuts* from 1925 to 1928 and *Animal Crackers* from 1929 to 1930. Their first films, beginning with *The Coconuts,* were made at Paramount. In those days, they performed on Broadway in *Animal Crackers* by day and shot the movie version of *The Coconuts* at night, at Paramount's East Coast studios in Astoria.

But after the films *Monkey Business, Horse Feathers,* and *Duck Soup,* the financially troubled Paramount studio released them from their contract, and they were picked up by MGM, headed by production chief Irving Thalberg.

Thalberg quickly restored the brothers to their glory days, inserting a romantic subplot into *A Night at the Opera* to expand the appeal of their movies to wider audiences. In fact, he took *A Night at the Opera* on the road, staging live performances of the script to hone the timing.

This was the first of two movies the boys would make under Thalberg's aegis; *A Day at the Races* followed in 1937, the same year of Thalberg's sudden death. On loan to RKO in 1938, they made one last grand comedy, *Room Service,* before moving on to two routine postwar efforts, *A Night in Casablanca* and *Love Happy,* a film notable today only for the appearance of a young starlet named Marilyn Monroe.

Margaret Dumont, who plays Mrs. Clayton, was a Marx brothers movie regular. She had the thankless task in seven of their films of playing the foil for the boy's antics. This is, however, her funniest performance.

Groucho Marx, the oft-imitated "lead" brother, was the source of numerous amusing stories, most of which centered around his irreverent outlook on life. When, for instance, a writer once noticed Groucho with a copy of Tolstoy under his arm, he asked him, "Do your brothers read, too?" "Just about," replied Groucho.

Of course, Groucho wasn't the only Marx born with a sense of humor. Harpo Marx's wife said that in more than twenty-five years of marriage, her husband tried to amuse her at least once a day, every day, successfully. His friend Salvador Dali once sent him an unusual gift: a harp with barbed-wire strings. Harpo sent Dali a photo of himself playing the instrument, with all ten fingers bandaged.

Chico, who as Forelo signs a contract with Driftwood in one of the most famous, funniest scenes in movie history, was in real life an accomplished card player. But one night, he was down on his luck and lost a small fortune. So he wrote a letter to the president of the American Playing Card Company, asking "Sir. Are you still manufacturing aces and kings?"

A disciple of Cecil B. DeMille, director Sam Wood would work with the boys again in *A Day at the Races*. One of the great directors in Hollywood history, he also made the original *Goodbye, Mr. Chips; For Whom the Bell Tolls;* and *Pride of the Yankees*. Although George Cukor was replaced as director on *Gone With the Wind* by Victor Fleming, Sam Wood finished up the epic masterpiece when Fleming fell ill.

Coscreenwriter George S. Kaufman was one of the great men of letters of his day. The best of the Marx brothers' humor is as much due to Kaufman's wit as the brothers' delivery and timing. Kaufman once attended a dinner party, after which he commented to his hostess: "You know, you have a good layout here. The food is good, the service is good, and if you can get enough people to talk about this place, you could do some business." His hostess, Eleanor Roosevelt, had just presided at the dinner at the White House.

With a rich history of humor and remarkable personalities, *A Night at the Opera* will delight young viewers and give them a rare look into an earlier style of comedy. All this in a film offering brilliant timing, a perfect script, and the funniest trio of actors ever to perform in front of a camera.

North by Northwest

Category: Drama. Starring Cary Grant, James Mason, Eva Marie
Saint, Martin Landau, Leo G. Carroll. Screenplay by Ernest Lehman.
Music by Bernard Herrmann. 136 minutes. 1959. MGM/UA Home
Video.
Director: Alfred Hitchcock.
Suggested Age Group: 11 and over.

**The
Story**
Roger Thornhill is a successful Madison Avenue advertising executive with two ex-wives and a penchant for fancy lunches. One afternoon in the Oak
Room at New York's posh Plaza Hotel, he is mistaken by some
strong-arm men for someone named George Kaplan, a mysterious figure involved in a complex scheme to smuggle something
vital out of the country, and abruptly kidnapped.

Despite constant protests and denials, Thornhill is taken to an
estate outside the city to meet Phillip Vandamm, the suave and
disdainful leader of the group, who refuses to believe him.
Thornhill is then drugged and put in a car that careens toward a
cliff.

This series of events occurs early in the movie, so it's obvious
that he will escape. The next day, after summoning the police
and his wisecracking mother to the house where he'd been held,
he finds completely different people are working there. Vandamm and his henchmen have gone, and consequently no one
believes Thornhill.

Later, he's followed again and is framed for the murder of a
diplomat at the United Nations. He boards a train headed for
Chicago and meets a beautiful woman named Eve Kendall, who
seems to be on to him. Shortly thereafter, he escapes gunfire
aimed at him from a crop duster plane in an isolated cornfield,
and eventually winds up dangling from the side of Mount Rushmore with the same mysterious woman, fleeing Vandamm and
his henchmen in one of the most famous and thrilling climaxes in
movie history.

Background: Every young movie fan should see at least one Hitchcock classic, and this is the best, combining thrills, excitement, danger, and romance all in a smooth, elegant style and featuring the classiest movie actor ever to grace a screen.

North by Northwest was Hitchcock's twenty-third American-made movie. He began his career in England in 1922 with *Number Thirteen,* followed by talking pictures such as *The Man Who Knew Too Much, The 39 Steps, Sabotage,* and *The Lady Vanishes.* He also helmed classics such as *Rebecca, Foreign Correspondent, Suspicion, Saboteur, Lifeboat, Spellbound,* and *Notorious.*

In the ten years between 1949 and 1959, Hitchcock's great movies came one after another, starting with *Rope* (that noble experiment which he filmed with long, single takes and only one camera). Others included *Strangers on a Train, Dial M for Murder, Rear Window, To Catch a Thief,* and *Vertigo.* Hitchcock was already the master of the genre, as much a star as any of his players. Audiences loved trying to spot his trademark cameo appearances, and in *North by Northwest,* it comes early in the film. In the scene outside the Plaza Hotel in New York, a bus stops at the corner and pulls away, just as a passenger is trying to board. The rotund passenger is, of course, Hitchcock.

Flawless though the $4 million movie is, there is one amusing visual gaffe left in the film, which has taken on a life of its own. It comes in the scene in which Eve Kendall pretends to murder Thornhill in a restaurant at the foot of Mount Rushmore. Keep your eyes on the little boy seated at the table behind her. Hitchcock obviously rehearsed the scene or has already shot a take, because the boy, knowing a gun will soon be fired, covers his ears in anticipation!

This, Cary Grant's fourth and last film for Hitchcock, is also his best. He'd already appeared in *Suspicion, Notorious,* and *To Catch a Thief.* And Eva Marie Saint plays the standard Hitchcock blonde, in the tradition of Kim Novak, Grace Kelly, and Ingrid Bergman before her and Tippi Hedren after. She is beautiful, cool, and mysterious.

Martin Landau, who here plays Leonard, Mason's principal henchman, years later won the Academy Award for Best Supporting Actor for his brilliant portrayal of Bela Lugosi in 1995's *Ed Wood,* looking more like the embittered, drug-ravaged old Dracula than Lugosi himself.

In *North by Northwest,* Hitchcock is at the top of his form. His style is sly, elegant, and suspenseful. The climactic sequence along the faces of Mount Rushmore is one of the most famous in movie history. Supposedly, Hitchcock had wanted Grant and Saint to run up and hide in Lincoln's nostrils, which would give credence to the story that the film had the working title *The Man in Lincoln's Nose,* but cooler heads prevailed.

Older children will be mesmerized by the film's suspense, admire Grant's suave delivery and Saint's elegance and mystery, and appreciate Hitchcock's ability to manipulate his audience by combining a complicated plot, amazing special effects, and a quintessential everyman who goes to extraordinary lengths in a dangerous situation.

Oklahoma!

Category: Musical. Starring Gordon MacRae, Shirley Jones, Gloria Grahame, Charlotte Greenwood, Eddie Albert, Gene Nelson, James Whitmore, Rod Steiger, Jay C. Flippen. Screenplay by Sonya Levien and William Ludwig, from the Broadway musical by Richard Rodgers and Oscar Hammerstein II, based on the play *Green Grow the Lilacs* by Lynn Riggs. Music by Rodgers and lyrics by Hammerstein. Choreography by Agnes de Mille. 145 minutes. 1955. CBS Fox Video.
Director: Fred Zinnemann.
Suggested Age Group: 7 and older.

 The Story   *Oklahoma!* is the exhilarating screen version of the 1943 Broadway musical that revolutionized the American theater. Prior to that show, musicals were mostly staid, formulaic affairs, with traditional structures and often plodding story lines and familiar numbers. But this show exploded off the stage, fusing the story, songs, and choreography into an operetta-like musical that enthralled audiences for years.

The plot itself is simple. Curly and Laurey love each other, but hired hand Jud Fry loves Laurey, too, and he tries to steal her away. When Curly and Laurey get married, Jud challenges Curly to a fight and is accidentally killed. Curly is exonerated, and the story ends happily as they go off on their honeymoon.

Background: There is another romance in the subplot, but the basic story is straightforward, relying on the beautiful songs and ballet-like choreography to win the audience. It did just that on Broadway, where, in the dark days of World War II, theatergoers were eager for something bright and hopeful. The show ran 2,212 performances, grossing some $7 million, an astronomical figure back then.

Instead of using Oklahoma, locations were filmed in the San Rafael Valley, northeast of Nogales, Arizona, which the producers found more in keeping with the way Oklahoma probably looked a century and a half ago.

Rules were broken from the beginning. Whereas most musicals begin with large production numbers, *Oklahoma!* begins with a lone singing cowboy, crooning a song about the weather. Even so, "Oh, What a Beautiful Morning" is just one of half a dozen songs from the show which would become standards of the American musical theater.

By 1955, the movie industry was trying all sorts of gimmicks to lure the first generation of television viewers back into theaters. Thus *Oklahoma!* was filmed in Todd-AO, the new wide-screen process devised by the flamboyant producer Mike Todd. Oddly, it was later rereleased in another wide-screen process, Cinema-Scope. The movie was made under the direct supervision and control of Rodgers and Hammerstein, who tried to make it some-what resemble the stage production.

The authors reportedly kept telling director Fred Zinnemann to keep the film intimate and theatrical. Indeed, the movie begins with a black background behind the opening credits, accompanied by an overture, a combination evocative of a Broadway musical.

One of the few concessions made by Rodgers and Hammerstein was the elimination of two songs from the original stage version. Gone were "It's a Scandal! It's an Outrage!" and "Lonely Room." Even with these changes, however, the 145-minute running time is still long.

Ironically, the film version of *Oklahoma!* seemed to reveal an almost conscious effort to form an entirely new company, retaining none of the original stage players. Though Howard Keel was considered for Curly, and a young Paul Newman and even the moody James Dean actually tested (imagine what that must've looked like!), the part eventually went to Gordon MacRae. And when it came to the female lead, the producers took a chance with the vivacious newcomer Shirley Jones, who won the part over Joanne Woodward.

Gloria Grahame replaced her Broadway counterpart Celeste Holm to become Ado Annie, and Howard da Silva, who played the sinister Jud on Broadway, fell victim to the shameful blacklisting of that time, so the part went to Rod Steiger, who was not known as a musical actor. Eddie Albert, falling into and out of his accent, played Ali Hakim, a Persian peddler.

Gordon MacRae had already made thirteen movies by the time he starred in *Oklahoma!* but it was this film that made him a star. His relatively brief screen career included another classic

Rodgers and Hammerstein musical the following year, *Carousel*. He is the father of actresses Meredith MacRae and Heather MacRae.

Shirley Jones, a onetime Miss Pittsburgh, known to younger fans as the mother on the TV series *The Partridge Family*, made her film debut in *Oklahoma!* then went on to star with MacRae in her next movie, *Carousel*. She later won the Oscar for Best Supporting Actress for her portrayal of a prostitute in *Elmer Gantry* and played Marian the librarian in *The Music Man*.

Rod Steiger, who played the sinister ranch hand Jud Fry, is best known for his title portrayal in his Oscar-nominated role of *The Pawnbroker* ten years after *Oklahoma!* His other famous role was as Marlon Brando's older brother in *On the Waterfront*, another performance for which he won an Oscar nomination. His performance as Police Chief Gillespie in *In the Heat of the Night* finally won him his statuette in 1967.

Gloria Grahame, who played Ado Annie, had already won an Oscar for Best Supporting Actress in 1952's *The Bad and the Beautiful*. Her other films of note include *In a Lonely Place*, *The Big Heat*, and *Odds Against Tomorrow*.

Fred Zinnemann, the Viennese-born director, had an impressive résumé by the time he helmed *Oklahoma!* Among his important credits are *The Member of the Wedding*, *From Here to Eternity*, *A Man for All Seasons*, *The Nun's Story*, *The Day of the Jackal*, and *Julia*.

Oklahoma! was the first collaboration between Richard Rodgers and Oscar Hammerstein, arguably the greatest musical songwriters of them all. Soon after the play opened on Broadway to smashing reviews, Rodgers and Hammerstein set up a corporation for their joint output, called the Williamson Corp. because both their fathers were named William. They insisted that no movie version of any of their shows could be made for at least ten years after the show opened, to ensure audiences for Broadway and the touring companies.

Oklahoma! became such a hit, spawning so many other Rodgers and Hammerstein collaborations, that audiences held them to a higher standard than any other composing team. When, for instance, they wrote *Me and Juliet,* the musical was considered a flop, even though it ran a year and earned 50 percent profits.

Oklahoma! is a thrilling version of a watershed musical that loses none of its charm and vivaciousness in the translation.

Oklahoma!

Shirley Jones is enchanting, and she and Gordon MacRae play their roles to the hilt. It won't be difficult for young viewers to understand why this timeless musical revolutionized the American theater and remains one of the best movie musicals ever made.

Old Yeller

Category: Drama. Starring Tommy Kirk, Dorothy McGuire, Kevin Corcoran, Fess Parker, Chuck Connors. Screenplay by Fred Gipson and William Tunberg, based on the novel by Fred Gipson. 83 minutes. 1957. Disney Home Video.
Director: Robert Stevenson.
Suggested Age Group: 8 and older.

The Story   This poignant story of a frontier family begins on a small farm in Texas in 1869. As we join the Coates family, the father, Jim, is about to leave for a three-month cattle drive and leaves his fifteen-year-old son Travis in charge of running things while he's away. Soon after the father's departure, the younger son, Arliss, finds a stray yellow Labrador retriever and quickly befriends him, naming him Old Yeller. They have some predictable but suspenseful adventures together, and slowly the lovable dog wins the confidence of both Travis and his mother, eventually becoming another member of the family.

One day, a friendly cowboy arrives and explains that the dog is his, and that he's been tracking the dog for a long time. But he quickly notices how much young Arliss loves Old Yeller and "trades" him for a horned toad Arliss had been carrying around in his pocket. Thus Old Yeller earns a permanent place in the Coates family.

Soon after, Travis is badly hurt when he falls off a tree into a herd of wild pigs, which Old Yeller bravely manages to fight off. But Old Yeller is injured as well, and must be confined after their neighbor tells them that a form of rabies has been spreading in their area and all animals must be watched closely.

Old Yeller is placed in a pen for a long period of observation to make certain he hasn't contracted rabies from the pigs. At first he seems normal, but slowly he becomes more vicious, frothing at the mouth and showing the classic rabies symptoms.

By this time, Travis has become quite attached to Old Yeller as well, and tries to deny the sad truth that Old Yeller has indeed contracted rabies and must be put out of his misery.

But all is not lost. The neighbor's daughter gives Travis one of Yeller's pups, which has been born to her dog. After initially rejecting the adorable little pooch, insisting that no dog could replace Old Yeller, Travis begins to come around. When his father returns from the cattle drive, he explains that such situations are a part of life, and he helps Travis understand that the hopeful thing about Old Yeller's death is the arrival of the puppy, which Travis then welcomes into the family.

Background: *Old Yeller* was made at a time when the Disney studio was the leader in family entertainment; no other studio consistently made wholesome movies with appealing young actors in dramatic situations that also taught valuable lessons about life.

Parents should be cautioned, however. I remember watching *Old Yeller* as a child and being disturbed at seeing the dog's master have to shoot him. Younger children—even those growing up in today's more cynical world—might need some preparation for this scene.

Though he has a relatively small part as Jim Coates, Fess Parker was the big Disney star of that era, having become a national sensation as Davy Crockett on Disney's popular TV show three years before. He would later assume the role of Daniel Boone in another popular TV series for Disney.

Dorothy McGuire, who played Travis and Arliss's mother, Katie Coates, was no stranger to Disney, as she had also appeared in *Swiss Family Robinson.* She also costarred in *Friendly Persuasion* and *The Remarkable Mr. Pennypacker.*

Director Robert Stevenson, though born in London, nevertheless captured the look and feel of the American frontier in *Old Yeller.* His other directorial credits include *King Solomon's Mines, Tom Brown's Schooldays,* and a slew of Disney favorites including *Kidnapped, The Absent-Minded Professor, In Search of the Castaways,* and *Bedknobs and Broomsticks.* But he is best known as the director of *Mary Poppins,* one of the great family classics of all time.

Old Yeller is a compelling coming-of-age story in which its young protagonist must learn that life sometimes takes some strange turns, some of which are unfair. But eventually he comes to realize that, despite life's necessary losses, there is always hope, and life must go on.

The Parent Trap

Category: Comedy. Starring Hayley Mills, Brian Keith, Maureen O'Hara, Charlie Ruggles, Una Merkel, Leo G. Carroll, Joanna Barnes, Cathleen Nesbitt. Screenplay by David Swift, based on the book *Das Doppelte Lottchen* (*Lisa and Lottie*) by Erich Kastner. 124 minutes. 1961. Walt Disney Home Video.
Director: David Swift.
Suggested Age Group: 5 and older.

The Story This is the charming story of two girls, Sharon McKendrick and Susan Evers, who, when they meet at a summer camp, learn that they are identical twins who were separated in infancy when their parents divorced. Sharon lives in Boston with her mother, while Susan lives with her father in Carmel, California.

After they stop feuding at camp, they quickly grow attached to one another and concoct a secret scheme to switch identities and return to the other twin's home. Naturally, they're both curious about their other parent and they pull off the ingenious plan with surprising ease. (Not so surprising, actually, since Disney movies of that era had little relevance to the real world.) Their goal, of course, is to reunite their parents.

The only fly in the ointment is their father's attractive fiancée, who, as it turns out, is really after his money and is determined, once she marries him, to send her stepdaughter off to a boarding school in Switzerland. Posing as her sister, Sharon overhears this plan and phones Susan to tell her to return home before it's too late. The secret plot spills into the open when Susan tells her mother the truth, and both hurry to California.

What follows is a series of predictable but funny preadolescent hijinks, as the twins and their mother conspire to wreck the upcoming wedding. The gold-digging fiancée is finally driven away, and the girls' parents eventually reunited.

Background: *Pollyanna* was such a success that Walt Disney, realizing that he had a major star on his hands with Hayley Mills, reunited her with her Pollyanna director to make this light-headed but charming comedy. Thanks to the efforts of camera-man Lucien Ballard, it is very difficult to see the tricks used to depict Mills as twins; early on, you'll stop looking for any telltale dividing lines on the split screen and just see the twins.

Viewed through contemporary eyes, *The Parent Trap* does paint a somewhat distorted picture of reality; life among the idle rich and all that. But Hayley Mills makes the picture work. For Hayley Mills, *The Parent Trap* was a tour de force. She manages to convince you she is two different girls with different personal-ities but who are similar enough to be believable as twins. She shows a remarkable presence in front of the camera, and inter-acts with the mostly adult cast superbly.

This was the only Disney movie Maureen O'Hara ever made. She is radiant as Maggie McKendrick, the twins' understanding and down-to-earth mother. One of the biggest stars in Holly-wood's so-called golden age, she worked frequently with John Ford, most notably in 1941's *How Green Was My Valley.* The Dublin-born actress came to America and first starred here in *The Hunchback of Notre Dame* in 1939. Her beautiful red hair was particularly suited to Technicolor, and it was never lovelier than in movies such as *The Quiet Man,* costarring John Wayne. By the time she appeared in *The Parent Trap,* she'd just finished *Our Man in Havana,* and ahead lay *Mr. Hobbs Takes a Vacation, The Long Gray Line, Magnificent Matador, Spencer's Mountain, McLintock!, Big Jake,* and her last film to date, 1991's *Only the Lonely.*

Ex-Marine Brian Keith, the son of longtime character actor Robert Keith, is convincing in *The Parent Trap* as the loving fa-ther of the twin girls. His other film credits include *Nevada Smith; The Young Philadelphians; The Pleasure Seekers; Kraka-toa; East of Java; The Russians Are Coming! The Russians Are Coming!;* and *Gaily, Gaily;* he also played Teddy Roosevelt in *The Wind and the Lion.* He is known to TV audiences for his role in the sixties series *Family Affair.*

The Parent Trap is bubbly, breezy fun, especially appealing to preadolescent girls who will delight in the twins' conflict, then growing affection and pursuit of a common goal. In our more cynical age, the movie may look naive, but it is a pleasant com-edy children will love.

Phar Lap

Category: Drama. Starring Ron Leibman, Tom Burlinson, Martin Vaughn, Judy Morris, Celia de Burgh. Screenplay by David Williamson. Music by Bruce Rowland. 118 minutes. 1983. Rated PG. Fox Home Video.
Director: Simon Wincer.
Suggested Age Group: 10 and older.

The Story   This is the true story of a New Zealand–born racehorse with questionable bloodlines who is discovered in 1928 by a down-on-his-luck Australian trainer. The trainer makes a deal with his unimpressed boss, an American racehorse owner, to lease the horse for three years while turning him into a champion.

Though Phar Lap, which in Aborigine means "lightning," finishes last in his first few races, the trainer and his handler teach the horse how to race and how to want to win. The trainer tends to work the horse too hard, while the handler relies more on Phar Lap's heart to guarantee victory.

Phar Lap soon begins winning, eventually crossing the wire first in thirty-three races. His victories lead to the coveted Melbourne Cup, but after he wins that, he becomes the victim of several attempts on his life, a target for frustrated gamblers. His owner accepts a lucrative offer to race him in America, but after he wins his first big race in California, Phar Lap mysteriously dies, plunging Australia into deep mourning for its fallen hero.

Background: While a household name Down Under, the legendary Phar Lap is relatively unknown in North America. The horse, though considered unattractive, quickly displays an almost mystical ability to beat any other horse, regardless of training or pedigree. His success, needless to say, did not sit well with the stuffed-shirts of the Australian racing establishment, who resented the horse's Jewish-American owner.

In one scene, Ron Leibman, who plays the owner, is summoned to the office of the racing association, where the head of the group disdainfully refers to the animal as "your horse," only to be quickly corrected by Leibman. "Phar Lap. His name is Phar Lap," yells Leibman, with indignation and justifiable pride.

Ron Leibman is usually considered a stage actor, but here he brings a tremendous energy to his role. Short-tempered, not unwilling to accept blame for defeat but eager to accept credit for victory, he comes close to stealing his scenes from the other actors. His other films include *Where's Poppa?, The Hot Rock, Slaughterhouse Five,* and *Norma Rae.* Onstage, he won the Tony Award for his brilliant portrayal of controversial attorney Roy Cohn in *Angels in America.*

Tom Burlinson, who plays the horse's groom (referred to as a "strapper" in Australia) and later his trainer in America, also starred in *The Man from Snowy River* and *Return to Snowy River.* Phar Lap's real groom, Tommy Woodcock, gave technical assistance on the film.

Director Simon Wincer also made *D.A.R.Y.L., Quigley Down Under,* and the popular TV miniseries *Lonesome Dove.*

Filmed on location in New South Wales, Australia, *Phar Lap* is a stirring story of a national hero who came out of nowhere to beat the odds. It is a testimonial on the strength of spirit, and one of the best stories about horse racing ever told.

Pocketful of Miracles

Category: Comedy. Starring Bette Davis, Glenn Ford, Hope Lange, Ann-Margret, Sheldon Leonard, Peter Falk, Mickey Shaughnessy, Thomas Mitchell, Edward Everett Horton. Screenplay by Hal Kanter and Harry Tugend, from Robert Riskin's screenplay *Lady for a Day*, based on Damon Runyon's story "Madame La Gimp." 136 minutes. 1961. MGM/UA Home Video.
Director: Frank Capra.
Suggested Age Group: 8 and older.

The Story   Based on the 1933 movie *Lady for a Day* (also directed by Frank Capra), taken from a story by Damon Runyon, the film concerns a superstitious but good-hearted gangster named Dave the Dude and the shabby street-corner vendor who sells him apples he thinks bring him luck.

Apple Annie, the apple vendor, has a daughter who has been living abroad at school whom she hasn't seen in years. Ashamed of her desperate plight, Annie has been using stationery purloined from a fancy hotel to write long letters to her daughter about the grand life she's supposedly living in New York. But when she learns that her daughter plans to visit her with her new fiancé, Apple Annie panics, for she doesn't want her daughter to learn the terrible truth about her.

Meanwhile, Dave the Dude is on the verge of making an important deal with an out-of-town member of the syndicate, and is also being pressured by his girlfriend—a beautiful nightclub owner—to give up the rackets, marry her, and live a quiet life on a farm. But Dave has faith in Apple Annie's lucky apples, and he comes up with an ingenious solution to both his dilemma and hers: why not turn Apple Annie into a "lady for a day," so she can impress her daughter and her daughter's fiancé? Her luck, he reasons, will rub off on him, and he'll be able to seal his big deal.

In typical Capra style, the plan works perfectly, just as Christmas approaches.

Background: *Pocketful of Miracles* was Bette Davis's seventy-first movie in a career that began with 1931's *Bad Sister* and ended with 1987's *The Whales of August*. She had just finished *The Scapegoat* and would yet see her career take a different, bizarre turn to the horror genre with *Whatever Happened to Baby Jane?* No actress in movie history has made more great movies, including *Dark Victory; Now, Voyager; The Little Foxes;* and *The Man Who Came to Dinner*. She reigned as the queen of Warner Bros., a star unequaled in Hollywood history.

Here, though just fifty-three, she is made up to look twenty years older, a pathetic street person selling her apples, living in a grungy basement apartment, and spending what little money she makes on gin. Like the typical Damon Runyon character, though, she has a heart of gold.

Her performance shows great depth and poignancy, and the viewer can almost visualize in her distant gazes her earlier life of elegance now long gone. She modulates from wistfulness to fear when she discovers that her long-absent daughter will visit and learn the terrible truth about her mother. While this is not one of Bette Davis's most famous roles, in working with Frank Capra on what would be his final film she gives one of her most noble and effective performances.

Glenn Ford, who plays Dave the Dude, had previously worked with Bette Davis, playing her widower in 1946's *A Stolen Life*. His other memorable films include *Affair in Trinidad, The Big Heat,* and *The Blackboard Jungle*. Ahead for Ford lay *The Four Horsemen of the Apocalypse, Midway,* and the role as Clark Kent's father in *Superman*.

Hope Lange, who plays Dave the Dude's girlfriend, won an Oscar nomination for Best Supporting Actress in *Peyton Place;* her other films of note include *Bus Stop* and *The Young Lions*.

This was the screen debut for Ann-Margret, who was born Ann-Margaret Olsson in Sweden and trained at Northwestern University, where many other future stars were nurtured. In addition to memorable performances in fluff like *Bye Bye Birdie* and opposite Elvis Presley in *Viva Las Vegas,* she was superb in the compelling *Carnal Knowledge,* which won her an Oscar nomination for Best Supporting Actress of 1971.

Sheldon Leonard, who plays Darcy, the sinister Chicago mobster swinging the deal with Dave the Dude, is a longtime TV producer of shows such as *The Dick Van Dyke Show, The Andy Griffith Show,* and *Gomer Pyle;* by casting Bill Cosby in *I Spy,* he gave the first starring role in TV history to an African-American. Leonard, who also appeared in the classic *It's a Wonderful Life,* was no stranger to gangster roles, for his acting résumé includes such films as *The Gangster* and *Guys and Dolls*. Ironically, he also portrayed J. Edgar Hoover in *The Brinks Job*.

Peter Falk is a hilarious scene stealer as "Joy Boy," righthand man to Dave the Dude. Falk, who was nominated for an Oscar for Best Supporting Actor, had been similarly honored the year before for *Murder, Inc*. That same year he also appeared in *Pretty Boy Floyd*. Before *Colombo* made him a star on TV, the diminutive New Yorker acted in *It's a Mad Mad Mad Mad World, Robin and the Seven Hoods,* and *Husbands*.

Thomas Mitchell, who plays a boozy philosopher–pool shark masquerading as one of Apple Annie's high-class friends, is best remembered as Scarlett O'Hara's father in *Gone With the Wind*. He won an Oscar for Best Supporting Actor in *Stagecoach,* also in 1939. His other films of note include *It's a Wonderful Life* and *Lost Horizon,* both for Capra, *The Sullivans,* and *High Noon*.

Frank Capra, who wound up his magnificent career with this film, had a unique style that has become part of the American consciousness. The terms "Capraesque" or "Capracorn" evoke images of goodness and homespun American values. The original *Lost Horizon, Mr. Smith Goes to Washington, Meet John Doe,* and *It's a Wonderful Life* reaffirm the best in all of us.

Pocketful of Miracles is an endearing movie that will warm the hearts of all who watch it.

Pollyanna

Category: Drama. Starring Hayley Mills, Jane Wyman, Karl Malden, Nancy Olson, Adolphe Menjou, Agnes Moorehead, Donald Crisp, Kevin Corcoran, James Drury. Screenplay by David Swift, based on the book by Eleanor H. Porter. Music by Paul Smith. 134 minutes. 1960. Buena Vista Home Video.
Director: David Swift.
Suggested Age Group: 5 and older.

The Story Orphaned Pollyanna, blessed with a sunny disposition and outlook on life, has come to the town of Harrington in 1912 to live with her well-to-do but stern aunt Polly Harrington. The house is filled with servants who have crabby natures, but Pollyanna soon sets out to change all that, as well as many of the people in the town. She befriends a boy from the nearby orphanage, and she keeps the secret of the housemaid's love for a handsome young man in town to herself.

The town minister preaches fire-and-brimstone sermons each week, but Pollyanna tells him that her late father, a missionary, taught her that when you look only for the bad in people, you will probably find it. Her simple words of wisdom change the reverend's entire outlook, and eventually the whole town comes around to Pollyanna's way of seeing things, making Harrington an infinitely better place to live.

A new orphanage is desperately needed, but Mrs. Harrington, the sponsor of the old one, objects. A fund-raising bazaar is planned anyway, and after the reverend lends his support, it is a sure success. All this time, Pollyanna plays matchmaker between her aunt and a doctor with whom she was once in love.

When an accident paralyzes Pollyanna's legs and she must travel to Baltimore for a delicate operation, the entire town turns out at the railroad station to wish her well. As evidence of her powerful influence, a once nasty and reclusive old man adopts her orphan playmate, a hypochondriac invalid is now cured, the reverend no longer sees only gloom and doom, and even Pollyanna's aunt realizes that she herself has a lot of love to give.

As Pollyanna's train pulls out, we see a new sign, now identifying the town of Harrington as "The Glad Town."

Background: *Pollyanna* was the second film version made of this story; the first one was made in 1920 with "America's Sweetheart," Mary Pickford. *Pollyanna* marked the starring debut of Hayley Mills, the bubbly young daughter of actor Sir John Mills (*Swiss Family Robinson*) whom Walt Disney himself had spotted the year before, acting with her father in the British movie *Tiger Bay.*

Hayley Mills would personify the Disney image of that era, in films such as *The Parent Trap, In Search of the Castaways,* and *That Darn Cat.* While she never became a major star (her affair several years later with producer-director Roy Boulting, thirty-three years her senior, didn't help her image), she also starred in *The Chalk Garden* and *Appointment with Death.* More recently, she portrayed a teacher on the popular after-school TV comedy *Saved by the Bell.*

Jane Wyman, who plays Pollyanna's stern Aunt Polly, is perhaps best known to later generations for her role on the eighties nighttime soap opera *Falcon Crest.* By the time she played Aunt Polly in *Pollyanna,* she'd had a career as a radio singer and a bit player under the name Jane Durell, and had given a superb performance in the ground-breaking movie on alcoholism, 1945's *The Lost Weekend.*

She was also memorable as the dour mother in *The Yearling,* and won an Oscar for Best Actress in *Johnny Belinda* as a deaf-mute rape victim. She also starred with Rock Hudson in *Magnificent Obsession.* She is the ex-wife of Ronald Reagan.

Karl Malden's role is a bit overbearing here, and his fire-and-brimstone sermon is allowed to go on too long. Nevertheless, he does make a believable transformation, thanks to Pollyanna. By 1960, Malden had already assembled a respectable résumé of stage and film work, including *They Knew What They Wanted, 13 Rue Madeleine,* an Oscar for *A Streetcar Named Desire, On the Waterfront,* for which he won an Oscar nomination as Best Supporting Actor, *Baby Doll,* and *Fear Strikes Out.* He would make *One-Eyed Jacks* that year with his friend Marlon Brando, and *Birdman of Alcatraz,* playing the jailer to Burt Lancaster. He was again a minister, Father Devlin, in *The Great Impostor,* made two films with Steve McQueen, *The Cincinnati Kid* and *Nevada Smith,* played General Omar Bradley in *Patton* and starred in the popular seventies' TV series, *The Streets of San Francisco*. A former president of the Screen Actors Guild, he has continued to enjoy a long and distinguished career.

Pollyanna might easily have been a sappy, sentimental movie that children would have quickly rejected. But although it didn't fare particularly well at the box office back in 1960, it has since become a family favorite for its endearing outlook on life, and its introduction to Hayley Mills, one of the great child stars in movie history.

The Prince and the Pauper

Category: Adventure. Starring Errol Flynn, Claude Rains, Billy Mauch, Bobby Mauch, Henry Stephenson, Barton MacLane, Alan Hale. Screenplay by Laird Doyle, based on the novel by Mark Twain. Music by Erich Wolfgang Korngold. 120 minutes. 1937. Black and white. MGM/UA Home Video.
Director: William Keighley.
Suggested Age Group: 10 and older.

The Story
Mark Twain's classic tale involves the young Prince Edward, who meets a look-alike beggar boy named Tom Canty outside the royal palace. Ignoring the guards, the prince invites the pauper into the palace to play, and after noticing their resemblance, they switch clothes and identities. When the prince, now in rags, is thrown out of the castle by the unknowing guards, the pauper soon finds himself on the throne of England, while the rightful young king is now living in the streets.

But the Earl of Hertford, a scheming advisor to the king, has figured out the mistake and makes plans to murder the king. Meanwhile, a devil-may-care soldier of fortune comes to the aid of the beggar boy, not realizing that he's telling the truth about being the true king. Inside the palace, the real pauper adjusts gradually and rather gleefully to his new station in life. But eventually their identities are set right.

Background: *The Prince and the Pauper* may be the only movie in Hollywood history which was guaranteed to "play in Peoria," as the saying goes, since stars Billy and Bobby Mauch, who had the respective title roles, were Peoria-born boys. Though they sound like graduates of the Freddie Bartholomew school of thirties child acting, they perform marvelously as the title players. Their performances are smooth and effortless, and they will quickly have viewers curious to find out their fates.

More interesting is the appearance, about half an hour into the story, of young Errol Flynn as soldier of fortune Miles Hendon.

Errol Flynn was not yet a major star in 1937, but had already made *Captain Blood* and *The Charge of the Light Brigade*. His next films would be the now largely forgotten *Another Dawn* and *The Perfect Specimen*. It wouldn't be until the following year when Flynn would play his signature role in *The Adventures of Robin Hood* and become a screen icon.

Claude Rains' portrayal of the Earl of Hertford, the evil advisor to the young ersatz king, is precisely on point. With a sinister-looking triangular beard and a cool, detached delivery, he seems born to wear the lavish costumes of a sixteenth-century nobleman and will soon have young audiences hoping he meets his demise.

Alan Hale, who plays the corrupt head of the palace guard, is the look-alike father of his namesake son, Alan Hale, Jr., who would play "Skipper," the costar of TV's *Gilligan's Island*. The elder Hale would make eleven more films with Flynn, who became a close friend.

The Prince and the Pauper takes a bit of time to get going, and some of the dialogue may be difficult for young American ears to understand at first. There are several sword fights and a murder, but they're all shot with a minimum of bloodshed in the swash-buckling style of that glorious era. The coronation ceremony at the end of the movie is almost as long as the real-life event itself, with all the splendor and circumstance you would expect. After all, 1936 was the year King George VI ascended to the throne, so any movie about one of his supposed ancestors had better look authentic.

The Prince and the Pauper is a timeless adventure story, sure to please adventure-minded young viewers.

The Red Balloon

Category: Fantasy. Starring Pascal Lamorisse. Written by Albert Lamorisse. 34 minutes. 1956. Columbia Home Video.
Director: Albert Lamorisse.
Suggested Age Group: 4 and older.

The Story   This is one of the strangest, most beautiful children's movies ever made. One day a lonely Parisian boy named Pascal finds a large red balloon stuck in a doorway just within his reach. He frees it, and then the balloon takes on a life of its own. It follows him to school, it follows him around the streets of Paris, and it eludes a taunting band of slingshot-flinging bullies. When the boy is denied permission to bring his balloon on a crowded bus, somehow the balloon finds him when he gets off at the other end.

With the exception of one brief utterance from the boy to his strange new friend, not a single word of dialogue is spoken in this timeless classic. Instead, a most unusual friendship is forged, until the balloon's unhappy demise. The movie ends on an upbeat note, however, with all the balloons of Paris pulling themselves out of the hands of children and vendors, towing Pascal skyward.

Background: Imagine you are Federico Fellini, sitting in your seat at the 1956 Academy Awards, confident that the screenplay you cowrote for *La Strada,* one of the great postwar Italian films, has an inside shot at the Oscar for Best Original Screenplay. Instead, presenter Deborah Kerr calls out the winner: somebody named Albert Lamorisse for *The Red Balloon,* a movie with no dialogue!

Of course no dialogue is required in this enchanting fable. The City of Light plays the third character in this unusual story of innocence and friendship between a disarming little boy and his unique balloon.

Albert Lamorisse was not a newcomer to moviemaking. A Paris-born photographer who turned to short subject films in the late forties, he won recognition for *Crin Blanc (White Mane)* at the Cannes Film Festival in 1952. In 1970, eight years after he was killed in a helicopter crash while filming a documentary near Teheran, his final film, *Le Vent des Amoureux (The Lovers' Wind)* was completed using his notes and went on to win an Oscar nomination for Best Documentary.

Visually haunting and atmospheric, *The Red Balloon* is an unforgettable and uplifting film for all ages.

The Red Pony

Category: Drama. Starring Robert Mitchum, Myrna Loy, Louis Calhern, Peter Miles, Shepperd Strudwick, Margaret Hamilton. Screenplay by John Steinbeck, based on his story. Includes music by Aaron Copland. 109 minutes. 1949. Republic Pictures Home Video.
Director: Lewis Milestone.
Suggested Age Group: 7 and older.

The Story A Florida farmboy named Tom Tiflin, who lives with his parents, his grandfather, and a hired hand, loves to hear the tales of the Old West his grandfather spins. One day, the boy is given a beautiful red pony he names Gavilan, and he cares for him with the help of the hired hand. His new responsibilities begin to bring him closer to his parents, especially his somewhat standoffish father, who's grown tired of the grandfather's repetitive yarns.

Soon, the horse takes sick, and the worried boy is distracted at school. Finally he runs home early to care for him, much to the dismay of his teacher. Tom blames the hired hand for the beloved pony's illness, but he eventually forgives his friend, as together they try to save Gavilan.

Parents should be cautioned about one scary sequence in which Tom, chasing after his pony, fights off several vultures who claw him on his arms and face with their talons. The sequence is brief, however, and the boy is soon rescued by his father and the hired hand. *The Red Pony* is one of those long-forgotten movies that children will enjoy because it shows a love for a simpler kind of life and a special pet, as well as a respect for an older generation.

Background: When he costarred in *The Red Pony* as the hired hand Billy Buck, Robert Mitchum had already begun to achieve his star status. After his debut in a Hopalong Cassidy movie, *Bar 20*, in 1943, just two years later he was nominated for an Oscar for Best Supporting Actor for *The Story of G.I. Joe*. His other movies of note include *Out of the Past, One Minute to Zero, River* *of No Return, The Night of the Hunter, Cape Fear,* and *Heaven Knows, Mr. Allison.* More recently, he played Philip Marlowe in *Farewell, My Lovely* and made a cameo appearance in the re-make of *Cape Fear.*

A fan once requested an autograph, but before Mitchum could sign, the fan started to show off. "Mr. Douglas, Mr. Douglas, I know all your movies," he said, breathlessly. Then he recited the names of twenty Kirk Douglas movies. Mitchum glared at him, grabbed the pen and paper, and wrote "Drop dead. Kirk Douglas."

Myrna Loy, who portrayed Alice Tiflin in *The Red Pony,* was best known for playing Nora Charles to William Powell's Nick Charles in *The Thin Man* series of films. Though she never won even one Oscar nomination, she received an honorary statuette in 1991. Her other films of note include *Manhattan Melodrama* (the movie that desperado John Dillinger saw just before he was gunned down by the F.B.I.), *The Best Years of Our Lives,* and *Cheaper by the Dozen.*

Louis Calhern, who plays Tom's grandfather, was one of the best-known character actors of his generation. He will forever be remembered for his title portrayal of Justice Oliver Wendell Holmes in *The Magnificent Yankee.* He also portrayed Buffalo Bill Cody in *Annie Get Your Gun* and was a foil for the Marx brothers in *Duck Soup.*

The Red Pony is based on a story by John Steinbeck, the Nobel Prize–winning author of *The Grapes of Wrath* and *Of Mice and Men,* and one of the twentieth century's towering literary figures. On a visit to Chicago one time, Steinbeck sought anonymity so he could see friends without being bothered by the local press. Reporters checked all the swank hotels looking for him, hoping for an interview, but overlooked a tiny hotel—which charged $9 a week for a room—where Steinbeck decided to stay.

Director Lewis Milestone won an Oscar in 1930 for *All Quiet on the Western Front* and also helmed *Hell's Angels, Rain, The Purple Heart,* and *The Strange Love of Martha Ivers,* Kirk Doug-las's debut film.

The Red Pony evokes a simpler time, focusing on strong family ties and the innocence of a boy about to become a man. It tells an extremely endearing story.

The Rocketeer

Category: Adventure. Starring Bill Campbell, Alan Arkin, Jennifer Connelly, Paul Sorvino, Timothy Dalton, Terry O'Quinn, Ed Lauter. Screenplay by Danny Bilson and Paul De Meo, based on a book by David Stevens. 108 minutes. 1991. Rated PG. Buena Vista Home Video.
Director: Joe Johnston.
Suggested Age Group: 11 and older.

The Story Right before World War II, a daredevil flyer and his mechanic stumble onto an amazing invention: a backpack rocket engine invented by Howard Hughes, which, if placed in the wrong hands, can wreak worldwide havoc.

The duo quickly find themselves in danger from the gangsters who've stolen the rocket from the government, intending to sell it to the Nazis. As it turns out, the gangsters are secretly in the employ of a dashing movie star working for the Germans.

Meanwhile, the daredevil pilot's girlfriend is an actress working in a new movie which happens to star the traitorous actor. Soon she unwittingly leads him to her boyfriend and the rocket. The climax of *The Rocketeer* offers superb special effects via George Lucas's Industrial Light and Magic, great suspense, and a happy ending.

Background: *The Rocketeer* has the wonderfully campy look of the old-time Saturday matinee movie serials that delighted generations before the advent of television. From the opening sequence, in which an old P-38 racing plane zooms into the screen and is then shot down by a bad guy with a tommy gun, the film has lots of action, some interesting dialogue, and terrific special effects.

Parents should be advised that there is plenty of violence in *The Rocketeer,* but it is all done in the fast-paced comic adventure serial style of films like *Raiders of the Lost Ark.* The spectacular flying sequences will certainly enthrall young viewers.

Bill Campbell, who plays Cliff, the handsome flyer who quickly masters the backpack rocket, played Luke Fuller on TV's *Dynasty,* and after other TV and stage work, made his screen debut in this film.

Alan Arkin gives his familiar but likable delivery as Pete, the mechanic who shares in Cliff's adventures. His film credits include *The Heart Is a Lonely Hunter, Catch-22, Freebie and the Bean, The Seven Percent Solution,* and *The In-Laws.*

Paul Sorvino, the burly actor-singer who plays the gangster Eddie Valentine, is a versatile performer whose credits range from *That Championship Season* to *Dick Tracy* and a starring role on the popular TV series *Law and Order.* He gave up much of his acting to pursue his first love, opera singing.

Timothy Dalton, who plays movie star Neville Sinclair, started on the stage after completing studies at the Royal Academy of Dramatic Arts. Best known for his James Bond portrayal, Dalton made his debut as King Philip of France in *The Lion in Winter,* then played Heathcliff in the 1970 remake of *Wuthering Heights.* The onetime significant other of Vanessa Redgrave, he played "Bond, James Bond" in *The Living Daylights* and *Licence to Kill.*

Jennifer Connelly, who plays Cliff's actress girlfriend Jenny Blake, made her screen debut at twelve in *Once Upon a Time in America.* She also starred in *The Hot Spot* and *Career Opportunities.* More recently she was seen in John Singleton's 1995 movie *Higher Learning.*

Although *The Rocketeer* was not a huge box-office success, it's good campy fun, with a wonderful sense of style and an authentic period look. The climactic sequence, a confrontation and fight on a huge flying dirigible, is worthy of any of the Indiana Jones movies, and it effectively wraps up a fast-moving, stylish comic-book adventure kids will love.

Rocket Gibraltar

Category: Drama. Starring Burt Lancaster, Macaulay Culkin, Bill Pullman, Suzy Amis, Kevin Spacey, John Glover, Patricia Clarkson, George Martin, Sinead Cusack. Screenplay by Amos Poe. 100 minutes. 1988. Rated PG. Columbia Home Video.
Director: Daniel Petrie.
Suggested Age Group: 8 and older.

The Story   This is a wistful, nostalgic movie about a writer named Levi Rockwell approaching his seventy-seventh birthday who's arranged for one last gathering of his children, their spouses, and his grandchildren. It's the Labor Day weekend, and unbeknownst to his family, he is suffering from a terminal illness known only to him and his doctor.

The children are all busy with their own lives. One son is a movie producer whose portable phone is permanently attached to his ear; his son-in-law is a nearly washed-up pitcher on leave from the New York Mets; another son is a struggling standup comic; and his daughter is a likable free spirit with lots of boyfriends.

The story is set at the widower's country home in the Hamptons, on eastern Long Island's south shore. The end-of-summer setting is an appropriate metaphor, for it represents a time of reflection on the season just passed, with the chill of autumn and the emptiness of winter lying ahead.

Ultimately, it's the grandchildren who learn of their grandfather's illness, as well as his admiration for the way the Vikings buried their dead in burning boats headed out to sea. Discovering this information in an endearing and ingenious manner, they proceed to carry out his wishes, while their self-absorbed parents try to sort out their own lives.

Background: Though the film deals with death, it's not the main thrust of the story. *Rocket Gibraltar* is really a celebration of life, a look back at grander times, and a subtle indictment of the tendency of grown children to ignore their parents' feelings and needs in pursuit of their own goals.

Young viewers will love the way Levi's grandchildren are depicted as the smarter generation, outthinking their parents in a delightful way. There are some references to the Suzy Amis character's sexual exploits, but they're minimal.

Rocket Gibraltar was one of Burt Lancaster's last films, made just before his final screen appearance in 1989's *Field of Dreams.* One of the great stars of the postwar era, he won the Oscar for Best Actor for *Elmer Gantry* in 1960. His other films of note include *Seven Days in May, Birdman of Alcatraz, From Here to Eternity, Sweet Smell of Success,* and *Field of Dreams,* among many others.

Given the number of his excellent films, it's easy to overlook *Rocket Gibraltar,* an underappreciated delight, but don't miss it. It gives viewers a glimpse of a great actor who, instead of simply fading from the screen as he got older, chose roles that were suited for his maturity.

Speaking of things quickly gone from theaters, soon after he became a star in the late 1940s, a life-sized poster of Lancaster was placed in the lobby of the old Capitol Theater on Broadway in New York. But after two days it had to be removed. Dozens of bobbysoxers had covered the cutout poster with lipstick-stained kisses.

Director Daniel Petrie, who also directed *A Raisin in the Sun,* coaxed a superb performance out of then-unknown seven-year-old Macaulay Culkin, especially in a tender scene in the kitchen with Burt Lancaster as the two prepare shrimp. In this scene of innocence contrasted with experience, you can clearly see the qualities which would soon make the blond tyke the biggest child star since Shirley Temple.

This is a good movie to see when you're in the mood for something subtle, offering a realistic and bittersweet look at life. George Martin is especially poignant as Lancaster's understanding doctor, who shares with him recollections of the woman they both loved years ago.

Sinead Cusack, who plays Levi's daughter Amanda, is the daughter of the famed Irish star Cyril Cusack. Suzy Amis, who plays Aggie, another of Levi's daughters, is a onetime model who trained at the Actors Studio and is married to Sam Robards, son of Jason Robards and Lauren Bacall. Her other films to date include *Fandango, Rich in Love,* and the title role in *The Ballad of Little Jo.*

Bill Pullman, who plays the son-in-law, appeared recently in *The Last Seduction.* His credits include *Spaceballs, Ruthless Peo-*

ple, A League of Their Own, Sleepless in Seattle, Casper, and *While You Were Sleeping.*

John Glover, who plays movie deal-maker Rolo Rockwell, may be familiar to younger audiences from *Gremlins 2;* he also appeared in *Annie Hall* and *Melvin and Howard.*

Kevin Spacey, who plays the struggling standup comic Dwane Hanson, won a Tony on Broadway for his role in Neil Simon's *Lost in Yonkers.* He has also appeared in such films as *Consenting Adults, Glengarry Glen Ross, Outbreak,* and *Swimming with Sharks.*

Some parents might not like the fact that the children act so independently, but it's all done with such a touching style that you might just shed a tear or two as *Rocket Gibraltar* and its principal character reach the sunset.

Rookie of the Year

Category: Comedy. Starring Thomas Ian Nicholas, Gary Busey,
Dan Hedaya, Daniel Stern, John Candy. Screenplay by Sam Harper.
103 minutes. 1994. Rated PG. Fox Home Video.
Director: Daniel Stern.
Suggested Age Group: 7 and older.

The Story   A twelve-year-old boy named Henry Rowengartner
loves baseball, in particular the Chicago Cubs. Running after a fly ball in a Little League game, he steps
on a baseball and injures his arm. But after surgery, he suddenly
finds that he can hurl a horsehide at more than 100 miles an
hour. When he catches a homerun ball hit by an opposing player
in the stands in Wrigley Field, in the tradition of the Cub fans he
tosses it back. To his great surprise, his throw is a line-drive bullet, belt high, all the way to the plate. Before he knows it, he's
signed to a contract, in uniform, and on the mound, hurling for
his beloved Cubs.

But although he can toss a baseball through the proverbial
brick wall, Henry isn't automatically a great pitcher. The manager
of the Cubs assigns an aging pitcher named Chet Seadman to
teach him the art of pitching, and perhaps a bit about life, too.

Another influence on him is goofy pitching coach Phil Brick-
man, who has never quite recovered from being beaned in the
head by a baseball. Meanwhile, Henry's stepfather is trying to
cash in on Henry's sudden prowess, while his best buddies Clark
and George realize that his newfound fame has placed their
friendships in jeopardy.

Henry has the usual ups and downs of any rookie pitcher,
magnified, of course, because of his tender age, unique ability,
and instant stardom. How he deals with it and performs on the
mound makes for a familiar but effective preteen fantasy.

Background: *Rookie of the Year* was inspired by the cult baseball
movie *Roogie's Bump,* a 1954 Republic film about a boy whose
bump on his arm allowed him to throw a baseball at the speed of

light. While that film was poorly received and suffers from some lapses in logic, this version is flawless. This is the feature film directing debut for actor Daniel Stern, best known as one of the bumbling "wet bandits" in the *Home Alone* movies, and for his work in films such as *City Slickers, Diner,* and *Breaking Away,* also reviewed in this book.

One of the things that makes this fantasy so effective is the film's realistic look. Actually filmed at Wrigley Field, it features one scene that was shot between games of a Cubs-Cardinals doubleheader, with 35,000 fans in the stands.

Thomas Ian Nicholas, who plays Henry, appeared in the awful *Radio Flyer* and some made-for-TV movies. Here he is more than up to the task of convincing you he suddenly has a million-dollar arm. He is a bright, engaging young actor who will instantly win the hearts of young viewers.

Gary Busey plays aging hurler Chet Seadman and handles the role convincingly, going from reluctant tutor and father figure to best friend. Busey's best-known roles are his Oscar-nominated turn in *The Buddy Holly Story* and the villains in *Lethal Weapon* and *Under Siege.* Surely the only actor ever to come from Goose Creek, Texas, he is a direct descendant of Black Bart, a legendary outlaw of the Old West, whose claim to fame was being the first bandit to use the term "Hands up!"

Curiously, the late John Candy made an unbilled appearance as the play-by-play announcer. Candy, who rose to fame on Canadian TV's witty *SCTV* series in the early 1980s, costarred in *Home Alone; Uncle Buck; Planes, Trains and Automobiles;* and *Cool Runnings.* He died suddenly on the Mexican location of *Wagons East* in 1994.

Baseball fans will note the presence of superstars Bobby Bonilla, Barry Bonds (in his old Pittsburgh uniform), and former star Pedro Guerrero, all of whom face the young pitching star with predictable but nevertheless funny results. This is a wholesome, funny, and well-crafted fantasy about a boy who gets the chance to live his dream.

The Russians Are Coming!
The Russians Are Coming!

Category: Comedy. Starring Carl Reiner, Alan Arkin, Theodore
Bikel, Eva Marie Saint, Brian Keith, Jonathan Winters, John Phillip
Law, Tessie O'Shea, Michael J. Pollard, Paul Ford. Screenplay by
William Rose, based on the novel *The Off-Islanders* by Nathaniel
Benchley. 126 minutes. 1966. Fox Home Video.
Director: Norman Jewison.
Suggested Age Group: 10 and older.

The Story

When a Russian submarine runs aground off a
small New England island, a group of sailors,
headed by an officer named Rozanov, comes
ashore for help. Their first interaction is with a vacationing
Broadway musical comedy writer named Walt Whittaker and his
family, who misinterpret the Russians' intentions and alert the
other townspeople that they are, in fact, invading. Immediately
the town rallies, grabbing their guns and forming a militia. Then
it takes an act of courage and cooperation on behalf of both par-
ties in saving a child's life to bring them together and to find a
peaceful, happy ending.

There are brief sequences of mild violence, when the townspeople fire at the fleeing Russians, but it's all handled in a slapstick, Keystone Kops–like manner. Young viewers will love the
silly townspeople, the writer's precocious children, and the way
the parents act heroically in the end.

Background: In 1966, tensions between the United States and the
U.S.S.R. were high. The movie was thus an effective and funny
call for understanding, a warning against the catastrophe that can
result from rumor and fear. Because the U.S. Navy refused to lend
the filmmakers a submarine, they had to construct one for the
pivotal scenes in the harbor.

Carl Reiner, who plays Walt Whittaker, is best known as Sid
Caesar's straight man, and as Alan Brady from *The Dick Van Dyke
Show,* the popular sixties TV situation comedy. He also appeared
in films such as *It's a Mad Mad Mad Mad World,* and in more re-

The Russians Are Coming! The Russians Are Coming!

218

cent years directed such films as *Where's Poppa?* and *Oh, God!* He is the father of Rob Reiner, the actor-director.

Eva Marie Saint, who plays Walt's wife, Elispeth, won an Oscar for Best Supporting Actress for 1954's *On the Waterfront,* going on to costar in *Raintree County, North by Northwest,* and *Exodus.* She also had a recurring role in the popular eighties TV series, *Moonlighting.*

Alan Arkin, who plays Rozanov, coincidentally played the young Carl Reiner character on Broadway in Reiner's autobiographical comedy, *Enter Laughing,* and won an Oscar nomination as Best Supporting Actor for this, his debut role. He would go on to star in such films as *Catch 22, Little Murders, Edward Scissorhands,* and *Glengarry Glen Ross.* His son Adam is a rising star, primarily on television shows like *Northern Exposure* and *Chicago Hope.*

Theodore Bikel, who plays the captain of the Russian submarine, appears briefly at the beginning and then at the end, both times speaking fluent Russian. A talented folk singer and theatrical performer, he was born in Vienna, raised in Israel, and, prophetically, starred on the stage there in *Tevye the Milkman;* years later he would star in several productions of *Fiddler on the Roof,* playing the same character in the beloved musical. He was the original Captain Georg Von Trapp in the Broadway version of *The Sound of Music.* His memorable movie roles include *The African Queen* and *The Defiant Ones,* for which he was nominated for an Oscar for Best Supporting Actor.

Brian Keith, who plays the sheriff of the tiny resort island, also appeared in *The Wind and the Lion* and *Nevada Smith,* as well as *The Parent Trap.*

Jonathan Winters, who plays the deputy sheriff, is one of the most original, creative comics of this generation, perfectly cast on TV's *Mork and Mindy,* the popular seventies TV comedy series, the show which made Robin Williams an overnight star. His other credits include *It's a Mad Mad Mad Mad World, The Loved One,* and *The Shadow.*

Director Norman Jewison also made *Fiddler on the Roof; Forty Pounds of Trouble; The Cincinnati Kid; In the Heat of the Night; Jesus Christ, Superstar; Moonstruck;* and *Only You.*

Viewing *The Russians Are Coming! The Russians Are Coming!* on tape nearly thirty years after its theatrical release, it still has a charm and a homespun quality about its look at New Englanders, as well as offering an overriding message that Russians and Americans could be friends—if only given the chance.

The Sandlot

Category: Comedy. Starring Tom Guiry, Mike Vitar, Patrick Renna, Chauncey Leopardi, Denis Leary, Karen Allen, Brooke Adams, James Earl Jones. Screenplay by Robert Gunter, David Mickey Evans. 101 minutes. 1993. Rated PG. 20th Century–Fox Home Video.
Director: David Mickey Evans.
Suggested Age Group: 7 and older.

The Story Scotty, a quiet, friendless boy, is the new kid on the block. He's just moved to town with his mother and stepfather, and he has no friends—until he goes to the nearby sandlot.

The setting is suburban Los Angeles in the summer of 1962, and the new kid on the block is reluctantly welcomed by a group of boys practicing baseball. The boys quickly discover that not only does Scotty have next to no ability at baseball, but he also doesn't even know who Babe Ruth is! He is, therefore, no shoo-in as the latest member of their motley crew. The boys practice in a field adjacent to a mysterious vacant lot, where a huge, unseen guard dog lives. The dog, lovingly nicknamed The Beast, makes any ball hit over the fence a lost cause.

When Scotty realizes that one ball hit over the fence is a Babe Ruth–autographed collector's item he'd borrowed from his stepfather's trophy case, he's determined to retrieve it no matter what. Of course, it's up to him to lead the foray over the fence before his stepfather realizes the prized ball is missing.

The boys employ all sorts of schemes, from using a catcher's mask attached to four vacuum cleaners, to sliding a pot under the fence, to building a contraption with an Erector set—all to no avail. They even try lowering one of the boys on a makeshift platform, supported by a catcher's chest protector. But the Beast prevails, and the ball remains in its lair.

As a break from their dangerous mission, the boys go to an amusement park. They then make the mistake of experimenting with some chewing tobacco just before boarding a flying saucer ride. The results are predictable but humorous.

The Sandlot

Back at the old sandlot, just when the prized baseball seems lost forever, we meet the Beast's master, who welcomes the boys into his home, spins some stories about his friend George (i.e., George Herman Ruth), and gives them some memories to treasure for a lifetime.

Background: *The Sandlot* is a nostalgic look back to a simpler time, one when baseball was pure and didn't involve strikes, drug abusers, agents, lockouts, or Astroturf. Some of the narration is a bit sappy but the young actors are all appealing.

Filmed in Salt Lake City and at Dodger Stadium, the cast includes James Earl Jones as the mysterious friend, a former Negro League star the boys meet late in the story. As usual, he lends a gentle, fatherly presence to the proceedings. Even though Jones is not a baseball fan—in fact, he's never even been to a big-league game—he has an extensive baseball résumé in movies, in films such as *Field of Dreams, The Bingo Long Traveling All-Stars & Motor Kings,* and as a narrator for the excellent TV documentary *When It Was a Game.* Denis Leary, who plays Scotty's stepfather, is a fast-talking, witty standup comic and screenwriter, as well as an actor, whose one-man shows, *No Cure for Cancer* and *Birth, School, Work, Death,* have won him a wide audience of young fans. His movies of note include *Strictly Business, The Ref,* and *Operation Dumbo Drop.*

No, that's not Babe Ruth, of course, in a brief dream sequence. It's Art LeFleur, who also starred in *Bull Durham* and was one of the ghostlike players in *Field of Dreams.*

Even though it's a bit difficult to believe that any fifth grader in suburban America hasn't heard of Babe Ruth, *The Sandlot* is a sweet coming-of-age movie, extolling innocence and friendship, and providing a delightful diversion for children.

Scrooge

Category: Musical. Starring Albert Finney, Sir Alec Guinness, Kenneth More, Dame Edith Evans, Lawrence Naismith. Screenplay by Leslie Bricusse, adapted from *A Christmas Carol* by Charles Dickens. Music by Leslie Bricusse. 118 minutes. 1970. Rated G. CBS/Fox Home Video.
Director: Ronald Neame.
Suggested Age Group: 6 and older.

The Story   This is the musical version of Dickens' *A Christmas Carol*, set on Christmas Eve 1860 in London. Ebenezer Scrooge, who owns a counting house and hates Christmas, thinks nothing of making his usual collection rounds on the most festive night of the year, demanding prompt payment. He even ducks into the tiny booth where one debtor is performing a Punch and Judy show, and threatens to confiscate the man's puppets if he doesn't pay up!

Most shocking of all, Scrooge pays his loyal clerk, Bob Cratchit, a mere fifteen shillings a week, despite the fact that Cratchit has five children, including Tiny Tim, a physically challenged child who nevertheless is always of good cheer.

But that night, Scrooge is visited by the ghost of Jacob Marley. Marley warns him to change his ways, lest he end up in the shackles and chains like him, wandering through the grim afterlife. Subsequently, Scrooge is visited by the ghosts of Christmases Past, Present, and yet to come, after which he sees how his life might've turned out much happier.

By morning Scrooge has reformed his ways and his outlook, and accepts an invitation to Christmas dinner at the Cratchits. Of course, a Merry Christmas is had by one and all.

Background: One look at this film and it's easy to understand why it was nominated for Oscars for Best Costume Design, Best Original Score, Best Song, and Best Art Direction. It has a beautiful, authentic look about it, faithfully re-creating the dreary interior of a Dickensian counting house, and the luminous glow of a mid-Victorian home at Christmastime.

Albert Finney, though just thirty-four when he made this movie, is nevertheless marvelous as Scrooge, the most infamous skinflint of them all, who at first calls himself "a martyr to my own generosity" simply for allowing his clerk to have Christmas Day off. One of the last members of the so-called Angry Young Man generation who came to prominence in the 1950s—O'Toole, Burton, Stamp, and Caine are among the others—Albert Finney is today regarded as one of the world's great actors.

Luther was one of his early signature roles, which he performed on the London and Broadway stages to great acclaim, and he won worldwide fame in movies such as *Tom Jones* and *Saturday Night and Sunday Morning.* His other notable films include *Two for the Road* opposite Audrey Hepburn, *Murder on the Orient Express,* in which he plays Hercule Poirot, *Wolfen,* the movie version of *Annie,* as Daddy Warbucks, *The Dresser, Miller's Crossing,* and more recently *A Man of No Importance, The Browning Version,* and *The Run of the Country.* He chooses his roles carefully, and it shows, for these are all quality films and performances.

As a young stage actor, Finney, a standby, was informed just before the curtain that the star was ill. Then he heard the audience groan after they got the news. After all, they'd come expecting to see the star, Sir Laurence Olivier. But Finney won a standing ovation that night, and Olivier later called him the finest actor of his generation.

Sir Alec Guinness, who plays the ghost of Jacob Marley, is best known to younger audiences as the Jedi Knight, Obi-wan Kenobi, in the *Star Wars* trilogy. He became a real Knight of the Realm in 1985 and when asked what went through his mind during the ceremony, he replied "I kept looking at the rear end of the anonymous banker from Bristol ahead of me, wondering, as he knelt down, what on earth he'd done to be knighted!"

Dame Edith Evans, who appears as the Ghost of Christmas Past, was one of the great actresses of her generation. Her small role in *Scrooge* doesn't begin to demonstrate her regal presence, which was especially in evidence when she was doing the classics. Though she was mainly a stage actress, her films of note include *The Importance of Being Earnest, The Nun's Story, Tom Jones* (with Finney), and *The Whisperers.*

If you ever come across a movie called *Genevieve,* by all means see it. It's a delightful 1953 comedy involving vintage automobiles on a cross-country race, and it starred Kenneth More, who plays the Ghost of Christmas Present in *Scrooge*. More had a thirty-year career which included *A Night to Remember*, the definitive movie about the sinking of the *Titanic, Sink the Bismarck!*, *The Longest Day*, and *Oh! What a Lovely War*, Richard Attenborough's directorial debut.

Director Ronald Neame's credits range from *The Chalk Garden* to *The Man Who Never Was, Tunes of Glory*, and *The Poseidon Adventure*.

Leslie Bricusse, who wrote the sparkling songs for *Scrooge*, was at his peak in the 1960s with hit shows such as *Stop the World, I Want to Get Off* and *The Roar of the Greasepaint, the Smell of the Crowd*. He has written a spiffy, captivating score here, highlighted by a song called "Thank You Very Much." It still holds up after a quarter-century.

I have a very special affinity for *Scrooge*, since it was the first movie I reviewed professionally back in 1970. A recent viewing demonstrates that it has lost none of its charm, and it deserves a place in any family library, to be dusted off every holiday season and enjoyed anew.

Searching for Bobby Fischer

Category: Drama. Starring Joe Mantegna, Joan Allen, Laurence Fishburne, Ben Kingsley, Max Pomeranc. Written by Steven Zaillian. 110 minutes. 1993. Rated PG. Paramount Home Video.
Director: Steven Zaillian.
Suggested Age Group: 9 and older.

The Story   This is the true story of a seven-year-old New York chess prodigy named Josh Waitzkin, whose understanding and playing of the game was discovered accidentally by his father, a New York baseball sportswriter. Josh's parents find themselves confronted by the dilemma of how to encourage the boy's talent for chess while also making sure he plays for the love of the game itself, rather than for the sake of winning. Moreover, they want to ensure that his social skills will not be affected by the nurturing of his special gift.

Josh begins playing two kinds of chess. One is the style learned from Bruce Pandolfini, a serious chess master his parents hire to tutor him. Bruce tries to instill in Josh the proper discipline for ultimate success, and in the process, he wants his parents to make chess the focus of Josh's life. The other style Josh picks up is street chess, which he plays with a chess hustler in New York's Washington Square Park. This informal tutor tries to teach Josh how to play to win, not simply to avoid losing.

Josh's parents are caught in the middle, struggling for balance. On one hand, they want to encourage him, but on the other, they want to make certain he doesn't become another troubled, dysfunctional soul like the eccentric chess champion Bobby Fischer. From time to time, to remind us of the glory and the risks a prodigy faces, the film shows old footage of Fischer accompanied by Josh's voice explaining the troubled genius's ascent to the top of the chess world. Josh refers to Fischer as "an American hero," then adds, "He bragged to the world that he'd beat the Russian, and he delivered. Then he made the most original, unexpected move of all. He disappeared."

Background: *Searching for Bobby Fischer* was released in the summer of 1993, a season when audiences preferred block-busters. It had only a modest theatrical run, but word of mouth has given this wonderful movie a second life on video. It was ar-gued that its title put people off, suggesting a story of the ob-sessed and obnoxious Ty Cobb of chess. What audiences missed was a compelling movie about a love of learning, an unusual dilemma, and the way two ordinary parents handled it.

Despite his native Chicago twang, Joe Mantegna is convincing as a New York baseball writer who is quick to pick up on his son's rare gift. Often associated with the work of playwright David Mamet, Mantegna got his start on the Chicago stage, where his adeptness at ad-libbing was well honed. Indeed, on the opening night of Mamet's play *Glengarry Glen Ross,* for ex-ample, he forgot his lines in the opening monologue, and smoothly ad-libbed. Backstage later, Mamet said he liked Man-tegna's "interpretation." Mantegna, a busy screen actor, is also a writer, and starred in his own play, *Bleacher Bums,* the Emmy Award–winning teleplay about a group of Chicago Cubs fans in a particular part of the bleachers at Wrigley Field. The name he cre-ated, incidentally, has stuck with that team's particular breed of long-suffering fans.

His other films include the unintentionally hilarious *Body of Evidence, Airheads, Offbeat, House of Games, Things Change, Homicide,* and Woody Allen's *Alice.*

Joan Allen, who plays Josh's mother, is primarily a stage actress who won a Tony for her Broadway debut in 1987's *Burn This.* Her films include *Compromising Positions* (with Mantegna), *In Coun-try,* and *Ethan Frome.*

Ben Kingsley, who plays Bruce Pandolfini, Josh's chess tutor, became an international star with his Oscar-winning portrayal of *Gandhi* in 1982. Born Krishna Banji, he was drawn to the theater while watching Shakespeare performed at Stratford-Upon-Avon, where, standing in the back of the hot theater, he became so en-grossed with what he saw onstage that he fainted!

Kingsley appeared in this movie just before his Oscar-nomi-nated performance as Best Supporting Actor in *Schindler's List.* His other films of note include *Turtle Diary,* a little-seen gem with Glenda Jackson, *Bugsy,* as gangster Meyer Lansky, *Sneakers, Dave,* as the Vice President of the United States, *Death and the Maiden,* and *Species.*

Laurence Fishburne, who plays the chess hustler Josh meets at the park, won an Oscar nomination for Best Actor for his portrayal of Ike Turner in *What's Love Got to Do With It?* Here, Josh's insistence that he be allowed to continue playing "street chess" with the hustler, even after Pandolfini forbids it, is touching, and a wise decision. Fishburne made his screen debut at twelve in *Cornbread, Earl and Me,* and his credits include *Apocalypse Now, Boyz N the Hood, Higher Learning, Bad Company,* and *Just Cause.* He then tackled the difficult role of Othello in another screen version of Shakespeare's classic.

Produced by Sydney Pollack, *Searching for Bobby Fischer* conveys a genuine understanding of the relationship between Josh and his parents as to how they will deal with his unusual and sometimes disturbing gift. Children will get to know a pair of caring, concerned parents who may have differences over how to raise their son but still share a deep concern for his well-being. Even if you don't know a pawn from a knight, you'll find this an exciting and poignant movie.

The Secret Life
of Walter Mitty

Category: Musical comedy. Starring Danny Kaye, Virginia Mayo,
Fay Bainter, Ann Rutherford, Boris Karloff, Thurston Hall, Florence
Bates. Screenplay by Ken Englund and Everett Freeman, based on
the story by James Thurber. 105 minutes. 1947. HBO Home Video.
Director: Norman Z. McLeod.
Suggested Age Group: 8 and older.

The Story

Based on a story James Thurber wrote in 1939, this
film focuses on chronic daydreamer Walter Mitty.
Working as a proofreader at a pulp fiction magazine,
he allows his dreams to go even further than the silly adventures
he edits. He can instantly transport himself to the deck of a sailing
ship in a raging storm; to the Old West, where he's a feared gunfighter known as the Perth Amboy Kid; or to the cockpit of a
British Spitfire fighter plane, shooting down an enemy aircraft. He
can become a surgeon performing a delicate operation, a conductor leading a symphony orchestra, or a Parisian milliner named
Anatole. In fact, we see seven characterizations in all.

Mitty's fantasy life doesn't sit well with his boss, nor the silly
woman he's supposed to marry but whom he doesn't really love.
Mitty's mother is also displeased. Mitty, ignoring them all, fixates
on his dream girl, who turns up in each fantasy and then in the
middle of a real-life jewel caper masterminded by a sinister crim-
inal. Soon Mitty is off on a series of wacky adventures, which
we're not sure are real or imagined, but which are far more exciting than anything Mitty dreams. His mother and fiancée think his
dreams have taken over his brain and send him to a psychiatrist,
but the doctor turns out to be the master jewel thief, who tries to
convince Mitty that his daydreams are nothing more than harmless fantasies.

Of course, Mitty manages to unravel everything in the end and,
after two hilarious scenes in which he disrupts a board meeting
at the magazine, he captures the thieves and wins his dream girl
at last.

Background: Danny Kaye was a unique talent, sort of a cross between Robin Williams and Michael Richards (Kramer on the *Seinfeld* TV series) but with his own combination of grace and limitless talent. You never know what to expect from one moment to the next in any Danny Kaye movie. He will break into song, do bizarre imitations, do a dance step in a style all his own, put on any accent, or make hilarious references to real-life situations.

Kaye was signed by Samuel Goldwyn, and perhaps because he was a star at an independent studio rather than one of the more established ones, his movie stardom never reached its full potential. Casting him proved difficult, because of his unique talents, but he did find some star vehicles, including *Hans Christian Andersen, Merry Andrew,* and *White Christmas.* He would later go on to achieve much greater fame as an international spokesman for UNICEF.

Though Goldwyn made him a film star, at heart Kaye loved performing before live audiences. After he began making movies, he'd make certain never to permit a single year to pass without his appearing on a stage. At the end of his one-man performances, Kaye would tell the audience "I'll let you in on a little secret: if you think you'll tire me out before I tire you out, think again. No one in the world enjoys hearing me entertain more than me."

The supporting cast of *The Secret Life of Walter Mitty* provides a cross section of some of Hollywood's busier character actors. Boris Karloff, who plays the psychiatrist who is really the jewel thief, had become famous for a role Bela Lugosi rejected because there was no dialogue. Little did he know that Frankenstein's creation would prove to be just as popular a screen monster as Dracula; to some extent, it typecast Karloff for the rest of his career.

Virginia Mayo, whose dream-girl character comes to life in the movie, had plenty of experience working opposite Kaye, having already costarred with him in *The Kid from Brooklyn.* She would also go on to make *A Song Is Born* with him the following year. Most of her movies were routine studio offerings, but she was a capable romantic foil for Danny Kaye and, in other movies, Bob Hope.

The Secret Life of Walter Mitty tells young viewers it's OK to be a dreamer. Sometimes the most gentle people can have the most exciting ways of looking at the world, even if their dreams occasionally cause havoc.

Seven Brides for
Seven Brothers

Category: Musical. Starring Howard Keel, Jane Powell, Russ
Tamblyn, Julie Newmeyer. Screenplay by Albert Hackett, Frances
Goodrich, and Dorothy Kingsley, from the story "The Sobbin'
Women" by Stephen Vincent Benét, suggested by Plutarch's *Lives*.
Music by Gene DePaul, lyrics by Johnny Mercer. 103 minutes.
1954. MGM/UA Home Video.
Director: Stanley Donen.
Suggested Age Group: 7 and older.

The Story

This is a rousing story, set in Oregon in 1850, about
Adam Pontabee, a fur trapper who comes to town
seeking a wife. He finds one quickly in a beautiful
woman named Milly, and he brings her back to his remote home
in the mountains, where he lives with his six loutish, love-starved
brothers. Though they are rough and uncivilized, they quickly
begin to learn manners from their new sister-in-law.

The brothers go to a barn-raising celebration during which
they both dance and stand up to the challenges from the men of
the town. Try as they might, they can't avoid getting into fights
with their rivals, and they return home to Milly, who dutifully
nurses their wounds. Taken with Milly's charms and female com-
panionship, they agree with all good intentions to kidnap six
girls from town to be their brides.

After they spirit the girls away, the brothers cause an avalanche
in a mountain pass near their home, leaving outraged townspeople behind for the winter. The six frightened women, reassured
by Milly, live separately from the men, cooped up in an adjoining
cabin. Over the long winter months, however, they grow restless
and increasingly attracted to the six brothers. By springtime, the
men from the town finally arrive to rescue the kidnapped
women, but it's too late. The women are hooked, and all six
marry the six brothers.

Background: Although this was one of the last movies made during MGM's domination of the musical genre, the musical num-

bers, including "Bless Your Beautiful Hide," "Wonderful, Wonderful Day," "Goin' Co'tin'," and "June Bride" are simply beautiful, while the "Barn-Raising Dance" is one of the liveliest, best-choreographed numbers ever captured on film.

Howard Keel, more familiar to younger audiences from his work on TV's *Dallas* in the seventies, worked his way up from his humble beginnings to a starring role in the movie version of 1950's *Annie Get Your Gun,* his first important movie role. His other memorable films include *Show Boat, Calamity Jane, Kiss Me Kate, Rose Marie, Jupiter's Darling,* and *Kismet.*

Jane Powell, who plays Milly, signed with MGM when she was just fifteen. Born Suzanne Burce in Portland, Oregon, she won an amateur contest on a radio show, and her prize was an MGM contract and a new name. After films such as *Song of the Open Road, Holiday in Mexico,* and *Three Darling Daughters,* she got her chance at stardom with *Royal Wedding.* Though the film was originally planned to star Fred Astaire and June Allyson, when Allyson became pregnant Judy Garland was then proposed for the starring role. But, as it turned out, Garland was physically and emotionally unable to do the film, so the studio turned to Jane Powell, who subsequently became a star.

After *Seven Brides for Seven Brothers,* undoubtedly her greatest film, Powell played Debbie Reynolds' sister in *Athena,* followed by her last musical at MGM, *Hit the Deck,* in 1955. This enchanting musical star has had a relatively short career, perhaps influenced by the decline in popularity of lavish musicals. Her last film was the forgettable *Enchanted Island* in 1958. She had a comeback of sorts in the eighties on the TV sitcom *Growing Pains.*

Julie Newmeyer, who plays Dorcas, one of the six women brought to the isolated cabin, later changed her name to Julie Newmar and became well known as Catwoman on the *Batman* TV series. Although her only other films of note are *Li'l Abner* and *Mackenna's Gold,* her name came back into the public consciousness in the 1995 comedy *To Wong Foo, Thanks for Everything, Julie Newmar.*

Russ Tamblyn, one of the seven brothers, is best known as the athletic, engaging dancer-actor of musical films such as *West Side Story* and *Tom Thumb,* although he won an Oscar nomination for Best Supporting Actor for his dramatic role in 1957's *Peyton Place.* In the late eighties he appeared with his *West Side Story* costar Richard Beymer in the strange, slightly eerie David Lynch TV series *Twin Peaks.* The sequence in *Seven Brides for Seven Brothers* in which he dances with an ax—jumping over the handle, then back again, as well as dancing on his hands—is one of the highlights of the movie's brilliant choreography.

Director Stanley Donen was a onetime dancer who was in the chorus of the 1940 Broadway musical *Pal Joey.* Besides codirecting (with Gene Kelly) classics such as *On the Town, Royal Wedding,* and *Singin' in the Rain,* Donen made *Funny Face, The Pajama Game,* and *Damn Yankees.* Among his nonmusicals are the stylish *Arabesque,* the delightful romantic comedy *Two for the Road,* and the hilarious *Bedazzled.* Another of his underrated comedies is *Movie Movie.*

Seven Brides for Seven Brothers was nominated for Best Picture but had the misfortune of running against *On the Waterfront,* which won the Oscar that year.

It is a measure of the greatness of *Seven Brides for Seven Brothers* that, unlike so many movie musicals, it was written directly for the screen; indeed, a Broadway stage version of the musical with Debbie Boone flopped, and a TV series retitled *Here Come the Brides,* starring then teen heartthrob Bobby Sherman was also short-lived.

This was one of Hollywood's last great studio-produced musicals, and its glow remains magical more than forty years later.

The Shaggy Dog

Category: Comedy. Starring Fred MacMurray, Jean Hagen, Tommy Kirk, Annette Funicello, Tim Considine, Kevin Corcoran, Cecil Kellaway. Screenplay by Bill Walsh and Lillie Hayward, suggested by the novel *The Hound of Florence* by Felix Salten. 104 minutes. 1959. Walt Disney Home Video.
Director: Charles Barton.
Suggested Age Group: 6 and older.

The Story   Fred MacMurray plays Wilson Daniels, a mailman who is allergic to dogs, though his wife and two sons feel otherwise. "Dogs don't like mailmen because sometimes they bring bad news," his wife explains. "Animals sense those things, you know."

Their older son, Wilby, is seen tinkering in the basement with a homemade missile interceptor (remember, this was filmed during the height of the Cold War), which goes off accidentally and nearly destroys their house. The rocket soars through the room into outer space, leaving a gaping hole in the roof.

The Danielses' new next-door neighbor, an assistant museum curator, has a beautiful seventeen-year-old daughter named Francesca with a pet sheep dog. After Wilby and his friend visit the neighbor's home and meet Francesca, Wilby wanders into a back room at the local museum and discovers a strange exhibit about the Borgias, an Italian family in the Middle Ages, who practiced an ancient art called shape shifting, borrowing other creatures' bodies. A friendly old professor explains the ancient practice to Wilby, who then accidentally carries off an ancient ring harboring a spell that transforms him into a large, shaggy dog exactly like his neighbor's.

Wilby, who retains the ability to speak, finds the old professor again and explains that it was the Borgia ring that turned him into a sheep dog. The professor informs him that an act of heroism can break the spell.

In his altered state, Wilby makes his way into his new neighbor's home, where he quickly learns that the curator is really a spy who's trying to steal plans for a new undersea hydrogen missile. Wilby keeps changing back and forth from form to form, and while in his canine form, Wilby convinces his father he's been transformed into a dog and thwarts the spy's plans, then changes back into human form. In the end, Francesca's dog gets the credit for capturing the spy.

There is a running gag throughout the film featuring a policeman, played by veteran character actor James Westerfield, who thinks he sees a talking dog but can't believe his eyes. It is timed for laughs, just as the boy changes back into a shaggy dog, and it will remind young viewers that underneath all that fur is Wilby.

Background: *The Shaggy Dog,* the Disney studio's first live-action comedy, unfolds slowly, with decidedly understated comedy.

This was the first of several effective light comedies Fred MacMurray would do for Disney in the 1960s. By the time he made *The Shaggy Dog,* the tall leading man from Kankakee, Illinois, had been making movies for a quarter century. Already on his résumé were movies like the film noir classic *Double Indemnity, The Egg and I, The Caine Mutiny,* and *The Far Horizons,* in which he played explorer Meriwether Lewis. He also reached new audiences during the twelve-year run of the popular TV sitcom *My Three Sons.*

Jean Hagen, who plays MacMurray's wife, Frieda, is best known for her unforgettable role in 1952's *Singin' in the Rain* as Lina Lamont, the high-pitched, empty-headed silent movie queen who can't make the transition to talking pictures. She also played Danny Thomas's wife in the TV series *Make Room for Daddy.*

This was the second film in the relatively short career of Annette Funicello, best known as the most famous of the Mouseketeers on *The Mickey Mouse Club* in the mid-fifties. By the time she appeared here as Allison, one of Wilby's friends, she had grown too old to be a Mouseketeer. She would, however, go on to make a slew of sixties beach party movies with Frankie Avalon.

The Shaggy Dog is an effective, unpretentious comedy with a pacing all its own. The special effects—which show Wilby changing into a dog, then losing his disguise at precisely the wrong moment—will have young viewers both laughing and nervously anticipating his fate at the same time. Of course, it's all so lighthearted and harmless that you won't have to worry about stressed-out kids or nightmares. Here's one shaggy dog story they'll love.

Sounder

Category: Drama. Starring Paul Winfield, Cicely Tyson, Kevin Hooks, James Best, Carmen Matthews, Janet MacLachlan. Screenplay by Lonnie Elder III, from the novel by William H. Armstrong. 105 minutes. 1972. Rated G. Fox Home Video.
Director: Martin Ritt.
Suggested Age Group: 7 and older.

The Story   In rural Louisiana in 1933, Nathan Lee Morgan, a poor sharecropper, is trying to make ends meet. He and his wife, Rebecca, have several children, the oldest of whom is David Lee, a curious student who is mature beyond his years.

Desperate, Nathan Lee steals some food for the family and is arrested by the sheriff. While taking him away, the sheriff's deputy takes a potshot at Sounder, the family's pet dog, but Nathan Lee kicks his shotgun just in time, so the dog is merely wounded.

Soon Nathan Lee is tried, convicted, and sentenced to a year at hard labor on a work farm, leaving David Lee to help his mother keep the farm going. Somehow, everyone in the family pulls together. But David Lee misses his father and is determined to visit him. So, given directions from a friendly neighbor, he sets off with Sounder to find his father.

David Lee learns his father has been transferred to another prison camp farther away. Undeterred, he continues his search. Along the way he meets a friendly schoolteacher who offers him shelter and a place in her class. She notices his love of books and his curiosity, and after David Lee returns home, his search having been in vain, he considers an offer to spend the following school year with the teacher.

After injuring his leg in a dynamite blast, Nathan Lee's sentence is shortened and he is finally allowed to return home. As *Sounder* ends, the family is making plans for David Lee to spend the coming year living with the schoolteacher.

Background: Shot entirely on location in rural Louisiana, replicating authentically the look of the Depression, *Sounder* offers a story so simple, so free of any self-conscious attempts to be noble, that it achieves a nobility and dignity far beyond any film of this type. As for Sounder, he doesn't do anything miraculous or even special; he's just a boy's best friend.

Though a small-budget film with no real stars, *Sounder* was nominated for a Best Picture Oscar. Unfortunately, against *The Godfather* it had little chance. Paul Winfield and Cicely Tyson were nominated as Best Actor and Best Actress for their roles in the film, but also lost out to the competition.

By the time he starred in *Sounder,* Paul Winfield, who was raised in the tough Watts section of Los Angeles, had made only three films, most notably *Brother John* with Sidney Poitier. His subsequent movies would not match the quality of *Sounder,* though they did include the box-office hits *Star Trek II: The Wrath of Khan* and *The Terminator.* Most of his later work has been on television, including a portrayal of Martin Luther King, Jr., in the miniseries *King.*

Cicely Tyson's career was at a similar point when she portrayed the mother in *Sounder.* She'd already appeared in *The Comedians,* with Richard Burton and Elizabeth Taylor, as well as in *The Heart Is a Lonely Hunter;* she would reteam with Winfield five years later in *A Hero Ain't Nothin' But a Sandwich.* The New York native has since been seen mostly on TV, beginning with the acclaimed *East Side West Side* with George C. Scott, and moving on to *The Autobiography of Miss Jane Pittman, Roots,* and the courtroom drama series *Sweet Justice.*

Sounder was perhaps the best film Martin Ritt ever directed. That's saying a lot, considering he made *The Long Hot Summer, Hud,* and *Hombre,* the last two among Paul Newman's most memorable films. He also directed *The Spy Who Came in from the Cold, The Great White Hope, Conrack,* and *Norma Rae,* which won Sally Field her first Oscar. Ritt, a survivor of the McCarthy-era blacklisting, also directed *The Front,* the Woody Allen movie about a writer fronting for a blacklisted colleague. His last film was 1987's *Nuts,* starring Barbra Streisand.

There is a humanity about *Sounder* which surely emanated from the original material and from Martin Ritt, who often directed socially conscious plays and films. *Sounder* provides a beautiful glimpse into a distant past, a look at a courageous family determined to survive.

The Spirit of St. Louis

Category: Drama. Starring James Stewart, Murray Hamilton, Patricia Smith, Marc Connelly. Screenplay by Billy Wilder and Wendell Mayes, based on the book by Charles A. Lindbergh. Includes music by Franz Waxman. 138 minutes. 1957. Warner Bros. Home Video.
Director: Billy Wilder.
Suggested Age Group: 9 and older.

The Story This is the true story of the famous solo flight of Charles A. Lindbergh from Roosevelt Field, New York, to LeBourget Field in Paris in May 1927. The film begins as the lanky flyer tries to get some sleep in a Long Island hotel the night before his famous flight. But his anxiety and the noise from the reporters' typewriters keep him awake all night, and he thinks back to events in his life.

Thus begins a series of flashbacks to Lindbergh's early years as a flyer, to the time he had to fly through a snowstorm carrying mail, was forced to ditch his plane, and complete his delivery by train. He eventually gets backing from a bank and a newspaper in St. Louis—hence the name of his signature airplane—and then has to find something to fly.

At first, Lindbergh encounters a potential manufacturer in New York, who insists he has the right to choose his own pilot; after that he treks out to San Diego, where he finds a company eager to build the plane for him to fly.

Tests in the desert go well, but just as he is about to embark for New York, news comes of two French flyers who are already en route over the Atlantic. But Lindbergh flies to New York anyway, and when the French flyers are reported overdue, he takes off on his own flight.

Just before he departs that fateful May morning, "the Lone Eagle," as he was known, finds he needs a mirror for the cockpit. He obtains one easily enough from a woman waiting in the crowd who volunteers her own from her purse. After affixing the mirror to the dashboard with a mechanic's chewing gum, he takes off in a light rain, just missing some trees and dragging an electrical wire.

Then this wonderful movie begins in earnest. Director Billy Wilder puts us in the cockpit with Lindbergh, as he spends the next thirty-odd hours trying to stay awake. Later, over the North Atlantic, he sees an iceberg and momentarily considers it a potential landing spot so he can get some sleep.

Then, shockingly, Lindbergh nearly loses his plane when he dozes off and heads into a spin, fighting the ice that weighs down his plane. Throughout his long solo flight, Lindy thinks back to earlier times in his life, including the time he traded a motorcycle for his first plane, landed at an army base for training just as his beat-up heap fell apart, and took passengers up for ten-minute spins in his biplane for a few dollars.

Every four hours, Lindbergh changes gas tanks to keep *The Spirit of St. Louis*'s balance intact, and after approaching Paris, he suddenly begins to lose altitude, realizing that he'd switched to an empty tank. Of course, he makes it safely, but this scene serves as one last reminder of the dangers the real Lindbergh faced and the courage he displayed. The accolades pour in as thousands come out to welcome him in the film's final sequence.

Background: The amazing achievement of the movie is its success in making the viewer feel as though he's inside the cockpit with Lindbergh. You feel the claustrophobia, the vastness of the ocean, the hour-by-hour droning of the engines, and the overwhelming sense of history in the making.

For Jimmy Stewart, portraying Lindbergh was just one of an incredible number of memorable roles unmatched by almost any other actor of his generation.

James Stewart's career began when he and his roommate, Henry Fonda, found work on the New York stage in the mid-1930s. He began in movies in 1935's *The Murder Man,* and after unforgettable roles in *Mr. Smith Goes to Washington* and *Destry Rides Again,* he won an Oscar for Best Supporting Actor in 1940's *The Philadelphia Story.* He was superb in several Hitchcock classics, including *Rear Window, Rope, The Man Who Knew Too Much,* and *Vertigo,* and in Westerns too, including *Cheyenne Autumn, Carbine Williams,* and *How the West Was Won.* Of course, his versatility also allowed him to succeed in films such as *Flight of the Phoenix, The F.B.I. Story, Strategic Air Command,* and his own favorite, *It's a Wonderful Life,* the greatest Christmas movie of them all.

The Spirit of St. Louis also boasts a marvelous score by Franz Waxman, the German Jewish refugee whose other notable scores include those for *A Christmas Story, Boom Town, The Philadelphia Story, Suspicion, Woman of the Year, Destination Tokyo, Sunset Boulevard, Stalag 17,* and *The Nun's Story.*

Although *The Spirit of St. Louis* was nominated for a Best Special Effects Oscar, the movie has a simple look to it. There is nothing fancy here, just a sense of adventure and risk, undertaken by a hero meeting the greatest challenge of his life.

Stand and Deliver

Category: Drama. Starring Edward James Olmos, Lou Diamond Phillips, Andy Garcia, Rosana de Soto. Screenplay by Tom Musca and Ramon Menendez. 105 minutes. 1988. Rated PG. Warner Bros. Home Video.
Director: Ramon Menendez.
Suggested Age Group: 11 and older.

 The Story This is the true story of Jaime Escalante, a remarkable man who, when he went to teach computer science at Garfield High School in South Central Los Angeles, was startled to find that there were no computers and that he'd been assigned to teach mathematics. His students, mostly Chicano, were inattentive and listless. Some were troublemakers and gang members. But slowly and forcefully, he got them to rediscover their self-esteem, to feel *gana* (the Spanish word for "desire"), and to begin to love learning.

Over the course of the school year, Escalante institutes a rigorous program of study, convincing his students to attend special classes on holidays, weekends, and even over the summer, all with the goal of passing standardized tests that no Latino students from that school had ever passed. Encouraged by their responsiveness, Escalante then begins teaching his students college-level calculus.

When every one of his students passes the difficult standardized math test, their integrity is doubted. Despite his vigorous protests to the Mexican-American examination official, the class is forced to take a second examination to prove no one had cheated. As expected, everyone passes again, kicking off a series of consecutive years during which an ever-increasing number of Escalante's students passed the examination and received college credit.

Background: When Oscar time rolled around, Edward James Olmos was nominated for Best Actor and Lou Diamond Phillips for Best Supporting Actor. For his brilliant film portrayal, Olmos stood with a stoop, shaved the top of his head, and seemed to age twenty years. The soft-spoken, dignified actor was first recognized in the late eighties for his leading role on the popular *Miami Vice* TV series. He also appeared in *The Ballad of Gregorio Cortez, Zoot Suit, Wolfen, Triumph of the Spirit, A Talent for the Game, American Me,* and *Mi Familia.*

Lou Diamond Phillips, who portrays Olmos's most reluctant but eventually most gifted student, was born in the Philippines, and is of Filipino, Native American, Irish, Scottish, Hawaiian, and Hispanic descent. His best-known role is that of the late rock star Richie Valens in *La Bamba.* His other notable films have been few, but they include *Young Guns* and its sequel, *Young Guns II.*

Andy Garcia is powerful in his few scenes toward the end of *Stand and Deliver,* playing a supervisor for the company issuing the examination. This movie came early in the Cuban-born actor's career, before he reached mainstream success in such movies as *The Untouchables, Eight Million Ways to Die, Black Rain, Internal Affairs, The Godfather Part III, Jennifer 8,* and *When a Man Loves a Woman.*

The inspirational value of *Stand and Deliver* is obvious. The students' increase in self-esteem and fierce pride in their achievements is heartwarming, and we see Escalante as a true American hero. Students and their parents will both care and be entertained.

Stand by Me

Category: Drama. Starring Wil Wheaton, River Phoenix, Corey Feldman, Jerry O'Connell, Kiefer Sutherland, Richard Dreyfuss, Casey Siemaszko, John Cusack. Screenplay by Raynold Gideon, Bruce A. Evans, based on the novella *The Body* by Stephen King. 87 minutes. 1986. Rated R. Columbia Home Video.
Director: Rob Reiner.
Suggested Age Group: 12 and older.

The Story   Set in the ordinary town of Castle Rock, Oregon, in the hot summer of 1959, this is a coming-of-age story about four twelve-year-old boys on the verge of junior high school, just before they discover girls. Told in a narrative flashback by Gordie, one of the boys, this is a look at an innocent time and place, when songs such as "Rockin' Robin," "Lollipop," and "Whispering Bells" filled the airwaves. The boys, whose home life is not exactly ideal, trek across usually deserted railroad tracks singing the lyrics to the TV Western *Have Gun Will Travel*.

One day, word comes that the body of a young man from the town has been sighted at a remote location, and the boys set out to find it. Their rivals for that dubious goal are a gang of older, more disorderly boys, headed by a bully named Ace Merrill and including one of the younger boys' older brothers.

As the boys camp out under the stars, Gordie, Chris, Teddy, and Vern exchange observations on life, punctuated and put into perspective by Gordie's narration, speaking from the present.

Finally the boys find the body, just as the older boys arrive, and Ace threatens to kill Chris with a knife, only to be saved by Gordie. It is a small adventure, to be sure, but one in which the boys learn lessons about life—particularly that the world is not so safe and innocent after all.

Background: Of course, there are some unintended ironies at work here, since one of the boys, Chris, is played by River Phoenix, who would die seven years later of a drug overdose, just as he was becoming a big star. His brief career included *Explorers, Running on Empty,* which earned him an Oscar nomination for Best Supporting Actor, *Indiana Jones and the Last Crusade, My Own Private Idaho,* and *Sneakers.*

Wil Wheaton, who plays the narrator, future writer Gordie Lechance, has made only a few films, including *The Buddy System, The Curse,* and *December.* Stoic and mature, he gives an effective, laid-back performance as a boy who loves storytelling—a portent of Gordie's destiny. Wheaton went on to play Wesley Crusher, a regular character on the popular TV series *Star Trek: The Next Generation.*

Rob Reiner had directed only two movies prior to this, *This Is Spinal Tap,* the brilliant rock documentary spoof, and *The Sure Thing,* but he has become the consummate director, helming such projects as *Throw Mama from the Train, When Harry Met Sally, Misery,* and *A Few Good Men.* As an actor, he shot to stardom on TV as Mike Stivic on the watershed situation comedy *All in the Family.* He has appeared recently in *Bye, Bye Love,* and his other credits include *Enter Laughing,* which was about how his father, director Carl Reiner, broke into show business, *Where's Poppa?,* and *Postcards from the Edge.*

Stand by Me remains one of the finest coming-of-age movies of the eighties. Parents should be cautioned about the generous use of obscene language that boys on the verge of manhood are wont to use, which earned the film an R rating. Nevertheless, the performances are first-rate, the evocation of the 1950s is wonderful, and the emphasis on self-reliance and independence make it very relevant for young viewers.

The Swan Princess

Category: Animated. Starring the voices of John Cleese, Sandy Duncan, Jack Palance, Steven Wright, Dakin Matthews, Howard McGillin, Michelle Nicastro. Screenplay by Brian Nissen, based on a story by Richard Rich and Brian Nissen and the ballet *Swan Lake*. 90 minutes. 1994. Rated G. New Line Pictures.
Director: Richard Rich.
Suggested Age Group: 6 and older.

The Story This is a gorgeously animated fairy tale about King William (the voice of Dakin Matthews) and Queen Uberta (Sandy Duncan), who have separate realms but are determined to unite by urging their children, who are friends, to marry.

The children, Prince Derek (Howard McGillin) and Princess Odette (Michelle Nicastro), spend summers playing, arguing, competing, and eventually falling in love. But when Derek tells Odette that he wants to marry her solely for her beauty, she rejects him, her love notwithstanding.

Meanwhile, Rothbart the Enchanter (Jack Palance), who has been banished from the kingdom, vows revenge, promising he will someday take over King William's realm. He kidnaps the princess and puts a spell on her, turning her into a swan whose human form can only emerge when the moonlight shines upon her wings.

The rest of the story concerns the prince's struggle to find her and proclaim his love, as well as to defeat the evil enchanter who, at the end of the movie, turns himself into a hideous monster the prince must fight.

Along the way, the princess befriends a helpful turtle (Stephen Wright), a delightful frog who thinks he is a French prince (John Cleese), and a puffin (Steve Vinovich), who all try to help her in her plight.

Background: Director Richard Rich, who left Disney to form his own company to do films such as this, took eight years to make this animated masterpiece, going through 12 drafts of the screenplay, more than 200,000 hand-painted cels, and some 880 different hues.

The characters offer the desirable combination of well fleshed-out images and endearing personalities, evocative of the best Disney characters. Even if you've never heard of the ballet *Swan Lake,* you will be enchanted by this dazzling fairy tale, with characters who seem much more real than the usual animated cutouts. Children will adore their human qualities, as well as the film's message that love—true love—conquers evil.

Jack Palance, who provides the voice of Rothbart, capped a long screen career with a Best Supporting Actor Oscar in 1992 for *City Slickers.* He'd been nominated in 1952 for *Sudden Fear* and again the following year for *Shane,* when he was still using his real first name, Walter. (He has yet to use his real last name, however. It's Palahnuik.) His other credits of note include *The Big Knife, Barabbas,* and *The Professionals.*

John Cleese, who provides the voice of the frog Jean-Bob, is perhaps best known as one of the members of the Monty Python Flying Circus comedy group. He earned an Oscar nomination for Best Original Screenplay for *A Fish Called Wanda*, in which he also costarred. As an actor, his best films include *And Now For Something Completely Different* and *Time Bandits.*

Sandy Duncan, who lends her voice to Queen Uberta, is a familiar face on TV and on Broadway, where her shows have included *Peter Pan* and *The Boyfriend.* She starred on TV in *Funny Face* and *The Hogan Family,* and (for better or worse) she hosted the original tapes of *Barney and the Backyard Gang* when the now-popular TV series was still available only on video.

The Swan Princess, a film which will delight children and mesmerize their parents, belongs in any family movie library. Parents of very young viewers should note that the scene in which the evil enchanter changes into a hideous flying dragon may be a bit frightening to some children. But the fight between the creature and Prince Derek is brief, with the predictable and hoped-for outcome.

Swiss Family Robinson

Category: Adventure. Starring Sir John Mills, Dorothy McGuire, James MacArthur, Janet Munro, Sessue Hayakawa, Tommy Kirk, Kevin Corcoran, Cecil Parker. Screenplay by Lowell S. Hawley, based on the novel by Johann Wyss. 128 minutes. 1960. Walt Disney Home Video.
Director: Ken Annakin.
Suggested Age Group: 6 and older.

The Story

A family survives a shipwreck in the South Seas late in the eighteenth century, and, after salvaging supplies from the ship, they set up a new life on a beautiful tropical island. The only apparent danger comes from a wandering tiger and marauding pirates. Curious and hearty, the two older sons, Fritz and Ernst, set sail to explore the island.

Their adventure begins in earnest when they rescue a young captive from the pirates and make their way back to the family compound. En route, Fritz and Ernst discover that the captive isn't really a cabin boy, as they'd thought, but a young woman in disguise, whose grandfather had to be left behind in the hands of the pirates. The trio returns to the family compound just in time for Christmas.

Eventually, the pirates find the family and a big battle ensues. The family is outnumbered but well prepared with booby traps, coconut bombs, falling logs, and cascading boulders—all of which hold off the pirates for a time. But just when the pirates begin to turn the tide and the family's doom looks to be sealed, a warship, with cannons booming, sails into the bay and chases the pirates away. As luck would have it, it is the ship captained by the girl's grandfather. Later, it is decided that one boy will return to England to complete his studies, while his brother will remain with the family and their new friend to continue life on the beautiful island.

Background: One can't blame the family for deciding to stay on the island after their rescue, since the movie was filmed on Tobago, one of the most beautiful places on earth. *Swiss Family Robinson* is the fulfillment of many childhood fantasies about living with one's family on a beautiful tropical island. No school, no teachers; just lots of warm weather, sand, family, and adventure.

Sir John Mills, who plays the family's fearless leader, is one of the most revered actors of stage and screen. His films include *Goodbye, Mr. Chips; Great Expectations; Hobson's Choice; Above Us the Waves; The Chalk Garden; King Rat;* and *Ryan's Daughter,* for which he won an Oscar for Best Supporting Actor.

James MacArthur, who plays the older brother, Fritz, is the adopted son of Helen Hayes—the "First Lady of the American Theater"—and playwright Charles MacArthur, who cowrote *The Front Page.* The same year he made *Swiss Family Robinson,* he appeared in Disney's *Kidnapped,* and would go on to costar in the underappreciated Cold War thriller *The Bedford Incident.* Of course, he's best known as Jack Lord's sidekick, Dano, on the TV show *Hawaii Five-0.*

The interplay between the actors and the animals in *Swiss Family Robinson*—including a zebra, baby elephant, ostrich, and faithful dogs, along with the family members' irrepressible spirit—makes this a first-rate family adventure with a rousing spirit.

Those Magnificent Men in Their Flying Machines

Category: Comedy. Starring Stuart Whitman, Sarah Miles, Robert Morley, James Fox, Alberto Sordi, Gert Frobe, Jean-Pierre Cassel, Terry-Thomas, Benny Hill, Red Skelton, Irina Demick. Screenplay by Jack Davies, Ken Annakin. 132 minutes. 1965. Fox Home Video.
Director: Ken Annakin.
Suggested Age Group: 7 and older.

 In 1910, a newspaper owner in London sponsors an air race between London and Paris, and the best flyers from Europe, the United States, and Japan arrive to participate.

The newspaper owner's daughter is about to be engaged to a British flyer in the race, but meets a cocky American hopeful to whom she is attracted. Other entrants in the race include another Englishman who tries to sabotage his competitors' planes, a stiff German flyer, and a French pilot who keeps meeting different women, all of whom look alike.

The race finally begins, with some amazing visual hijinks and misadventures, as inevitably the pilots fly onward toward their destination near the Eiffel Tower in Paris.

Background: This movie takes a while to get off the ground, but hang on during the early plot exposition and introduction of the characters. Once the pilots get into their rickety airplanes and into the air over the English Channel, it becomes a rousing adventure with a real sense of the thrill, danger, and joy of flying in those primitive aircraft. The duration of the winning flight, twenty-five hours and eleven minutes, is punctuated by two flyers downed in the English Channel, another landing in the field outside a nunnery, and another daredevil placing his plane and himself in jeopardy by attempting a daring midair rescue.

Sarah Miles, who plays Patricia Rawnsley, daughter of the newspaper tycoon, made her screen debut in 1962's *Term of Trial*. With her appearance opposite Laurence Olivier, the film propelled her to stardom in such movies as *The Servant, Blow-*

Up, Ryan's Daughter, The Man Who Loved Cat Dancing, The Sailor Who Fell from Grace with the Sea, and *Hope and Glory.*

James Fox, who plays Richard Mays, a top British aviator in the race, is the older brother of actor and look-alike Edward Fox. In 1973 he left acting to become a minister, then returned and wrote a book about his experiences. His films of note include *The Lavender Hill Mob, King Rat, The Chase,* and *Thoroughly Modern Millie.* More recently, Fox appeared in *Patriot Games* and *The Remains of the Day.*

Terry-Thomas, who plays Percy Ware-Armitage, the English flyer who tries to wreck his opponents' aircraft, was one of the most delightful screen comics of his time. His mustache and gap tooth were his trademarks in *It's a Mad Mad Mad Mad World, Strange Bedfellows, Those Daring Young Men in Their Jaunty Jalopies,* and the forgotten but delightful little comedy *A Matter of WHO.*

When Robert Morley, who plays newspaper tycoon Lord Rawnsley, was filming *Cromwell,* he was addressed by costar Richard Harris as "Sir Robert." "My dear boy," replied the delightfully pompous Morley, "that is premature. . . but likely." Morley would never be knighted, but his long list of memorable movies includes *The Story of Gilbert and Sullivan, The African Queen, Beat the Devil, Around the World in 80 Days, Nine Hours to Rama,* and *The Great Muppet Caper.*

Stuart Whitman, who plays Orville Newton, the American aviator, has been mostly a B actor despite earning an Oscar nomination for Best Actor in 1961 for *The Mark.* His other films include *When Worlds Collide* and *Murder, Inc.*

Those Magnificent Men in Their Flying Machines is a breathtaking escapist romp, featuring a gaggle of sixties stars having the time of their lives. But the real stars, of course, are the period-authentic airplanes, which are amazingly graceful, despite their primitive design. Children will love the movie's colorful sense of adventure and its engaging cast.

Three Godfathers

Category: Drama. Starring John Wayne, Harry Carey, Jr., Pedro Armendariz, Ward Bond, Ben Johnson, Mildred Natwick, Jane Darwell. Screenplay by Laurence Stallings and Frank S. Nugent, based on the story by Peter B. Kyne. 105 minutes. 1948. MGM Home Video.
Director: John Ford.
Suggested Age Group: 10 and older.

The Story A trio of desperados robs a bank in a small Western town, appropriately named Welcome, near the Mexican border. They flee into the desert, pursued by the town marshal. Along the way, they find a woman who dies in childbirth, leaving the infant in their care. Naturally, this event changes the men, who are determined to save the baby and bring it back to civilization. Their lives and perspectives on right and wrong are drastically altered by the responsibility of caring for their tiny charge.

Background: After years of toiling away in forgettable B Westerns, John Wayne made his breakthrough movie in 1939's *Stagecoach*, directed by John Ford, who would become a lifelong friend. The duo went on to make many movies together, including *The Long Voyage Home, The Quiet Man,* and *The Wings of Eagles.*

But it was in the Western genre that the director and actor made their marks together. *Three Godfathers* is just one of their great collaborations, along with *She Wore a Yellow Ribbon, The Searchers,* and *Rio Grande.* No other actor was more closely associated with the Western genre than was John Wayne, and no other director would master that movie form as would John Ford. *Three Godfathers,* Wayne's ninety-ninth film, by far the least-known Wayne-Ford collaboration, was made around the middle of Wayne's career, after memorable films such as *Tall in the Saddle, Back to Bataan,* and *Red River,* and preceding *She Wore a Yellow Ribbon, The High and the Mighty,* and *The Man Who Shot Liberty Valance,* all part of the greatest and most legendary screen career in movie history. John Wayne would finally win a Best Actor Oscar in 1969 for *True Grit,* beating out some stiff competition that year from Dustin Hoffman and Jon Voight, both in *Midnight Cowboy,* as well as from Peter O'Toole and Richard Burton.

Costar Pedro Armendariz had just worked with Wayne and Ford in *Fort Apache.* A veteran of many Mexican movies, his other notable role was in his last film, *From Russia with Love,* in which he played James Bond's ally, Kerim Bay.

Although in general *Three Godfathers* is a heartwarming story about the transformation of bank robbers into keepers of the most precious treasure in the world, there is one scene that may disturb some young viewers. Armendariz, hobbled by a broken leg and unable to continue his trek across the desert, shoots himself, content in the knowledge that Wayne has the baby safely tucked in his arms and is pressing on. His suicide takes place off-camera, but some parents may want to warn impressionable children.

Three Godfathers was dedicated to the memory of Harry Carey, Sr., John Ford's first Western star. The third member of the outlaw band was played by Harry Carey, Jr., who had appeared with Wayne in *Red River* the year before and would reteam with Wayne and Ford in *She Wore a Yellow Ribbon* and *Rio Grande.*

The other prominent member of the cast was Ward Bond, one of the most durable character actors in Hollywood history. A drinking buddy of Ford's, he first worked with the director and a young Wayne in 1929's football *movie Salute.* Bond, in fact, had played football at USC with Wayne, where Ford found them in the late twenties and convinced them to try acting. While TV viewers of the fifties remember Bond for his popular role as the wagon master Major Seth Adams on *Wagon Train,* his films ranged from *Dead End* to *Dodge City, Gone With the Wind* to *The Grapes of Wrath, It's a Wonderful Life,* and, at the end of his life, *Rio Bravo.* In all, he appeared in more than 200 movies.

Ben Johnson, who has a small role as one of the deputies in the posse, would go on to win a Best Supporting Actor Oscar for *The Last Picture Show* in 1971 as "Sam the Lion." A frequent costar in Wayne and Ford films, he had doubled for Wayne in earlier movies. Johnson's other memorable movies include *Shane, She Wore a Yellow Ribbon, The Getaway,* and *Dillinger.*

Director John Ford had made Westerns as far back as 1917's *Straight Shooting. Young Mr. Lincoln, My Darling Clementine, The*

Informer, The Grapes of Wrath, and *How Green Was My Valley* are just a few of the movies which solidified his place in the pantheon of great American directors. He understood his characters and their conflicts with society in a way that allowed him, unlike any other director, to capture his singular vision of American history.

Winton C. Hoch and Charles Boyle's outstanding cinematography, in glorious Technicolor, brilliantly displays Wayne etched against the Western sky, making his screen presence seem larger than life.

Corny? Sure, just a bit. Sentimental? To the hilt. After all, this picturesque and touching film is one of Hollywood's unsung gems, sure to delight family audiences. And to add to it all, the climax of the movie comes just at Christmastime!

To Kill a Mockingbird

Category: Drama. Starring Gregory Peck, Mary Badham, Phillip Alford, Rosemary Murphy, Robert Duvall, Brock Peters. Screenplay by Horton Foote, based on the novel by Harper Lee. Music by Elmer Bernstein. 129 minutes. 1962. Black and white. MCA Home Video.
Director: Robert Mulligan.
Suggested Age Group: 12 and older.

 Set in Alabama during the Depression, *To Kill a Mockingbird* tells the story of Atticus Finch, lawyer and gentle, noble widower father of two. His life is turned upside down when he defends a black man accused of raping a white woman.

Narrated in retrospect by the now grown-up "Scout" Finch, Atticus's precocious daughter, the story focuses on the children's perceptions formed as their father stands up for what he knows is right.

Background: The phrase "to kill a mockingbird" refers to Atticus Finch's father's admonition never to kill a mockingbird, which provides sweet music. The metaphor extends to Atticus's choice to defend a black man. Most of the small town's residents are all too eager to presume his client's guilt, but Atticus, feeling in his heart that the man is innocent, cannot stand by and allow an unjust lynching.

Gregory Peck once said that an actor is lucky to have one or two great roles in his career. This movie, along with *The Guns of Navarone, The Big Country, Spellbound, Mirage, Cape Fear, On the Beach,* and *The Boys From Brazil* are more great films than most actors even dream about making. The part of Atticus Finch afforded Peck the chance to deliver his Lincolnesque performance as a man who makes an unpopular choice in a small southern town, a place where a black man has virtually no chance of justice.

Peck's thirty-third movie found him in the role he called the most well-rounded character he ever portrayed. Hollywood obviously agreed, since he won an Academy Award as Best Actor for this role, beating out some of the stiffest competition of all time: Jack Lemmon for *Days of Wine and Roses,* Marcello Mastroianni for *Divorce—Italian Style,* Peter O'Toole for *Lawrence of Arabia,* and Burt Lancaster for *Birdman of Alcatraz.*

Horton Foote's adapted screenplay won him an Oscar, and Mary Badham won a nomination for Best Supporting Actress for portraying Scout. It took a titanic performance by Patty Duke for *The Miracle Worker* to deny her the prize.

Robert Duvall made his movie debut in *To Kill a Mockingbird* as the mysterious Boo Radley. Ahead lay memorable roles in *The Godfather; The Great Northfield, Minnesota Raid,* as Jesse James; *The Seven Percent Solution; Network;* his Oscar for Best Actor for *Tender Mercies;* and *Colors.*

Director Robert Mulligan has made several notable movies, including *Fear Strikes Out, Up the Down Staircase,* and *Summer of '42.*

Parents should be advised that there is a frightening coda to the movie, in which the children are attacked in the woods at night. Younger viewers should be forewarned.

With its segregated courtroom confrontation between the alleged victim's racist father and the accused, *To Kill a Mockingbird* is a powerful, deeply moving call for justice. A poignant, intense drama about a dignified man and his children—who come of age during some tempestuous times—it is a film every family should see.

Treasure Island

Category: Adventure. Starring Bobby Driscoll, Robert Newton, Basil Sydney, Walter Fitzgerald, Denis O'Dea, Robert Truman. Screenplay by Lawrence E. Watkin, based on the book by Robert Louis Stevenson. Music by Clifton Parker. 96 minutes. 1950. Buena Vista Home Video.
Director: Byron Haskin.
Suggested Age Group: 9 and older.

The Story Young Jim Hawkins comes upon a pirate treasure map and soon accompanies Doctor Livesey and Squire Trelawney on a hunt for the treasure aboard the ship *Hispañola.* They hire a one-legged cook named Long John Silver to recruit a crew, but the men who come aboard are really pirates planning to take over the ship and find the treasure for themselves. The relationship between the boy and the colorful pirate is at the crux of the story, which evolves into a series of thrilling adventures.

On Treasure Island, Jim is taken prisoner by Long John Silver, but he keeps his word not to try to escape, as the strange bond between them grows. Silver returns the favor when no treasure is found and the rest of the crew is about to vent its wrath against them when he gives Jim a gun to facilitate their escape.

The treasure is finally found, and, when Silver makes an attempt to make off with it, Jim thwarts his efforts. In the end, however, he still winds up helping his friend.

Background: Robert Louis Stevenson's classic tale of buried treasure and pirates had been filmed in 1934 with Wallace Beery, Jackie Cooper, and Lionel Barrymore, and again in 1972 with Orson Welles. Charlton Heston starred in a made-for-TV version in 1990. Nevertheless, this 1950 version is clearly the best of the lot, a film with lush colors, a true sense of adventure, a likable young lead, and a palpable atmosphere of danger.

Younger viewers may find some of the Cockney accents and old-style dialogue a bit hard to understand, but the action and the story move along so swiftly that they won't mind.

The real life of Iowa-born Bobby Driscoll, who played Jim Hawkins, is as dramatic and far more tragic than anything that befalls his character in *Treasure Island.* The only American actor in the cast, he won a special Academy Award as the outstanding juvenile actor of 1949. Driscoll was a young Disney contract player who, by the time he made *Treasure Island,* had appeared in *The Sullivans, O.S.S., Song of the South,* and *So Dear to My Heart,* among others. He also provided the voice of Peter Pan. But when his career faltered, Driscoll drifted into drug addiction and died at thirty-one, in an abandoned New York tenement. It took a year for his body to be claimed after he'd been buried in a pauper's grave.

Robert Newton's rolling, wide-eyed portrayal of Long John Silver ranks as one of the screen's most famous characters. Even though Wallace Beery played the salty old buccaneer well in the 1934 version, Newton defined the part with his performance in this movie. But it both made and limited his career, since he later returned to the character, playing the title roles in *Blackbeard the Pirate* and the *Long John Silver* TV series. His other films include *Odd Man Out, Oliver Twist, The High and the Mighty,* and *Around the World in 80 Days.*

The violence in this movie is only sporadic and even then largely bloodless, although Jim Hawkins does take a knife in the shoulder. Despite this minor injury, Jim is courageous and ready for action, leading young viewers through this timeless adventure classic.

20,000 Leagues Under the Sea

Category: Adventure/Science fiction. Starring Kirk Douglas, James Mason, Paul Lukas, Peter Lorre, Robert J. Wilke, Ted De Corsia. Screenplay by Earl Fenton, based on the book by Jules Verne. 127 minutes. 1954. Disney Home Video.
Director: Richard Fleischer.
Suggested Age Group: 8 and older.

The Story   Taken from the famous Jules Verne novel, the tale begins with stories about a fearsome monster that has been attacking warships in the Pacific in 1868. The monster is really the *Nautilus,* a futuristic submarine commanded by the well-intentioned but disillusioned Captain Nemo, a man who has devoted his life to the sea and to destroying all ships that might endanger it.

The navy sends out its frigate, the *Abraham Lincoln,* to find the "monster" and destroy it. Aboard the vessel is a genial harpooner named Ned Land who entertains the crew with a song enumerating his many female conquests. The ship is rammed and sunk by the *Nautilus* and only Land, a famous marine scientist, and his assistant survive.

After Land puts up a brief struggle, the trio is picked up by the crew of the *Nautilus.* Thus begins an adventure aboard Nemo's submarine as the unlikely trio tries to thwart his plans to change the world.

Nemo is a fascinating character. He has mastered atomic power decades before the rest of the world and has managed to harness the sea's limitless resources to a degree unimagined by others. Everything on the *Nautilus,* in fact, comes from the sea. After Nemo has invited his captives to dinner, he reveals in graphic detail what is really on their plates. Not surprisingly, these delicacies do not sit well with the unsophisticated palate of the harpooner Land.

While the scientist is fascinated by Nemo's discoveries about the sea, Land only wants to escape. He even resorts to putting distress letters in bottles and tossing them into the ocean, hoping they will bring help.

Parents should know that at the end of the movie, there is some violence during a fight between Nemo and his men and the crew of pursuing warships. But in an adventure such as this, featuring fascinating scenes of underwater exploration and intrigue, it is entirely appropriate viewing. Separately, a confrontation between Land and the scientist's assistant and a horde of pursuing cannibals is as funny as it is exciting, and no blood is shed. Similarly, the visual highpoint of the movie, a battle with a giant squid, will enthrall rather than scare young viewers. Given the limits of special effects forty years ago, the scene is quite remarkable.

Background: By 1954, Kirk Douglas, who plays harpooner Ned Land, was already a star. This was his twenty-first film, and his résumé already boasted such memorable films as *Champion, Young Man with a Horn, Ace in the Hole,* and *Detective Story.* Still ahead lay his great performances in *Lust for Life; Gunfight at the OK Corral; Paths of Glory; The Vikings; Spartacus; The Devil's Disciple;* his own favorite, *Lonely Are the Brave;* and *Seven Days in May.*

James Mason, who plays Captain Nemo, made his mark with films in England such as *Thunder Rock* and *Odd Man Out.* American audiences had seen him as Field Marshal Rommel in *The Desert Fox* and as Diello, the real-life Nazi spy, in *Five Fingers.* His other films include *Julius Caesar, A Star Is Born, North by Northwest,* and *Lolita.*

Paul Lukas, who plays Professor Aronnax, was a great Hungarian star best known here for movies such as *Watch on the Rhine, Dodsworth,* and *The Four Horsemen of the Apocalypse.*

His costar, who portrayed his assistant, was another Hungarian, Peter Lorre. He is best remembered for such classics as *M, The Maltese Falcon, Casablanca,* the *Mr. Moto* series of films, and *Beat the Devil.*

Director Richard Fleischer is the son of the great animator Max Fleischer, who gave the world Betty Boop and Popeye. His other movies of note include *The Narrow Margin, The Vikings, Barabbas,* and two chilling films based on true stories, *10 Rillington Place* and *The Boston Strangler.*

Had *20,000 Leagues Under the Sea* been made today, its special effects, which won an Oscar in 1954, would undoubtedly have been computer-enhanced. But that would surely have been at the expense of the film's powerful performances and the compelling sense of adventure unmatched by any other movie of its time.

WarGames

Category: Drama. Starring Matthew Broderick, Ally Sheedy, Dabney Coleman, Barry Corbin, John Wood. Screenplay by Walter F. Parkes and Lawrence Lasker. 110 minutes. 1983. Rated PG. Fox Home Video.
Director: John Badham.
Suggested Age Group: 10 and older.

The Story

WarGames begins with a fascinating look at the nerve center of NORAD, the North American Air Defense Command missile launching complex, where two Air Force officers receive orders via computer to launch intercontinental ballistic missiles aimed at Russia. Just before they turn the key which will launch the ICBMs, one officer gets cold feet.

So begins the argument—waged between Defense Department computer whizzes—that lies at the heart of this film, on the merits of having such globally significant commands come from computers instead of human beings.

Meanwhile, in faraway Seattle, a wide-eyed high school student named David demonstrates to his friend Jennifer his proficiency with his home PC by breaking into the school's computer and changing the grade in a course she'd failed. She insists he change her grade back, but when she leaves, he changes her grade again to an A.

David's next computer hacking session takes place when he tries to get an advance sneak peek at a soon-to-be-released computer game by breaking into the game company's computer. When the computer asks him which game he wants to play, he chooses "Thermonuclear War." But instead of the game company's secret code, he unwittingly breaks into the computer center at NORAD, the North American Air Defense Command. Of course, his actions inadvertently increase the DEFCON ("Defense Condition") alert system level to the point at which the U.S.'s intercontinental ballistic missiles are preparing to launch.

The situation room at NORAD is under the command of four-star General Beringer and Defense Department computer wizard McKitrick, who had, ironically, just been debating the merits of human versus computer command of missiles. With the help of FBI agents, David is soon caught, arrested, and brought to NORAD headquarters. By this time, David has discovered that a Professor Falken, a former NORAD computer wizard who designed the Defense Department's war game, is now dead. David doesn't give up, though, and soon has the NORAD computer revealing that Falken is, in fact, still alive, and located in a remote area of Oregon.

Accompanied by Jennifer, David tracks down the reclusive Falken who, it turns out, had left NORAD in disgust over the emphasis on military domination. He tells them that—like a game of tic-tac-toe—there can be no winner in a thermonuclear war.

David and Jennifer convince Falken to return to NORAD headquarters to shut down the war-games program, which is, by now, counting down to the moment when it will begin launching missiles. The radar screens at NORAD then indicate a first strike by the Russians, so American bombers are readied for takeoff, and submarines armed with nuclear warheads are deployed. The fate of humanity hangs in the balance as David and Falken try to stop the machine.

Background: Matthew Broderick's earnest portrayal of David in *WarGames* will quickly win over young viewers. Now, years after the movie was made, the computers in the film look ancient, but there is a definite sense of danger and excitement in the knowledge that the harmless computer-hacking of a high school student could wreak such worldwide havoc.

Matthew Broderick is the son of character actor James Broderick, who died in 1982, just before his son made his film debut in *Max Dugan Returns.* That movie was filmed just before he starred in *WarGames,* one of the top-grossing films of 1983. He also had the title role in the teen hit *Ferris Bueller's Day Off.*

But it was as Neil Simon's alter ego on Broadway in *Brighton Beach Memoirs* in 1983 and *Biloxi Blues* four years later that Broderick solidified his stardom. He worked continually throughout the next decade. One of his best films is *Glory,* about a gallant brigade of African-American soldiers in the Civil War. He remains a big star who works constantly, most recently returning to Broadway in a revival of *How to Succeed in Business Without Really Trying,* for which he won a Tony Award.

Ally Sheedy, who plays David's friend Jennifer, was a member of the so-called Brat Pack of young actors who came to the fore in the 1980s, particularly in John Hughes–directed and produced movies. Her films include *Oxford Blues, St. Elmo's Fire, Maid to Order, Short Circuit,* and *Betsy's Wedding.*

Dabney Coleman, who plays McKitrick, the government computer expert, made his debut on screen in the tense thriller *The Slender Thread,* with Sidney Poitier and Telly Savalas. By the time he made *WarGames,* Coleman had appeared in dozens of movies, such as *Downhill Racer, Cinderella Liberty,* and *North Dallas Forty.* His other films include *9 to 5, On Golden Pond,* and *Tootsie.* Coleman, who became a star on TV in the mid-1970s on *Mary Hartman, Mary Hartman,* has also appeared on several television sitcoms, including the ill-fated *Madman of the People.*

John Wood, who plays Falken, has done most of his work on the stage in London and Broadway. He was in the original Broadway production of *Deathtrap,* and his film work has only been occasional. Recently, he played a stuffy professor in *Shadowlands;* his other films of note include *Jumpin' Jack Flash, Lady Jane,* and Sydney Pollack's remake of *Sabrina.*

Barry Corbin, who plays the tobacco-chewing General Beringer, is best known for his role on the long-running television series *Northern Exposure.* But he's been around in movies for years, with credits including *Career Opportunities, The Hot Spot, Nothing in Common, Short Time,* and *Urban Cowboy.*

Director John Badham (who happens to be the brother of Mary Badham, who portrayed Scout in *To Kill a Mockingbird*) was born in England, raised in Alabama, and educated at the Yale Drama School. He began in the business in the mail room at Universal studios, moving later to tour guide before finally getting his chance to direct. His other credits include the wonderful baseball movie *The Bingo Long Traveling All-Stars & Motor Kings, Saturday Night Fever,* and *Dracula.*

WarGames has an exciting premise, and even though the computers are considered low-tech dinosaurs by modern standards, the movie is a harrowing, hang-on-for-dear-life adventure that computer buffs and illiterates alike will enjoy.

Where the Red Fern Grows

Category: Drama. Starring Stewart Peterson, James Whitmore, Beverly Garland, Jack Ging. Screenplay by Douglas Stewart and Eleanor Lamb, based on a novel by Wilson Rawls. 90 minutes. 1974. Rated G. Family Home Entertainment.
Director: Norman Tokar.
Suggested Age Group: 7 and older.

The Story This is the heartwarming story of a boy named Billy Coleman, who lives with his impoverished parents and young siblings on a small farm in Oklahoma during the Dust Bowl era of the Depression. More than anything else, Billy wants a pair of hunting dogs. Not any dogs, mind you, but dogs he can train to hunt raccoons and be his dearest companions.

Billy's grandfather advises him to save his money and go to a nearby town where he can buy two redbone hounds. He does as his grandfather says, and on the way home, he notices two names, "Dan" and "Ann" carved inside a heart on a tree trunk. He thus gives his new dogs those names and starts his trip home. On the way, he has an unpleasant encounter with two boys who bully him. One of the boys is accidentally knocked over and hits his head, causing a fatal injury. Luckily, Billy is exonerated.

Once he gets home, Billy slowly and patiently trains his dogs, then enters them in a raccoon-hunting contest. When his grandfather falls behind and is lost during the contest, Billy leads a search for him, costing him his certain victory. The eventual winner realizes this predicament and nobly gives Billy the trophy and prize money, which his family plans to use to move to Tulsa. Before they can decide what to do with Billy's dogs, however, a mountain lion confronts them, killing one dog and severely wounding the other.

Soon after, the surviving dog dies as well, and the family leaves the farm to move to Tulsa. But not before an emotional farewell scene at the dogs' graves, over which a red fern now grows as a sign of eternal life.

Background: This is a little-known, heartwarming family classic. Never overly sentimental or sappy, it is the story of a boy simply determined to achieve his dream. But in the process of its telling, it provides an absorbing portrait of Depression-era life, a life that demanded a courageous outlook on the world.

Nothing much ever came of the career of young Stewart Peterson, who plays Billy, but James Whitmore, who plays his grandfather, is one of movies' most versatile supporting players. A Yale graduate who served as a marine in World War II, he earned an Oscar nomination for his work in *Battleground,* which led to a slew of solid performances during the 1950s.

Films such as *Above and Beyond, Them, Battle Cry,* and *Oklahoma!* followed. Whitmore's career was revived in 1975 when he garnered another Oscar nomination for his brilliant portrayal of Harry Truman in *Give 'em Hell, Harry!,* which re-created his onstage triumph. More recently, he appeared as a lifelong inmate who can't deal with his newfound freedom in 1994's *The Shawshank Redemption.*

The only other notable cast member is Beverly Garland, who plays Billy's mother. The costar of the popular TV series *My Three Sons,* her films include *The Desperate Hours, The Joker Is Wild,* and *Airport.*

Although virtually no one knows about this wonderful, understated movie, it is instantly absorbing, and nothing is more powerful than the love of a child for his pets. In the end, though, despite his feelings, Billy accepts his dogs' fate stoically, with the calm and maturity that tough times require. It is this maturity— along with Billy's strong ties with his parents—that makes viewing *Where the Red Fern Grows* a special family experience.

Yankee Doodle Dandy

Category: Musical. Starring James Cagney, Joan Leslie, Walter Huston, Richard Whorf, Rosemary DeCamp, Jeanne Cagney, Eddie Foy, Jr. Screenplay by Robert Buckner. 126 minutes. 1942. Black and white. Fox Home Video.
Director: Michael Curtiz.
Suggested Age Group: 6 and older.

The Story The story begins just after a performance in the early 1940s of a musical called *I'd Rather Be Right,* in which George M. Cohan portrayed President Franklin Roosevelt. Backstage, he receives a telegram summoning him to the White House.

As Cohan enters the Oval Office and begins to tell FDR his life story, we see his life played out in words, song, and dance—from his birth on the fourth of July in 1878 (actually Cohan was born on July 3) and his formative years performing with his parents and sister, as the Four Cohans, to the years when his precociousness got the family in trouble. He matured, of course, and the Cohans continued to travel across the country. Through the years their reputation grew, and while they were subject to changing times, triumphs and flops, ups and downs, they nevertheless endured.

By the time Cohan finishes telling FDR his life story, the Chief Executive awards him the Congressional Medal of Honor, making him the first civilian to be so honored. Cohan leaves the White House, does a tap dance down the stairs, and encounters a parade of soldiers outside. They're singing "Over There," the clarion call of World War I that Cohan wrote. He joins the soldiers in step, and when he marches without singing, a soldier asks him if he knows the words. "I should think so," replies Cohan, as he joins in.

Background: By 1942, James Cagney had made thirty-eight films, including his 1930 debut in *Sinner's Holiday, The Public Enemy,* which made him a star the following year, *Footlight Parade, Devil*

Dogs of the Air, A Midsummer Night's Dream, Each Dawn I Die, and *The Bride Came C.O.D.* While Cagney won his only Oscar for *Yankee Doodle Dandy,* ahead lay classics including *White Heat, The Seven Little Foys, Tribute to a Bad Man,* and *The Gallant Hours.* No star in the history of Hollywood was so versatile as Cagney. Along with Edward G. Robinson and Paul Muni, he created the genre of the screen gangster. But he also appeared in Westerns, musicals, dramas, and comedies.

It is impossible to watch *Yankee Doodle Dandy* and not be inspired to feel good about being an American—so stirring and thrilling is its effect. Coming when it did, during the depths of the early months of World War II, when the enemy had the upper hand, this film helped boost morale to a home front which desperately needed it.

While some elements of the film are dated (there are some vaudeville performers in blackface, and "Battle Hymn of the Republic" is sung by a group of African-American actors in an old-fashioned Uncle Tom style), such moments are brief and not pivotal to the story.

Cagney gives one of the greatest performances in the history of the movies, singing, dancing and acting brilliantly as he enacts forty years of Cohan's life. His own style of stiff-legged dancing, and his kicks, twists, and method of climbing the walls are part of what made him a legend.

The real George M. Cohan had sold the rights to his life story to Warner Bros. for $50,000, a considerable sum back then. Since he also had script and casting approval, he chose Cagney for the part, although Jack L. Warner claimed it was he who had pegged Cagney for it. Cagney agreed—but only reluctantly—to the script Cohan had approved, and after risking a suspension from the studio, was convinced to do the part as written only because it would help the career of his sister, Jeanne, who played his sister in the film.

Once, during a rehearsal for a fight scene in a movie, Cagney spoke his lines in a subdued manner, gently nudging the actor who played his opponent. Amazed at the low-key effort by Cagney, the other actor wondered to himself "Why on earth is he a star?" Then the cameras rolled and Cagney, now yelling his lines, slammed the other actor against a wall, his eyes bulging. "Now I know," the actor thought, picking himself up off the floor.

Walter Huston, who plays Cohan's father, was one of the giants of his generation of actors. Born Walter Houghston, he was the father of director-actor John Huston and is the grandfather of actress Anjelica Huston, heading the only family with three generations of Oscar winners. A onetime vaudevillian himself, Huston starred on Broadway in the 1920s, then became one of the great character leads in Hollywood. *Abraham Lincoln,* D. W. Griffith's 1930 movie, was an early success, followed by *The Maltese Falcon, Dodsworth, The Treasure of the Sierra Madre* (directed by his son), and *The Great Sinner.*

Yankee Doodle Dandy is such a powerful, inspiring musical that its images and songs will stay with you long after the movie is over. Young audiences will be enthralled.

The Yearling

Category: Drama. Starring Gregory Peck, Claude Jarman, Jr., Jane Wyman, Forrest Tucker, Chill Wills. Screenplay by Paul Osborne, based on the novel by Marjorie Kinnan Rawlings. 128 minutes. 1946. MGM/UA Home Video.
Director: Clarence Brown.
Suggested Age Group: 7 and older.

The Story Set in the Florida Everglades in the 1870s, the story takes place mostly on a small farm where a lonely boy named Jody Baxter lives with his parents. His father is a strong, brave type, but his mother is embittered and humorless, probably due to the fact that she had lost four previous children.

The early part of the movie involves the pursuit of a marauding bear that had killed one of the family's dogs. After they chase the bear away, the father is bitten by a rattlesnake. He must shoot a young doe, as he needs her heart and liver to stem the swelling in his arm. After Jody summons the doctor, they discover a tiny fawn, obviously the offspring of the fallen doe.

Soon Jody adopts the deer, against his mother's wishes, and names him Flag. At first his father stands by Jody's decision to raise the fawn, as Jody's affection for his new pet helps to temper his grief over the death of a young friend.

Gradually, however, the deer becomes more of a problem. Six days of rain confine the deer and the family's dogs inside their small house, making the mother even more annoyed. After the storm passes, the deer starts destroying crops, despite the family's attempts to pen it in. When the father is injured trying to move a large tree stump, Jody tries to take over the chores of the farm, but to no avail. The deer leaps over the high fence and for the second time destroys the family's corn crop.

Finally the father has no choice. Still bedridden, he tells Jody to take the deer, now a growing yearling, out to the woods to shoot him. But the boy can't do it, so his mother does, wounding the deer. Jody is forced to finish the job, after which he runs away in anger.

Several days later, alone and unconscious in a small boat, Jody is picked up by the crew of a ship on a faraway river. Eventually he returns home and reaches an understanding with his father, who explains that every man is lonesome, but once he gets knocked down, he's got to take his share of lumps and go on.

At last, after almost losing him, Jody's mother opens up to her son, urging him to get well.

Background: This wasn't the first attempt to film *The Yearling*. Five years earlier, Spencer Tracy, Anne Revere, and young Gene Eckman started on one version, but it never got beyond a few weeks of filming. This version, which, like the first attempt, was made by MGM, was actually filmed in the Florida Everglades, but the location shoot proved too difficult, so interiors and some exterior shots were done on the studio lot. Nevertheless, some exteriors are unmistakably authentic, with gorgeous backdrops and dense, verdant undergrowth.

The Yearling is an eerily beautiful story of a boy's love for his pet, and his father's determination to make his small farm a success. Children will love the interplay between the boy and the deer, and his efforts to keep his pet as long as possible, against some tough odds.

The Yearling came early in Gregory Peck's career. In fact, it was his fifth movie, made just after the Hitchcock classic *Spellbound,* and he was simultaneously making his sixth film, *Duel in the Sun.*

Peck came to New York from La Jolla, California, working for a time as a page at Radio City Music Hall, after which he studied at the Neighborhood Playhouse and debuted on Broadway in *The Morning Star* in 1942. A spinal condition kept him out of World War II, so, as with Van Johnson, Peck's stardom rose rapidly while other stars were away in the military.

Very few actors have had so many memorable roles, and Peck's career is studded with fine films such as *The Man in the Gray Flannel Suit, Twelve O'Clock High, Moby Dick, The Big Country, Gentleman's Agreement, To Kill a Mockingbird,* for which he won an Oscar for Best Actor, and *The Boys From Brazil,* with a rare appearance as a villain.

As for Claude Jarman, Jr., who plays Jody, his career was something else again. Though given a special Academy Award for his debut in *The Yearling,* he would make only ten more movies, the only memorable one being *Rio Grande* four years later. When his brief film career ended, Jarman returned to school and wound up as executive director of the San Francisco Film Festival. He also produced the 1972 rock concert movie *Fillmore.*

The only weakness of *The Yearling* is the character of the mother, played by a dour Jane Wyman. She is constantly depressed, and unwilling to bend or to soften her disposition. At the time of *The Yearling,* Jane Wyman was married to the second of her four husbands, Ronald Reagan. Her other movies of note include *Brother Rat,* with Reagan, *The Lost Weekend, Magnificent Obsession,* and another movie discussed in this book, *Pollyanna.*

Like *Old Yeller* a decade later, *The Yearling* is an unconventional boy-and-his-special-pet movie. It takes us through emotional highs and lows, but still provides a happy ending. The result is a movie of incredible tenderness and incandescent beauty.

About the Author

The son of the late renowned Broadway columnist Leonard Lyons, Jeffrey Lyons took over in 1982 as cohost (with Michael Medved) of PBS' *Sneak Previews,* television's longest running movie review program. He began his career in New York television in 1970 and has since reviewed more than 6,000 films and 500 Broadway plays. The film critic for ABC's *World News Now* and host of *The Lyons Den,* the nationally syndicated radio report on entertainment, he has also written about movies for *Inside Sports, Video Review,* and other publications. He resides in New York with his wife and two children, and conducts a weekly film seminar in New Jersey called "Coming Attractions." He hopes to live long enough to see the Boston Red Sox win the World Series.